Assets in Common

Stories of business and community leaders remaking the economy from the ground up.

Written by:

Charity May
Jay Standish
Chelsea Robinson
Zoe Schlag
Derek Razo

Edited by:

Chelsea Robinson

Produced by:

Infrastructure for Shared Ownership (sharedownership.us)
Common Trust (common-trust.com)
Purpose Foundation (purpose-us.com)

Supported by:

One Project (oneproject.org)

© 2024 Infrastructure for Shared Ownership

All rights reserved. No part of this publication may be reproduced, distributed, or transmitted in any form or by any means, including photocopying, recording, or other electronic or mechanical methods, without the prior written permission of the publisher, except in the case of brief quotations embodied in critical reviews and certain other non-commercial uses permitted by copyright law.

Please contact the authors to discuss repurposing or using these materials.

Print ISBN: 979-8-35095-654-2
eBook ISBN: 979-8-35095-655-9

Table of Contents

Part I – Opening 1

    Foreword 3

    Introduction 7

    How to Read This Book 15

    A Glimpse into the Future 19

Part II – Living Proof:Case Studies 25

    The Calvert Community Investment Note 27

    Clegg Auto: A Steward Ownership Transition 37

    Credit Union Service Organizations 45

    Enspiral's Financial Commons 55

    Goodworks Evergreen: A Rural Rollup 73

    The Industrial Commons 79

    Mondragon Corporation 91

    Obran: A Cooperative Holding Company 113

    Rotating Savings and Credit Associations 123

    Sardex: A Complementary Currency 133

    Savings Pools: A Mutual Lending Practice 147

    Sumitomo Group: A Keiretsu 159

    Urban Wealth Funds 177

Part III – Patterns, Mechanisms, and Challenges:
An Analysis 189

    Purpose & Stewardship 191

    Structures, Governance & Ownership 197

    Shared Services 213

    Holding Companies 225

    Liquidity, Resource Sharing & Risk 235

    Marketplaces & Value Chain Integration 249

    Relationships, Capacity & Culture 261

Part IV – Opportunities for Action 271

Launching Shared Services Cooperatives 273

Building a Steward-Owned Holding Company 287

Opportunities for Funders 303

Part I –

Opening

Foreword

Zoe Schlag & Derek Razo – Common Trust

Dirt Under Our Nails

Business owners work with us every day to define the structures and processes that shape the destiny of their businesses and communities. We at Common Trust have worked with everyone, from farmers to financial institutions. We believe the American economy is overdue for structural changes that put people and communities first, and we have been using an innovative set of legal instruments and financing models to make it happen one business at a time.

We have directly managed the financing and deal structuring of companies from the seed stage to going public while retaining their mission and values. We have had the privilege of supporting community leaders and nonprofits to put privately held assets into the commons. We have worked on protecting and creating some of the largest affordable housing projects and food system businesses in the country. Furthermore, we have designed and deployed funds as fund managers, LPs, and grant makers. We have pioneered legal and tax research that led to the adoption and scaling of new ownership models, sector-wide. We made an investment in Organically Grown Company that enabled their steward ownership transition in 2018. Recently we were privileged to lead Clegg Auto's shared ownership roll-up process, establishing the nation's first employee ownership trust (EOT) holding company. We also conducted Text-Em-All's steward ownership transition. We're deep in the work we do, and so as we explain why this book is such an important read, keep in mind that we're not in the business of selling ideas, we are in the business of making real progress in our field. We rarely consider a research and writing effort to be as valuable as this one.

Ideas Worth Devoting Your Career To

We at Common Trust greatly respect the team behind this book and the supporting organizations, Purpose US[1] and One Project[2]. We believe these topics will only grow more relevant as this field matures. This book showcases the next wave of opportunities for growing the shared ownership movement. Transitioning ownership structures one by one is not the only path to economic change. There is a long history of evidence demonstrating that when networks of individuals and businesses collaborate, leveraging their assets, they can outcompete financial actors over the long term. This takes shared ownership to another level. The enmeshment of multiple entities that share values and vision can offer real efficiencies, resilience, and assets to each other over time. The alternative economic future outlined here is not a hobbyist's intellectual stimulation or a passing fad, but something that has quietly existed in our communities for generations, and we're dedicating our lives to scaling it. You will not be disappointed by the quality and diversity of possibilities spelled out here.

Our excitement extends to the caliber of this book's authorship. We've had the pleasure of working alongside Charity May, Jay Standish, and Chelsea Robinson. In their careers, they have led income-sharing pools, real estate portfolios, and cooperatives, as well as impact funds and startups, and consulted to organizations undergoing structural change. They have discovered insights and opportunities by studying long-running case studies. They have revealed both cultural history and practical recommendations for the current economy. They have given us all the gift of this book, which we see being required reading for our teams, clients, and allies for years to come.

Scaling What's Working

The rationale for this book emerged in the thick of running the Emerging Fund Manager Fellowship at Purpose US in 2021-2022. We supported these leaders to raise new funds to invest in stewardship and shared ownership

---

1   Purpose. https://www.purpose-us.com/

2   One Project. https://oneproject.org/

growth, and it was challenging. While there are many courageous and generous donors and investors pioneering this field, every dollar raised is done so in negotiation between existing ideologies and those not yet widely accepted. What's needed next is a roadmap that enables shared ownership to get to scale while building resilience.

While today's capital structures optimize for greater returns by shifting risk, time-tested models of shared ownership prioritize long-term success and resilience. Today's capital structures optimize for greater returns while shifting risk onto companies and their workforce. This is all done without taking into account any negative externalities to the company, community, or planet as long as those materialize beyond the life of a fund. This is simply not compatible with shared ownership structures that are designed for the long haul.

Many business owners and investors maintain the belief that real operational examples of shared ownership at scale don't exist yet. This couldn't be farther from the truth. There are full-scale shared ownership business networks that have existed for hundreds of years. Many are stuck thinking there are no valid examples because instead of raising an eye-popping round, they might acquire new businesses into their shared ownership holding company off their balance sheet or hit 200 years of private, profitable operations while giving back to their community. Success looks different.

This book showcases a diversity of approaches to inspire your thinking around alternatives, and we believe these examples are just the beginning of a Cambrian explosion of new shared ownership models.

Bring an Open Mind

When reading this book, you should expect to be challenged by what seems achievable and invest-able. Although many shared ownership structures may seem new, untested, or risky to you, it does not mean that they are. In comparison with recent creations such as LLCs and mortgages, some case studies in this book illustrate approaches that have been well-used for many generations, on many continents.

We showcase examples that already work at scale, led by people who had the odds stacked against them. These leaders have taken risks few have been willing to take, and have done so at the rugged interface between communities in need and modern regulatory environments. Expect to be inspired by their ingenuity, and to learn new ways of thinking.

We urge you to consider how this book could influence the work you do. Many of the principles here are not only suitable for many sectors, but they also apply even more broadly across multiple asset classes. Reflect on the transferable insights from each story, and pull yourself out of the details of their specific use case to transpose the concepts into your use cases and communities.

Let's Get Into It

We see groups of 'builders' and 'doers' around us who are ready to identify a shared opportunity to build something collectively and dig in. This is a call to action for those of us with assets or communities ready to operate differently.

Furthermore, we know that it's possible to get started without waiting for permission, and without waiting for norms to change on their own. We know that there is a community of leaders who don't need to see large institutions writing shiny reports to make this approach feel de-risked and credible.

Let's connect, and start trying some ideas in this book with the assets in our control today. We don't have to wait for thirty years, or for any one particular group to give the green light. We can look to our left and our right and see who's next to us, and start.

Talk soon,

Derek & Zoe.

Introduction

Chelsea Robinson

Infrastructure for Shared Ownership

The United States economy is overdue for a shift towards equity and democratic wealth building. As authors, we set out to reveal lesser-known corporate forms and financial structures that leaders can use to enable widespread transformation. We have compiled a curated selection of case studies that demonstrate outstanding examples of an alternative economic paradigm in action. In particular, we are excited about the potential of using shared ownership forms as the core instrument for business ownership and community asset stewardship.

This body of work is an attempt at figuring out how to scale steward ownership and shared ownership. Given that many leaders are already aware of the potential of tools such as trust-owned corporations to protect their values long-term, this work offers a next step; to grow this movement through infrastructure that connects assets for greater resilience and competitiveness. Throughout this book, we describe this in several ways. We use language like 'connective entities' and 'networked businesses' to describe what we call Infrastructure for Shared Ownership.

Shared ownership and steward ownership are key concepts throughout the book, so let's define them for you up front:

- Shared ownership refers to business and property ownership structures that distribute equity and control among a wider group of stakeholders, such as employees, customers, or community members. Shared ownership models create more equitable and engaged economic participation through structures like cooperatives, employee stock ownership plans (ESOPs), and community land trusts.

- Steward ownership is a corporate governance model that ensures enduring independence and mission-driven focus by placing a company's shares in a trust or foundation. This preserves the organization's purpose and values beyond the involvement of any individual leaders. Central to steward ownership is the strict separation of economic interest and governance. Rather than being privatized, profits are either reinvested in the business and its stakeholders or donated to charity.

When shared and steward ownership are combined, we protect assets and businesses for the long term, align financial interests with mission and values, incentivize reinvestment instead of extraction, and build wealth for all stakeholders.

This book extends the powerful concepts of shared ownership and stewardship by envisioning the integration of these units into something greater. If we work together to build infrastructural institutions between our entities and assets, we can create competitive ecosystems that more and more entities can opt into. Building infrastructure for shared ownership will promote the development of an economy running on different incentives and principles. If matured, these kinds of ecosystems could offer resilient, scalable alternatives to the default financial system.

Leaders face enormous friction when prioritizing reinvestment over extractive incentives. Business owners and community leaders are often ready to prioritize the health, well-being, and wealth of their people and places. Even after leaders restructure their community assets or company into a stewardship format, they still experience the hostile pressures of the extractive economy. Because of this edge effect between shared and steward ownership formats and the rest of the economy, this book shows how we can build corridors of connection between institutions.

Unlocking mutual support between entities can buffer against adverse pressures to place profit above all else. It is possible to build and share banking systems, currencies, employer-of-record companies, no-interest loan pools, warehouses, and heavy machinery libraries. It is also possible to run entire value chains within collaborative networks of allied organizations. Competitiveness can thrive alongside interdependence. Together, networks of institutions operating on different economic principles can buffer each other from the winds of the default economy as it crumbles.

The groundswell of attention on good governance in finance and corporations is driving a movement towards shared ownership and stewardship forms. Perpetual Purpose Trusts, Employee Stock Option Plans, Cooperatives, and Employee Ownership all share a big tent: Corporate models for an equitable economy. This book contributes to the next step in scaling up these modalities by emphasizing connectivity. This movement needs infrastructure to help these shared ownership models grow, become resilient, and eventually outpace the existing economy.

In this book, we not only break down the nuts and bolts of real examples, but we also elaborate on the patterns, success factors, and nuanced issues across each. Though an individual case study may seem relevant to some audiences and less so to others, the principles from each specific instance can be transferred and reapplied in many other environments. We hope that between all the stories you'll see the big opportunity.

A Highlights Reel

We've collated some key ideas up front. We hope this can be an enticing starting point and a point of reference. You may want to come back to this once you've read more of the book to allow these key points to sink in deeper. The following is a selection of patterns and concepts. We believe that combining these concepts in practice could help you successfully build infrastructure for shared ownership from the bottom up. These concepts can foster economic revitalization and build shared surplus for communities, regions, or sectors suffering from the long-term damages of over-extraction, and growth at all costs.

Conscious Consolidation

Many leaders are aggregating assets into unifying entities like holding companies or multi-stakeholder cooperatives. Achieving this via typical structures can be a slippery slope to monopoly and cartel behavior. However, when designed with shared ownership and stewardship, these can create value for stakeholders and long-term missions. Conscious consolidation can help with efficiency gains and greater influence in the market.

Shared Balance Sheets

Pooling assets in shared legal containers can create mechanisms for resilience and liquidity at scale. Putting many buildings, employees, business units, funds, or loans onto shared balance sheets enables pre-tax internal trade. These larger balance sheets can be leveraged for growth, acquiring capital, extending credit to allies, or buffering against losses and layoffs.

Pragmatic Leaders

A motivated, practical leader is often behind infrastructure for shared ownership. These leaders typically have an operational mindset and a vision to create win-wins for their people, customers, and stakeholders while staying in line with regulators.

Companies Cooperating

Connected entities create infrastructure for shared ownership. Methods like cross-shareholding, or co-investment in co-owned services companies create connective tissue between businesses and assets. Entrepreneurship typically focuses on developing and leading one project, but infrastructure projects require entrepreneurial creativity in managing relationships between entities.

Monetary Policy and Sovereignty

Monetary policy is typically considered the role of the state. It determines how the central bank controls the money supply and promotes price stability. It involves managing interest rates, setting bank reserve requirements, and influencing credit availability in the economy. These kinds of policies can be generated within networks of businesses with shared resources. Complementary currencies or internal network trade can be opportunities to redefine the role and value of money. Sovereign economic spaces can encode new incentives and imbue meaning to money itself.

Municipal & Civic Integration

Municipalities and citizen-led initiatives can benefit from infrastructure for shared ownership. Connected business networks enhance worker empowerment and agency. Empowered people participate more actively in local developmental efforts. Community leaders can use shared ownership and stewardship for community assets, while local governments can aggregate regional resources onto shared balance sheets. These concepts are relevant and beneficial for regions and cities alike.

Regionalism and Place

Each locale has a history of how economic and cultural development occurred in that area. These historical drivers, such as settlements created among mining, shipping, or fabrication, can be sources of economic revitalization. Looking at the endogenous sources of economic development in a region can inspire a purpose for networks of business activities to grow from. Linking the past activities of a place to its desired future state can provide a strategy for developing infrastructure for shared ownership.

Trust and Purpose

A culture of trust and mutual support often helps networked entities thrive. While the motivation to aggregate assets for resilience can stem from desiring efficiency gains, it is strongest when driven by parties that have a desire to help each other succeed over time. However, if mutual care consistently outweighs purpose, the culture can stagnate and become an 'in-crowd'. Cultures that balance trust and purpose, individuation and mutualism, are generative and can take risks together.

Pools and Closed Circuits

Infrastructure for shared ownership frequently emerges within walled gardens. Limiting partici-pants can help mitigate the downside while gener-ating shared benefits. In the default economy, this is achieved through systems like credit scores. In contexts of shared ownership and stewardship, there may be criteria of 'fit' for participating in a pool. One business' performance profile may make it more or less suited to joining a group of other businesses.

Shared Economic Destiny

Relationships of long-term interdependence are a strong bedrock for operating network infrastructure. While short-termism is transactional, long-termism is purposeful and relational. Many of our case studies showcase business-to-business or intergenerational relationships, which prioritize the strength of the long-term relationship over short-term profitability. This does create tension; however, it is a developmental approach. Investing in the person, company, or rela-tionship is expected to pay dividends indirectly over time. This is couched in a deeper stance that collective flourishing leads to individual flourishing.

Well-Managed Commons

The opposite of a tragedy of the commons is a well-managed commons. Rather than seeing cooperative enterprises as a cost center, co-investing in shared services and utilities can protect against challenges and accelerate growth. Investing in the management and governance of the shared systems is necessary for their success. Just as a building needs a facilities manager and a budget, projects bridging entities need leadership.

Reciprocity Mindset

Enlightened self-interest helps people understand that they will receive dividends on their generosity to shared pools of resources. Reciprocity is often thought of as a direct trade. However, in many cases of infrastructure for shared ownership, reciprocity is indirect. Fostering a mindset that places value on processes of indirect reciprocity aligns day-to-day acts of generosity with individual gain and overall collective thriving.

Seed Assets

In multiple case studies, people have used a seed company or an asset base to start a network of entities. Seed assets may be a fully functioning, existing entity such as a profitable business or a piece of land. Seed assets may already have monetary value in the default economy, which allows them to convert that value into starting a shared utility. Seed assets may also be of sufficient size and stability to invite other smaller entities to join their fray. Many business owners could consider whether their business can play this role. Many municipalities could consider whether their public assets can be carefully financialised for regional development.

Shared Services Groups of people or organizations often set up services between them to share costs. This can take the form of setting up an accounting company that is dedicated to back-office services for a network of businesses. It is important to differentiate between privately owned services companies that are extracting value from a network and shared services that have been structured to ensure the network benefits from the success of that shared services venture.

Diving in

We anticipate that you are reading this book because you are interested in stories of cooperative and shared ownership models. You might be a business owner, community leader, or an enthusiast within the movement. There are many examples of businesses that, individually, have demonstrated alternatives. Beyond the 'one business at a time' model, how do we snowball the positive effects of shared ownership and stewardship?

This book focuses on how businesses and communities can work together to scale impact through coordination. We explore how to create connective entities that offer resilience and growth to shared and steward-owned institutions. We see a path to transform the entire economic system by building interconnected networks wired for reinvestment. We see the potential of building coordinated infrastructure to protect and advance shared ownership and stewardship.

How to Read This Book

Chelsea Robinson

Navigating the Sections of this Book

This book has four sections. This outline can help you decide which parts interest you most. You can read this chronologically or jump around and dip into different topics and case studies at your own pace.

Part I – Opening	The opening is an orientation. We provide a framing narrative and explain our motivations. You will get important key concepts from the opening which you won't get elsewhere. Even if you read only a handful of other chapters, the opening is necessary for understanding the other sections.
Part II – Living Proof: Case Studies	Twelve in-depth case studies demonstrate diverse examples of infrastructure for shared ownership. We have focused on the mechanisms and gritty details of how these operate internally. We have also captured their context, history, and use case. Almost all case studies were informed by those directly involved in the projects. These are stories of pragmatic leadership and succeeding against the odds.
Part III – Patterns, Mechanisms, and Challenges: An Analysis	Our analysis covers topics that have recurred across case studies. We unpack issues like mitigating the downsides of cooperation and explicate success factors like governance and culture. We have outlined trends such as shared service provision and liquidity through resource pooling. The analysis discusses the nuances of the case studies and also adds more examples.

Part IV – Opportunities for Action	We identify valuable strategies worth adopting. In this section, you will find recipes for action. We cover how to build a shared services company and how to design a holding company founded on stewardship. Finally, we advise on how funders can invest wisely in this space.

Our Bias, Angles, and Ideologies

Here, we describe our decisions regarding the ideas represented. We explain our emphasis on the untold side of stories and our pragmatism.

For Builders, Alongside a Wider Movement

The work builds upon the efforts of countless individuals and communities who have pioneered alternative economic models for decades. We acknowledge and celebrate the leadership shown by economists within underrepresented groups, who have long been at the forefront of these discussions. In recent years, the ecosystem of alternative ownership and finance has experienced tremendous growth, with many organizations and individuals playing vital roles in its development. We know that our contribution is just one part of an ongoing, multi-faceted dialogue taking place.

Our contribution is to coalesce the ideas presented in this book as a platform for action, particularly for business and community leaders seeking pragmatic steps to build infrastructure for shared ownership. The case studies and concepts explored in this book draw from various ideological influences. We believe that no single paradigm or belief system holds a monopoly on truth, and we adopt a pragmatic focus on the mechanisms and practical "how-to" aspects of building alternative economic models. As a book written by builders, for builders, we recognize the crucial role played by individual and small group leadership in driving change.

A Spectrum of Economic Worldviews

The sociopolitical contexts of the case studies span both Western and Eastern countries, encompassing a mix of immigrant, indigenous, and colonial cultural concepts. For some communities, mutualism is a way of life and a default mode of operation. For others, private gain and extraction are the norm. Writing primarily for U.S. audiences, we use terms like "typical," "default," or "normative" to refer to the currently dominant extractive economic system prevalent in the United States. Some examples may be unconventional or surprising, while others may invite healthy critique. There is an inherent tension between market forces and coordination and a tendency in Western colonial viewpoints to perceive cooperation as anti-market behavior. However, for communities that have experienced oppression, suppression, and systematic extraction, shared ownership, and resource sharing have served as vital means of protection and survival in the face of economic violence. The Keiretsu case study illustrates this tension. Some view Keiretsu as having been set up for the Japanese elite to circumvent anti-monopoly policies. Others see it as a culturally coherent defensive move against American imperialism during the post-war restructuring of the Japanese economy for international market integration. As authors, we believe that valuable insights can be gained from every example, even if they may not align perfectly with our preconceptions.

Nuance Over Narrative

We have deliberately chosen to focus on aspects that may have been overlooked in other analyses, seeking to add value to the existing ecosystem of knowledge. Rather than rewriting the well-known and sometimes romanticized elements of case studies like the Mondragon Cooperative, we've aimed to dig deeper and uncover the underlying factors contributing to their success or challenges. This has led us to surprising findings, such as the intergenerational job guarantees within Mondragon — a testament to their long-term perspective — as well as the reasons why some of their companies chose to leave the cooperative.

Our selection of case studies represents a diverse range of approaches and concepts. Spanning from contemporary U.S. examples like Obran and the funder-driven stewardship model of Goodworks Evergreen, to ancient international practices like loan pools. By highlighting these, we hope to demonstrate that the ideas of shared ownership and alternative economic models are not foreign or impossible but are operating successfully around the world. While the examples included in this book are not exhaustive, we believe they provide a compelling cross-section of the possibilities within this space. Our aim is to catalyze further interest and exploration rather than suggesting that these specific instances are the only ones worthy of attention. As the movement toward infrastructure for shared ownership continues to grow, we eagerly anticipate the emergence of many more inspiring stories and innovative models.

Finally, most of our case studies have been informed by direct interviews and discussions with project or company leaders. We worked to produce the most realistic and detailed information we could achieve.

A Glimpse into the Future

Chelsea Robinson

Change happens faster than you might think. If something seems impossible today, it does not mean that it will remain that way. Keep in mind that LLCs, perhaps the most common legal entity in the country, were only invented in 1977[3]. Do not forget that 30-year mortgages only became legislated and widely used in the 1930s. Until the Great Depression, loans beyond 5-10-year periods were unthinkable[4]. A new financial product was designed to meet the day's needs, creating a new normal within just decades. We can build new legal and financial products that serve today's needs, and if done right, they do have the potential to generate transformative change for the American economy.

When trying to make changes in society, it can be easier to point to the fact that we're trying something 'different' rather than naming what we're building. The tendency is to say 'alternative economics" or "new economy". This can be problematic. Equitable economic infrastructure isn't just an "alternative", and it's not all "new". There are plentiful implementations of these models being competitive, lasting, and scalable. What is harder is to give it a name and a compelling story. We will offer some brief framing of how to conceptualize the bigger picture economic future that could be possible if we scale up infrastructure for shared ownership and unlock its widespread positive ripple effects.

---

3   Feldman, S. (2022, September 30). Understanding LLC law: Its past and its present. https://www.wolterskluwer.com/en/expert-insights/understanding-llc-law-its-past-and-its-present

4   Highfield, M. J. (n.d.). A brief history of the mortgage, from its roots in ancient Rome to the English 'dead pledge' and its rebirth in America. The Conversation. https://theconversation.com/a-brief-history-of-the-mortgage-from-its-roots-in-ancient-rome-to-the-english-dead-pledge-and-its-rebirth-in-america-193005

Beyond Cooperative Commonwealth to Stewardship Commonwealth

During our research, we were delighted to explore the work of political economist Jessica Gordon Nembhard[5]. We will briefly explain her work and ideas and how they offer a relevant vision. We will then add another dimension.

Nembhard is a scholar and activist whose work focuses on cooperative economics to empower marginalized communities and promote racial and economic justice. Her research highlights the often-overlooked history of African-American cooperative economic practices and their role in the struggle for civil rights and equality. Nembhard advocates for the development of cooperative businesses, credit unions, and other forms of collective ownership as strategies for fostering resilience. We appreciate how practical and urgent her voice is about what's possible: "One of my pet peeves is that we keep thinking we don't know what to do, but we do know because we have lots of models that have succeeded over the centuries, even over the last 20 years. There are lots of examples of cooperative solidarity economics that work, that deliver to people, that provide people a say, a piece, that operate in a business model that can make money for people. What we don't have is enough will and enough education about how to do it."[6]

One of her proposals is the vision for a Cooperative Commonwealth. The Cooperative Commonwealth is one of the few 'full stack' visions for a networked, equitable economy that we've found to be aligned with our ideas. The cooperative commonwealth implies many levels of society incentivized towards democratic participation, wealth building,

---

5 Wikipedia contributors. (2024, April 4). Jessica Gordon Nembhard. Wikipedia. https://en.wikipedia.org/wiki/Jessica_Gordon_Nembhard

6 Gordon Nembhard, J. (2015, September 28). Thinking about a next system with W.E.B. Du Bois and Fannie Lou Hamer. TheNextSystem.org. https://thenextsystem.org/thinking-about-a-next-system-with-w-e-b-du-bois-and-fannie-lou-hamer

reinvestment, and stakeholder control. To paraphrase Elias Crim[7], the Cooperative Commonwealth includes financial reforms such as the development of public banking and the widening of credit unions, processes to convert existing businesses to shared ownership, networks of affiliated businesses, and a lifestyle that "gives people time for caregiving, volunteering, and continuous learning."

In Nembhard's own words, "Risks are collectivized, skills are perfected, learning is continuous, and surplus is shared in equitable ways, through real democratic decision-making. In a system of shared prosperity, shared decision-making, and collective economic activity can spill over into other social and political spaces, and enrich civil society, families, and individual wellness. We do have examples of some of this. We have examples of sort of cooperative commonwealths where you have interlocking systems: a credit union that helps to develop worker co-ops and gives the first loan to the co-op store to buy its own building. And then the co-op store deposits its money in the credit union. And the credit union also helps the neighborhood to start a housing co-op. And the housing co-op members run their own security company and maintenance company as worker-owned companies that also service the credit unions and the co-op stores. The residents also have a co-op sewing factory, catering company, child care center, etc. So that's the kind of idea we have: that everybody is part of several different co-ops, which service each other and provide products and alternative financing. Some of the surplus from one co-op venture can then be put into something else, like affordable housing or other kinds of provisions, like collective utilities. So the notion is that we don't really have any one group, or one person running off with all the

---

7   Crim, E. (2024, January 16). Three Guides to navigating 2024 (#3). Solidarity Hall. https://solidarityhall.substack.com/p/three-guides-to-navigating-2024-3

spoils, right? The spoils are truly recirculating in the community. And the community itself is the one who decides what happens to those resources"[8]

The risk here is an over-emphasis on the 'cooperative' legal structure. We're advocating for a wider variety of legal structures. The interconnectedness of entities in Nembhard's vision is aligned with ours. However, we believe that although coops have been a popular choice for shared ownership, they are not without issues. For example, coops are structurally incentivized to serve the wealth and health of their own members due to their governance arrangements. In our vision, we would like to see the vitality and resilience of communities and landscapes become part of the success criteria of business activity. Rather than the priority being the wealth-building of worker-owners, we see the priority as being an economy that generates public goods.

For this reason, there is immense value in utilizing steward ownership. If a local utility company is owned by a trust that legally requires it to provide high-quality services and advance the environmental protections of the region, that business will extend its mission far beyond optimizing for profit share of its members. We admire and want to highlight Nembhard's extensive work in this area and also use this as an opportunity to distinguish the differences between a cooperative economy and a stewardship economy. For this reason, we offer the phrase 'stewardship commonwealth' as a possible iteration on this framing. We're not claiming this concept to be the most memorable or memetically powerful phrase, but it could be a useful description in the interim as we all collectively articulate a vision for a better economy.

A Better Monday

This next segment is a short story. It's a painting of how infrastructure for shared ownership can create positive effects on quality of life. It can

---

8 Gordon Nembhard, J. (2015, September 28). Thinking about a next system with W.E.B. Du Bois and Fannie Lou Hamer. TheNextSystem.org. https://thenextsystem.org/thinking-about-a-next-system-with-w-e-b-du-bois-and-fannie-lou-hamer

connect local, regional, and national institutions. It can normalize ethical and equitable conduct. We can add human and planetary health into the purpose of our economic logic. The result? A better Monday.

Imagine you wake up on a Monday morning in a house that you own and bought with low-interest rate community mortgage fund assistance. You roll out of bed and eat a breakfast of food products created by companies whose farmers, processors, and management all have a stake in those corporations and take pride in their work. You take a shower knowing your water company is a regionally owned and operated, municipality-co-funded company with a trustee board representing diverse community members. There's a bill to pay on the kitchen table from the power company, but it's only a small amount because your dividend covers most of the cost this month. You shudder to think how gas and electric companies used to cause wildfires through neglected line maintenance and cost-cutting. Never again.

You're getting ready for work, combing your hair, tying your shoes. You're commuting to a company you've worked with for eight years, where you've been accruing an increasing profit share every year as part of your compensation package. At work today, there will be a lunchtime discussion to input into the plans for a new regional warehouse via the employee representatives on the board of the holding company. You were rotated into the committee last year, but now you know someone else is handling the board process, and you're grateful to defer to them and just give them your two cents.

One of your projects at work is going incredibly well because of a partnership with a local bank that is backed by the public bank of your region. The bank is co-owned by a few large trust-owned companies in your area and a larger banking group. The bank's governance includes a set of stakeholders with a balance of interests. Their loan terms will allow you to invest in more environmental sustainability measures for your project because the municipality has set up a muni-bond product to offer subsidies to businesses that invest in environmental impact mitigation. A healthy balance sheet backs the bond due to the creation of an Urban Wealth Fund at the local government level.

To end the day, you have a doctor's visit at 4 pm, so you'll leave early. Your healthcare package is managed by the HR company within the broader HoldCo. Your healthcare provider is structured as a purpose trust, and their number one priority is quality of care. Paying a portion of your premiums doesn't feel like extortion like it used to because your profit share in the HoldCo's insurance scheme means that when the shared services do well, you do well.

Part II –

Living Proof:
Case Studies

The Calvert Community Investment Note

Jay Standish

Summary

Operating since 1995, the Calvert Impact Group is one of the most important pioneers in socially responsible investing. Calvert Impact drives meaningful social and environmental change with a portfolio spanning nine impact sectors. In this piece, we will explore their flagship product, the Community Investment Note, a debt investment product that has channeled $2.5 billion over nearly 30 years. With a 100% lifetime investor repayment rate on the Note, the group has earned a trusty-worthy reputation through a conservative investment approach and rock-solid cash management.

The Community Investment Note is a retail financial product that anyone can buy from their brokerage account. The Notes provide below-market returns with full principal repayment upon maturity.

The Calvert Community Investment Note showcases how a nonprofit corporation can issue a public finance instrument to channel a significant amount of capital in advancing positive impact goals.

Key Characteristics:

- $2.5 Billion deployed over 30 years.
- Below market rate of return: 1-3% APR.
- Provides capital in the gap between market rate and philanthropy.
- Issued and managed by a nonprofit.

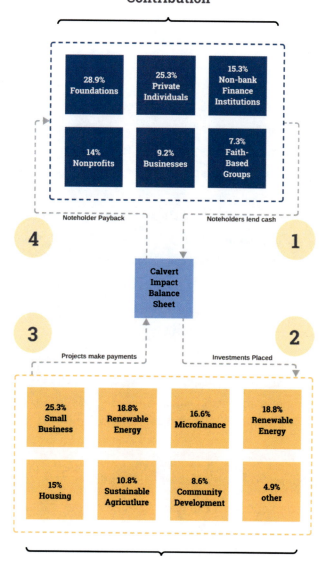

Capital Sources and Uses of the Calvert Community Note: Roughly 75% of capital is contributed by institutions, which is then invested across a variety of impact areas, both as debt and equity placements.

28 | Assets in Common

Context

Impact Investing

In the 1970s and '80s, the origins of the Socially Responsible Investing (SRI) movement emerged as activist investors sought to divest from companies complicit with social ills such as South African apartheid and the use of Agent Orange by U.S. forces in Vietnam. Over the last four decades, the concept has flourished and grown branches of related fields like Corporate Social Responsibility (CSR), Environmental, Social and Governance (ESG) factors, and Impact Investing.[9] While some branches of the SRI movement focus on activist investments in publicly traded companies, Calvert Impact Capital and their Community Investment Note are driven to provide capital to projects whose core mission is to make a positive impact. The Note bridges the chasm between market-rate investment and philanthropic grants.

The Community Investment Note is a form of Impact Investment that focuses more on private markets. Impact Investment funds are explicitly organized for the sole purpose of making impact-driven investments.[10] As a non-profit, Calvert Impact Capital makes investments in projects that have a business model but produce a below-market return. These projects don't need massive philanthropic grants to subsidize their operations, they just need patient capital that is willing to accept a lower return in exchange for the knowledge that the capital helped to make a positive impact.

The Many Faces of Calvert

Calvert Investments is one of the early pioneers of Socially Responsible investing. Calvert Investments, founded in 1976, began by offering mutual funds and other investment products focused on positive impact. In 1988, the founders of the Calvert Investment mutual funds launched the

---

9   Townsend, B. (2020a). From SRI to ESG: The Origins of Socially Responsible and Sustainable Investing. The Journal of Impact and ESG Investing, 1(1), 10–25. https://doi.org/10.3905/jesg.2020.1.1.010

10   Foroughi, J. (2022). ESG Is Not Impact Investing and Impact Investing Is Not ESG. Stanford Social Innovation Review. https://doi.org/10.48558/5K24-4Q54

non-profit Calvert Foundation (now renamed Calvert Impact) to make direct investments in underserved communities.

Calvert Investments was later rebranded as Calvert Research and Management, the for-profit group that manages mutual funds. It was purchased by Eaton Vance in 2017, which was then acquired by Morgan Stanley, so Calvert Research and Management is wholly owned by Morgan Stanley.[11]

While they share the same founders, Calvert Impact is legally independent of Calvert Research and Management. Calvert Impact, Inc. is the new parent of the Calvert Impact group, serving as the umbrella organization for multiple impact products, including the original Community Investment Notes issued by Calvert Impact Capital, Inc. and the Cut Carbon Note issued by Calvert Impact Climate, a new investment-grade security funding the greening of buildings.

For this case study, the balance sheet of Calvert Impact Capital is the most relevant, as the issuer of the Community Investment Notes.

Motivation

Driving Impact

The Note is an Impact Investing vehicle that makes direct investments into projects whose operation makes a positive social or environmental impact. The motivation for designing the Note is to put money to work to create more impactful outcomes in the world. Calvert Impact focuses on "impact additionality", meaning they try to invest in projects that may not otherwise attract capital. Thus, the Note fuels projects that are unlikely to happen without them, such that "additional impact" occurs due to Calvert Impact's investments. This doesn't mean their investees are weak or early stage, rather, it indicates their ideal projects don't match the criteria of other capital sources. Most commonly, traditional investment return expectations

---

11   Calvert. (2021, March 1). Morgan Stanley closes acquisition of Eaton Vance [Press release]. https://www.calvert.com/press-releases.php

are incompatible with the lower rate of return offered by these impact-driven enterprises.

Bridging the Chasm Between Market-Rate and Philanthropy

On one end of the spectrum, we have the massive world of for-profit, market-rate investing, where actors compete on a global stage to produce the highest returns possible inside an acceptable window of risk. On the other end of the spectrum, we have a relatively limited pool of philanthropic dollars available each year to drive charitable intentions. In between lies a chasm, projects that cannot produce market-rate returns, but also don't need free money from charities. The Note injects capital into that chasm, funding projects that are out of criteria for both philanthropies and market-rate investors. Many borrowers are projects working to bring financing to people and places currently underserved by capital markets.

Partial Philanthropy

As a nonprofit, Calvert Impact Capital operates the fund primarily to be of service, not as a scheme for money managers to earn fees. Buyers of the Community Investment Note can donate all or a portion of the interest payable on their Note. So, for buyers, instead of donating $1,000 to a charity and have their money put to work once, probably in a single year, that $1,000 can be used for multiple years, and then returned to them. Also, by placing capital into enterprises with underlying business models capable of returning capital, the Note amplifies durable, reliable approaches to creating impact that doesn't become dependent upon philanthropic grants.

How it Works

Structure + Scale

The Note is senior unsecured corporate debt issued by the non-profit Calvert Impact Capital, Inc. The Notes represent a general exposure to the balance sheet of Calvert Impact Capital as a whole. Essentially, you lend them money, and they can use it to invest in a wide array of socially impactful projects and companies. Although the Notes lack specific collateral, Calvert Impact Capital maintains over $150 million in capitalization through net assets, subordinated investments, and guarantees, safeguarding investors against potential portfolio losses.[12]

This retail product allows non-accredited investors to invest as little as $20, the Note's minimum. It can be bought directly from Calvert Impact Capital or through most brokerage accounts. Calvert used a clever legal structure, typically employed by churches, to be exempt from heavy SEC oversight and enable the public to invest. As a non-profit, Calvert Impact Capital can issue debt directly if it registers directly with each of the 50 states. About 26% of 2022's outstanding notes came from private individuals.

Terms

The Notes range in term from 1 to 5 years, and interest rates are fixed for each Note, and vary based on the rate environment when they were issued. The Notes are below-market-rate and have 6 months and 20 years, with interest rates from 1-5% (currently 3.5-5% as of early 2024). Interest-only payments are made annually, with a reinvestment option, with all principal repaid at the end of the term once the note has fully matured.[13]

Investment Program

Calvert Impact Capital invests in mature, mission-driven organizations with established track records, not risky startups. Their investment strategy includes both debt and equity investments in both for-profit and nonprofit entities. They invest half their capital in the U.S. and half internationally. As of Q4 2023, the Note had 95 active investments across 113 countries.[14]

There are 9 impact sectors in the Note's $520M impact investing portfolio of Q4 2023, with: Microfinance (15% of portfolio), Health (1.3%),

---

12   Jain, V. (2006). Investing in Change. Stanford Social Innovation Review, 4(1), 61–63. https://doi.org/10.48558/5VVX-P595

13   Calvert Community Investment Note. https://calvertimpact.org/investing/community-investment-note

14   Calvert Community Investment Note Portfolio.https://calvertimpact.org/investing/portfolio/community-investment-note-portfolio

Education (0.2%), Community Development (8.1%), Affordable Housing (18.1%), Renewable Energy (20.7%), Sustainable Agriculture (5.3%), Environmental Sustainability (2.5%) and Small Business (28.8%).

Balance Sheet Breakdown

As of the end of 2022, the entire balance sheet of Calvert Impact Capital had assets of $660 million, 58% of which was invested as debt and 18% as equity, with about 22% in cash and equivalents and 2% miscellaneous. The Notes amount to a meaningful portion of that balance sheet, but the group has other sources of capital.[15]

Cash Flow Highlights	2022	2021	2020	2019	2018
Notes issued	$ 108,499,371	$ 172,334,590	$ 183,306,940	$ 142,883,710	$ 91,349,071
Notes redeemed	$ (142,382,298)	$ (114,353,400)	$ (107,549,435)	$ (96,633,092)	$ (61,507,183)

Balance Sheet Highlights and Selected Data	2022	2021	2020	2019	2018
Cash, cash equivalents, CD's and readily marketable securities	$ 144,630,310	$ 176,181,661	$ 196,382,868	$ 115,418,721	73,886,116
Total loans receivable, net ("Portfolio-related investments")	$ 383,816,693	$ 400,815,427	$ 351,544,086	$ 349,405,849	342,063,384
Total Portfolio Investments	$ 116,961,233	$ 92,214,334	$ 54,939,181	$ 60,508,738	52,264,178
Amount of unsecured/unguaranteed loans receivable	$ 196,563,326	$ 248,843,183	$ 201,644,351	$ 195,278,796	174,837,111
Percent of unsecured/unguaranteed loans receivable	49%	48%	57%	55%	50%
Delinquencies – 30 Days	$ 165,465	$ 0	$ 4,000,000	$ 517,806	$ 0
30-Day Delinquency Rate	0.04%	0.00%	1.13%	0.15%	0.00%
Delinquencies – 90+ Days	$ 7,421,428	$ 4,000,000	$ 0	$ 0	$ 1,061,073
90+-Day Delinquency Rate	1.93%	1.00%	0.00%	0.00%	0.30%
Loan delinquencies (total)	$ 7,586,893	$ 4,000,000	$ 4,000,000	$ 517,806	$ 1,061,073
Total Loan delinquencies and Loans in Non Accrual Status	$12,414,030	$10,791,842	$6,000,000	$517,806	$1,061,073
Loan delinquencies and Non Accrual Rate	3.12%	2.63%	1.67%	0.15%	0.30%
Total Assets	$ 660,206,073	$ 680,509,844	$ 614,888,662	$ 533,806,306	475,670,717
Total Notes Payable	$ 556,510,674	$ 593,496,911	$ 532,342,148	$ 457,460,714	410,102,873
Amount of Notes redeemed during the fiscal year	$ (142,382,298)	$ (114,353,400)	$ (107,549,435)	$ (96,633,092)	$ (61,507,183)
Other long-term debt: Subordinated loans payable	$ 25,350,000	$ 20,350,000	$ 18,169,525	$ 13,169,525	9,169,525
Other long-term debt: Refundable and recoverable grants	$ 12,300	$ 12,300	$ 12,300	$ 108,800	418,800
Total Liabilities	$ 599,781,680	$ 622,377,707	$ 558,497,913	$ 478,425,225	426,378,834
Net Assets	$ 60,424,393	$ 58,132,137	$ 56,390,749	$ 55,381,081	49,291,883

Investee Highlights

The largest borrower in Calvert Impact Capital's portfolio is Benefit Chicago, a $100 million community development fund tackling economic inequality. In 2022, Calvert Impact Capital had $45 million in outstanding loans to the

---

15   Calvert Impact Capital, Inc (May 16, 2023.). Supplement to Prospectus https://assets.ctfassets.net/4oaw9man1yeu/35fnMQFEiRqGkXtQRedpMU/ 86bafbd082558a7535c241043fc650b8/cic-community-investment-note-prospectus.pdf

fund which is a partnership between the MacArthur Foundation, Calvert Impact Capital, and The Chicago Community Trust. It invests in underserved entrepreneurs through business loans, enables affordable housing, and backs CDFIs (Community Development Financial Institutions) bringing financial institutions to underserved populations.

Calvert Impact Capital's second-largest investment of $18 million is in Cut Carbon Notes issued by their sustainability-focused sister nonprofit, Calvert Impact Climate. These investment-grade rated secured notes are earmarked for upgrading commercial buildings to reduce carbon emissions.[16]

Beyond the U.S., a $13M loan has been made to a bank in Costa Rica to provide business loans to small and sustainable businesses.

Takeaways

Low Risk, Low Return

The Community Investment Note doesn't pretend to be a competitive investment that will make you independently wealthy. They market themselves as a way to put your cash to work toward good causes and keep up with inflation. They have been issuing the notes since 1995 and have shown a 100% repayment record of principal and interest. As a debt product, investors provide capital that is deployed by professional managers into projects driving real impact, and generating regular earnings. Remarkably, Calvert has responsibly invested over half a billion dollars into initiatives that drive real change. The Community Investment Note allows investors to earn a return while aligning their capital with honorable causes.

Boring is Sexy when it's Long-Term and Large Scale

Calvert Impact Capital's nearly 30-year portfolio is a testament to investing in unheralded efforts driving environmental and social progress. Over

---

16   Calvert Impact Climate, Inc. (September 15, 2023) PROSPECTUS. Cut Carbon Notes. https://assets.ctfassets.net/4oaw9man1yeu/7rrKq8UBmXrZup5s34b nel/70321b12136877882f89662a00eb9459/Calvert_Cut_Carbon_Notes_-_ Preliminary_Prospectus_9.15.23__exhibit_attached_.pdf

34 | Assets in Common

the history of the Note, Calvert Impact Capital has invested $2.5 billion into initiatives like solar projects, affordable housing developments, and small business lending programs — unglamorous work that takes years or decades to come to fruition. In the last 5 years, the note balance has grown by 36%, a testament to the reputation that Calvert Impact has earned.

Building an Institutional Track Record

Calvert Impact has focused on the fundamentals of a safe balance sheet, and delivering consistent, long-term results to foster trust with investors and borrowers. The risk rationale for the investment is built on the proven institutional trustworthiness of Calvert Impact, as well as its conservative investment approach and responsible capital management policies. With a 99% repayment rate from borrowers, Calvert Impact Capital has responsibly managed its finances to be able to absorb some losses and still have a 100% repayment rate to its investors. Calvert Impact Capital maintains a minimum 10% liquidity buffer on its balance sheet. It holds plenty of cash, cash equivalents, and readily marketable securities in reserve to pay out old loans coming to maturity, and to buffer any losses from any underperforming borrowers.

Once considered "nonstandard assets", the Community Investment Notes gained mainstream accessibility in 2005 when included in standard electronic securities clearinghouses. Now, investors can purchase these notes through brokerage accounts, consolidating their socially responsible investments alongside other assets.

Clegg Auto: A Steward Ownership Transition

Jay Standish

Summary

Clegg Auto is a group of four auto repair shops in Utah. It transitioned to employee ownership in August 2022 using a Perpetual Purpose Trust (PPT) structure.[17] In just their first year post-transition, the group of businesses doubled profits, had their highest customer satisfaction ever, and increased employee satisfaction, all while distributing record profit sharing with employees. The CEO, Kevin Clegg, had envisioned this transition for years prior and was motivated by the social impact of employee ownership. The cultural rollout and communicating the "ownership-mindset" were critical in the performance results of the transition. This is an example of how an existing company with multiple locations can convert to employee ownership. Clegg retained the original CEO and exited the founder at a fair price while allowing employees to participate in the business's success.

---

17   Price, D. (2023, June 5). A Utah auto shop demonstrates a pathway to worker ownership via a perpetual purpose trust. ImpactAlpha. https://impactalpha .com/a-utah-auto-shop-demonstrates-a-pathway-to-worker-ownership-via-a-perpetual-purpose-trust/

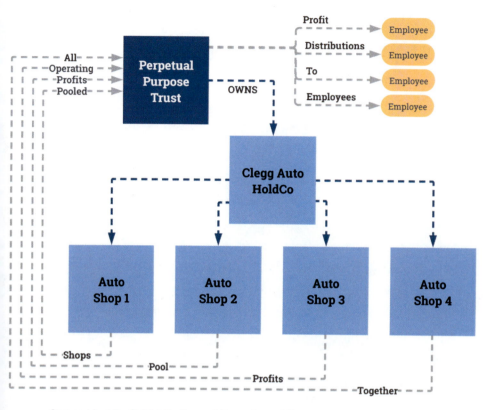

Ownership + Profit Distributions of Clegg Auto: A Perpetual Purpose Trust owns a holding company which subsequently owns the auto shops. Employees receive profit distributions quarterly and have elected to split profits equally rather than based on shop performance.

Context

Two brothers, Steve and Kevin Clegg, started their first auto repair shop in 1998. After the success of the first shop, Kevin went to graduate school and furthered his career in HR and leadership roles. In 2012, he returned to the business and eventually took over as CEO. The company grew to 3 auto shops and 1 body shop in Utah.

Perpetual Purpose Trusts are a form of trust that exists to fulfill a certain purpose, rather than financially reward individuals as the beneficiaries.[18] Most trusts have a limited shelf-life, while PPTs can exist indefinitely. This makes them a great tool for ensuring and institutionalizing the mission or purpose of an organization. There are many ways to set up a PPT and broad flexibility in defining their purpose. Like in the case of Clegg, PPTs can be designed as de facto worker ownership models, whereby the dividends of the company are directed to workers, while the actual stock ownership of the company is held by the trust.[19]

Motivation

Early on when Steve brought Kevin in to run the businesses, Kevin was clear about his long-term goals: to eventually transition the businesses to employee ownership.

Kevin has a background in HR and is a "people person" driven to serve and support the development of those around him. In 2021, with a track record of growing the businesses, including being named the Top Auto Repair Shop in Utah Valley for six years, Kevin began to explore their options to become employee-owned. Kevin initially explored the Employee Stock Ownership Plan (ESOP) and worker co-op structures but found issues with both. ESOPs were too expensive to set up and would require a lot more ongoing compliance headaches. Worker cooperatives tended to have pre-baked governance models that weren't a fit for Clegg. He eventually discovered the purpose trust structure. Which was a better fit due to its flexibility, ability to customize incentive structures, and ability to ensure that the business would remain employee-owned over the long term.[20]

---

18   Team, P. (2021, July 22). Understanding the perpetual purpose trust — purpose. Purpose. https://www.purpose-us.com/writing/whats-a-perpetual-purpose-trust

19   Bove, A. A., Jr, & Langa, M. (2021). The Perpetual Business Purpose trust: the business planning vehicle for the future, starting now. ACTEC Law Journal, 47(1), 3. https://scholarlycommons.law.hofstra.edu/acteclj/vol47/iss1/3

20   Zoe Schlag, personal communication, January 30, 2024

"Back when I re-partnered up with my brother, it was important that what we built was for all of our people. When I watched different transactions in the corporate world take place I was left almost every time with the feeling that when businesses transact... the people that usually benefit the least are the most important and that's the employees and the customers." [21]

-Kevin Clegg

How it Works

Prior to the employee ownership transition, each shop had distinct owner-ship structures. Key employees at each of the shops had minority equity stakes as management incentives, and all but one of these managers elected to roll their equity into the purpose trust.

Restructuring Ownership

The new ownership structure has three layers. At the top is the Perpetual Purpose Trust, which is functionally the sole shareholder of a HoldCo. This HoldCo then has subsidiaries which are each of the shops.

The ownership structure was designed for smart incentives at multi-ple levels – incentivizing the performance of the individual subsidiaries, as well as the overall holding company. One mechanism through which this plays out is the profit-sharing scheme, which allows managers to adjust how profits are shared both at the level of the HoldCo and at the level of the individual subsidiaries.

For instance, if one garage brought in more profit than the other, its employees would receive higher dividends commensurate with their contribution to earnings. While profit sharing with employees is codified and protected by the trust, its specific allocation pattern is determined by management, to accommodate for long-term dynamism and growth.

---

21   Interview with Kevin Clegg from Clegg Auto: From Family-Owned to Employee-Owned (Z. Schlag, Interviewer). (2023, August 31). [Video]. Common Trust.https://www.common-trust.com/exits/ clegg-auto-transition-to-employee-ownership

This flexibility was an important feature to Kevin Clegg and came into play in their first year as an EOT, due to how the business performance and profit-sharing allocations played out, one of the businesses would have distributed significantly less than the other three. The leadership team enlisted the support of key leaders across the four businesses to discuss how to handle the situation, and the teams unanimously requested that profits be shared equally across all four businesses due to the fact that they were "in this together".[22]

Performance Uplifted in First Year, Post-Transition

One year after the transition, Clegg has doubled the profits of the previous year.[23] It's important to note that the group had two auto shops shift from being young "startups" to becoming profitable. For a fairly small group of companies with 55 employees that had previously seen steady but slower growth, this is a major increase in a single year. Kevin attributes this performance surge to the impact of employee ownership, not just on the company's operations but on the quality of service delivered. Once employees truly stepped into the role of owners, he watched as they took a level of ownership on the floor to find efficiencies and improve quality in a way he hadn't seen in the two decades prior. In contrast to other buyout approaches like private equity, which often rely on layoffs and cost-cutting measures that can compromise quality, Clegg Auto's employee-ownership model aligned incentives and yielded equal or superior performance gains.

These profit increases were not at the customer's expense. In the first year under employee direction, the company also posted the highest customer satisfaction ratings in its history. The company also rolled out health insurance to all employees, which is rare in the industry for auto technicians.

---

22   Kevin Clegg, Personal Communication, March 17th, 2024

23   Schlag, Z. (2024, April). Clegg Auto doubles profit after shift to employee ownership. Common Trust. https://www.common-trust.com/blog/clegg-autos-employee-ownership-trust-benefits-for-employees

"Our last full year (2021) prior to going employee-owned we did about 500k of profit. [In] our transition year (2022) we spiked to about 1 million in profit. And our first full year (2023) as employee-owned was about 1.3 million in profit." – Kevin Clegg[24]

Takeaways

Leadership + Culture

Clegg has fostered an inclusive leadership style, even telling the staff that an employee buyout was in the works before the deal was ironed out. Clegg has emphasized "200% accountability" where team members are accountable to themselves and to each other. This underlies a genuine culture of teamwork, which is further reinforced by employee profit sharing. No one wants to be the weakest link in the chain, because their performance actually impacts the financial outcomes for their coworker's family.

"You have to commit 100% for your own actions and behaviors to own your life...then you commit the other 100% to those you are in the program with, to support them in their own personal desire to own their lives. If you see them doing something contrary to what is expected...you need to be curious and ask them about it and support them in living up to the changes required to have accountability." – Kevin Clegg[25]

Seller Evangelism

Kevin Clegg came from an HR background and wanted to pursue employee ownership from when he first joined the company. As a genuine evangelist for the social merits of employee ownership, Kevin's initial interest in employee ownership is largely tied to the benefits of employee ownership to workers. For instance, employees at employee-owned firms have 33% higher wages, on average[26], and 4x greater access to childcare, compared

---

24   Kevin Clegg, personal communication, March 17th, 2024

25   Kevin Clegg, personal communication, March 17th, 2024

26   National Center for Employee Ownership. (2017). Employee Ownership & Economic Well-Being. https://www.ownershipeconomy.org/wp-content/uploads/2017/05/employee_ownership_and_economic_wellbeing_2017.pdf

to their non-employee-owned peers.[27] Only later did Kevin discover the research on the performance benefits of employee ownership, and just in the last year did he experience those himself.

Mindset or Incentives – What Drives Performance?

Unlike extrinsic motivation which is about offering carrots to entice people to perform, intrinsic motivation is based on internal feelings, meaning, satisfaction, and relationships. In the case of Clegg, a significant portion of the doubling of profits was due to two shops maturing from the "startup" phase to profitability. But the increase still marks a notable uplift, and the improved morale of the team has undeniably improved the operations of the company.

---

27   Kevin Clegg, personal communication, March 17th, 2024

Credit Union Service Organizations

Jay Standish

Summary

A Credit Union Service Organization (CUSO) is a third-party entity that is formed to support and enhance the offerings of credit unions. They range in function from pooling capital for larger investments, to expanding member services, reducing operational costs, and increasing revenue. As of 2021, roughly 42% of all credit unions participated in a CUSO, with about $4B invested.[28] As of January 2024, there were 1,066 CUSOs registered in the US[29]

CUSOs allow small credit unions to band together and compete against big banks.

They provide a way for credit unions to pool resources, lower costs, and offer more services to their members. They also allow credit unions to partner with capital sources outside of member deposits.

This case study provides an overview of the CUSO concept, history and use in the United States. In most cases, CUSOs provide shared services – a concept we've explored later in this book.

Common CUSO Functions:

- Technology + IT Solutions
- Loan Origination + Servicing

---

[28] K. Wrapp, M. (2021). The Next Generation CUSO: New CUSO Models for Growth and innovation (No. 554). Filene Research Institute. https://www.filene.org/reports/the-next-generation-cuso-new-cuso-models-for-growth-and-innovation

[29] NCUA CUSO Registry Search. (2024, January). NCUA. https://cusoregistry.ncua.gov/Search/Search

- Regulatory Compliance + Risk Management
- Human Resources + Staff Training
- Marketing + Business Development
- Shared Branches + ATM Networks
- Payment Processing + Card Services
- Investment + Wealth Management
- Insurance + Benefits Solutions
- Legal + Consulting Services

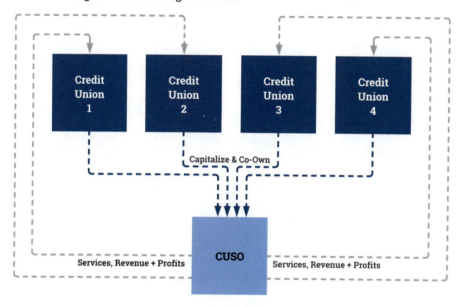

Typical Structure of a CUSO: Multiple credit unions make capital contributions to become members of a CUSO. The CUSO runs specialty operations that benefit members, and financial returns may come in the form of cost savings, cash distributions or both.

Context

Credit unions are nonprofit banks. In the U.S., they have been federally provisioned and regulated since President Franklin Delano Roosevelt signed them into law in 1934. In 2023, there were over 4,604 credit unions in the

U.S., with a combined balance sheet of $2.26 trillion.[30] For comparison, Goldman Sachs had assets of around $1.64 trillion as of March 2024.

Most credit unions are small, local, operations that lack the scale and resources of large commercial banks. Despite their modest size, credit unions must find ways to meet all their members' banking needs to stay competitive with for-profit banks.

Motivation

CUSOs are used to solve different types of problems. Most are created by either a single credit union or a collaborative group of multiple credit unions facing similar problems. However, some CUSOs are founded by independent entrepreneurs seeking to partner with the credit union industry.

New Revenue Streams

In the 1990s and 2000s, rising operating costs and dropping interest rates made it challenging for credit unions to sustain themselves solely on deposit interest. New regulations in 1987 allowed credit unions to work with broker-dealers through CUSOs, which they were barred from doing directly. As a result, the use of CUSOs increased greatly in the 90s. CUSOs became a vehicle for credit unions to earn additional revenue through networking arrangements with investments and insurance broker-dealers.[31]

Through an investment CUSO, credit unions can receive a share of commissions from brokers/dealers for insurance or investment sales. These are also relevant services that credit unions want to offer to their members. So, investment CUSOs serve to extend the credit union's business model – providing more customer value and earning more income.

---

30   National Credit Union Administration. (2024, March 12). Credit union assets and delinquencies grow in the fourth quarter [Press release]. NCUA. https://ncua.gov/newsroom/press-release/2024/credit-union-assets-and-delinquencies-grow-fourth-quarter

31   Messick, G. (n.d.). Credit Union Service Organizations ("CUSOs"). NACUSO. https://www.nacuso.org/wp-content/uploads/2018/02/History-of-CUSOs-2-7-18.pdf

Expanding Product + Service Offerings to Members

Many credit unions partner with CUSOs to offer more financial services to their members, most commonly business lending, home mortgage lending, and auto lending. A small credit union with a staff of five would not have the time or the expertise to underwrite risk for three very different kinds of loans. Instead, they would typically outsource the underwriting and operational processes to a CUSO that specializes in issuing loans of a given type. Since a CUSO can receive capital from multiple credit unions as well as take on outside capital, each member credit union benefits from this broader access to capital. This way, a small credit union can provide loans to its members it otherwise would not have been able to fund on its own.

Partnering for Specialty Expertise

The rise of online banking presented a significant challenge for credit unions. Developing a secure online banking platform is a complex and costly endeavor, requiring sophisticated systems capable of conducting financial transactions securely. Most small credit unions lacked the resources to build such systems independently. CUSOs emerged as a popular way for a group of credit unions to share in the cost of building and maintaining modern tools for digital finance. In addition to IT expertise, CUSOs are used to access consulting underwriting, research, legal, and compliance expertise.

Reducing Operating Costs

With the rising cost of labor and the increase in financial regulation, operating costs have increased for credit unions. Credit unions can outsource some of their operations and back-office functions to CUSOs. Some of these services include loan document processing, customer call centers, and database management. Although a few CUSOs offer a comprehensive suite of back-office services, most credit unions assemble an "a la carte" stack of services from specialized CUSO vendors.

Beyond operational support, CUSOs enable credit unions to reduce costs by accessing economies of scale and leveraging the expertise of specialized teams focused on driving efficiency improvements.

How it Works

Structure + Ownership

The most common structure for a CUSO is a for-profit LLC, but a range of structures are deployed. To qualify as a CUSO, they must be majority-owned by credit unions. Some CUSOs are only owned by one credit union, others by multiple, and some CUSOs also have non-credit union minority owners. Based on 2018 data, it is estimated that 65% of these are wholly-owned by a single credit union and the remaining 35% are owned by multiple credit unions. The initial investment from a credit union into a single CUSO cannot be greater than 1% of that credit union's capital surplus, but it can make additional investments of a greater amount.

Some CUSOs focus more on driving cost savings to their members than producing a dividend. Others are structured as cooperatives, with one-member-one-vote governance policies to ensure smaller credit unions have a voice.

Regulation

While for-profit banks are regulated by the FDIC and other departments, credit unions are regulated by the National Credit Union Administration (NCUA). The NCUA's purview extends to CUSOs as well, effectively regulating how credit unions can interact with these organizations.

The activities expressly permitted for CUSOs are:

- Checking and currency services
- Clerical, professional, and management services
- Electronic transaction services
- Financial counseling services
- Fixed asset services
- Insurance brokerage or agency
- Leasing
- Loan support services
- Record retention, security and disaster recovery services

- Securities brokerage services
- Shared credit union branch (service center) operations
- Travel agency services
- Trust and trust-related services
- Real estate brokerage services
- Loan origination, including originating, purchasing, selling, and holding any type of loan permissible for Federal credit unions to originate[32]

Large CUSO Examples

PSCU Services

Originally called Payment Systems for Credit Unions, PSCU was founded in 1977 by five credit unions. PSCU primarily offers online banking software, ATM management systems, and cardholder support call centers. It was already the largest CUSO in the country before merging with Co-op Solutions (formerly, CO-OP Financial Services) in 2023. The combined organization has over 5,000 employees and $1.3 billion in annual revenue.

CO-OP Financial Services

Co-op has an ATM network with over 30,000 locations. By comparison, Bank of America has around 15,000 locations in the US.[33] Credit Union members of Co-op gain access to these ATMs, allowing customers access to cash in a much broader geography than if each credit union only directly serviced a few local ATMs. Co-op also provides many other services, like credit and debit card network Point of Sale (POS) transactions and shared branch support. This shared branch arrangement allows customers of one credit union to do business at the branch of another credit union.

---

32   CUSO Activities. (2022, March 2). NCUA. https://ncua.gov/regulation-supervision/cuso-activities

33   ATM Network. Co-op Solutions. https://www.coop.org/Solutions/Engage/Co-op-ATM-Network

Takeaways

Evolution of Use

Prior to the 1980s, CUSOs were rare. The first wave of meaningful adoption was really as a legal workaround, allowing credit unions to indirectly contract with brokers-dealers through CUSOs, which they were prohibited from doing directly.[34] This initial use case was also driven by the increased revenues achieved through referral fees to these same third-party brokers and insurance companies.

The second wave of CUSO activity was driven by a desire to lower operating costs. CUSOs were repurposed as a shared services vehicle for collaboration across multiple credit unions. Call centers, lending due diligence, and back-office compliance work could increasingly be "outsourced" to a specialized CUSO.

The third CUSO wave arose from a need to deliver a modern, digital-friendly customer experience akin to commercial banks. Credit unions turned to CUSOs to jointly access sophisticated and expensive digital banking systems, digital payment reconciliation, ATM logistics, and other complex technology required to remain relevant and competitive. Even venture-backed fintech companies started to spin up special CUSOs to cater to the credit union community as a customer segment.

Barriers + Challenges

A key inherent strategic risk for credit unions is that when they use a CUSO, they are entrusting a critical function to an outside entity. In many cases, this is addressed by the CUSO being owned and governed by its constituent credit union. However, for very large CUSOs like PSCU/Co-op, smaller credit unions have a limited individual say in customizing major nationwide digital systems. Instead, they must rely on the collective voice of the sector to shape these nationwide platforms.

---

34   That legal discrepancy has since been cleared, and credit unions can work directly with broker/dealers now.

Consolidation challenges small credit unions and a mixed bag for CUSOs. While CUSOs can aid small credit unions to survive by banding together and sharing costs, the growth of larger credit unions could result in a decreased need for multi-stakeholder CUSOs.

Collaborative Culture

Credit unions are typically very collaborative, driven in part by their non-profit status. Despite competing as an entire industry against large banks, they foster internal collaboration. It is rare to see an industry collaborate so closely across organizations and implement such deep shared operations and financial investments. It begs the question of whether other industries would be more collaborative if the firm-level profit motive was less of a dominant driver.

Bank consolidation is rampant, and the credit union industry is not immune. However, CUSOs can help buck the trend by making it easier for small credit unions to band together to lower costs and expand member services and offerings.

Shared Services Cooperatives

Most CUSOs are prime examples of shared services cooperatives. This is particularly true for CUSOs owned and managed by multiple credit unions, formed jointly to lower operating costs, outsource back office functions, and share technology expenses. From this vantage point, PSCU/COOP may even represent one of the largest shared services cooperatives in the U.S.

Application Toward Infrastructure for Shared Ownership

Steward Ownership HoldCos (discussed later in this book) could partner with credit unions to launch a CUSO fund that provides working capital or equipment loans to portfolio businesses. Profitable steward-owned businesses could invest alongside credit unions in these CUSOs, recirculating their profits to promote the health of their peers.

Such a fund could also provide acquisition loans or even equity to companies looking to exit into steward ownership or employee ownership. With expertise in these models and equipped with the lending powers of a bank, CUSOs could play a major role in maturing the financial infrastructure needed to expand these purpose-driven enterprises.

Participating as an actor in networked organizations, such as multi-stakeholder cooperatives or keiretsu-like networks, the CUSO model offers insights into how financial shared services can enhance collaboration and mutual support among diverse entities. By addressing the unique banking and liquidity needs of concepts like keiretsu and multi-stakeholder cooperatives, the CUSO model could serve as a specialty banking partner to enable cross-organizational collaboration, and could even serve as the venue of a shared balance sheet.

Enspiral's Financial Commons

Chelsea Robinson

Disclosure: The author of this article has direct experience as a member of Enspiral.

Summary

Enspiral is a network of entrepreneurs and businesses connected with legal and financial infrastructure and shared services. The stated purpose of Enspiral is to get "more people working on stuff that matters"[35]. People in Enspiral help each other make money doing socially and environmentally positive work. Enspiral fosters personal development by enabling members to invest in each other's growth for long-term mutual benefit. The kinds of businesses operating within this network include software companies, professional services firms, design agencies, events companies, and more. Enspiral offers shared services that social entrepreneurs can access by becoming members.

In this case study, we focus on the financial model and virtual bank accounts used to run the network. A piece of software called My.Enspiral was one of multiple software products created for internal use within the network to track, allocate, loan, and transfer money within the network. If this case study piques your interest and you'd like to learn more about the history and evolution of Enspiral, you can do so via a book hosted at this link: betterworktogether.co.

Key attributes of this case study:

- Centralized legal and financial infrastructure for collective use
- Stewardship governance model with member-shareholders of an LLC
- Shared services for network members including office, legal, and accounting

---

35   Enspiral. https://www.enspiral.com/

- Unlocking overhead-reducing efficiencies
- Software and process design as an enabler of collaboration

"I don't care what you work on, whether it's climate change, global poverty, self management, social enterprise, planting trees, gender equality, decolonisation, or steady state economics. If your primary mission is to make the world a better place, your personal success is the reason Enspiral exists. There is a trickle of human energy going into the most important issues of our times. Enspiral exists to help turn that trickle into a river."

Joshua Vial, Founder of Enspiral.

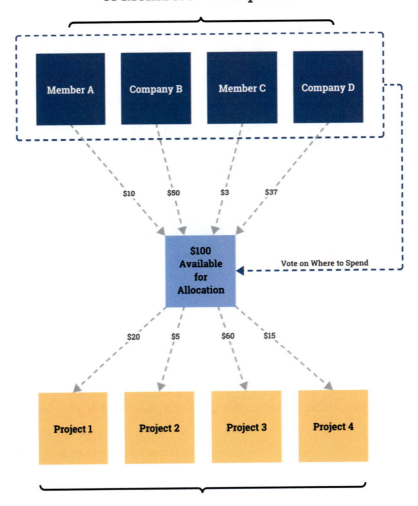

Fundable Projects Per Round

Enspiral Network's Project Funding: Enspiral offers services to its members (accounting, biz ops, office space, etc.). The members are both people and companies. Members contribute financially to a shared funding pool. After the costs of operating the network services are covered, the remaining funds are allocated to projects through "CoBudget".

Enspiral's Financial Commons | 57

Context

Enspiral was founded in Wellington, New Zealand in 2010. A that time there was an early but growing popular awareness of the climate crisis and other global issues, as part of the emerging polycrisis[36]. The 2010s were a decade when many young professionals became disenchanted with the traditional economy and were looking for ways to connect their professional lives to a greater sense of meaning. Offerings like international volunteering, giving 1% income to charity, hackathons such as Good For Nothing[37], and platforms listing impactful jobs like Escape the City[38] were becoming popular. Additionally, international uprisings such as the Occupy movement and the Arab Spring were inspiring new kinds of decentralized organizing. This wave of interest in making a difference fueled the growth and adoption of Enspiral's systems.

Simultaneously, building companies of the future was in vogue, and the availability of talent, tools, and passion for this was soaring. Publications like the Valve Employee Handbook[39] were circulating rapidly. Software-driven industries and open-source software communities were growing, and software developers were earning high compensation. The 'startup' craze had hit New Zealand and there were active discussions about how to make Wellington more like Silicon Valley without compromising values. Many professionals sought meaningful work that allowed them to create something impactful alongside like-minded peers. This coincided with the growing number of people who could command high hourly rates and give either their time or money surplus to an impactful project. Importantly,

---

36 Whiting, K., & Park, H. (2023, March 7). This is why "polycrisis" is a useful way of looking at the world right now. World Economic Forum. https://www.weforum.org/agenda/2023/03/polycrisis-adam-tooze-historian-explains/

37 Good for Nothing. https://goodfornothing.com/

38 Escape the City. http://www.escapethecity.org

39 Valve's Handbook for New Employee, https://www.valvesoftware.com/en/publications

software development became more accessible, enabling developers to swiftly create community-focused tools.

Motivation

> "I [was] searching for something I could not describe. I knew I couldn't go on doing "just a job", but I didn't know what was next for me. I wanted meaning and connection. I wanted to bring my whole self to work. I wanted to grow."
>
> Alanna Irving, Enspiral Member.

Joshua Vial, a senior software developer and serial entrepreneur, is the founder of Enspiral. At first, Enspiral was a self-managing services coop operating under an LLC wholly owned by Joshua called Enspiral Limited. As Enspial grew, it became less about a collective of individuals and more about offering infrastructure for a network of businesses and their respective employees. Alanna Irving and Joshua Vial were central to setting up the systems showcased in this article, and you'll hear both of their perspectives throughout.

Enspiral's growth was driven by diverse motivations that attracted a variety of participants. Some were professionals like bankers, accountants, and lawyers seeking a fulfilling career outside the extractive economy. Others were founders trying to build impact projects that needed support. Existing business owners joined for the sense of community and friendship gained by running companies alongside like-minded people. Outside the network, a wider group of interested allies emerged to partner with Enspiral out of admiration for the unique talent pool and approach. Government and corporate intrapreneurs were looking to partner with innovative allies and Enspiral became a preferred service provider for the delivery of new kinds of projects such as public-private partnerships. This wider group of allies often brought client projects to the network which allowed Enspiral to grow financially.

How it Works

"We consciously decentralise money, information and power, and use rich information systems to coordinate our actions. We borrow old social technologies from cooperative organising and integrate them with modern technologies to explore new ways of working together."

Joshua Vial, Founder of Enspiral

Legal Structures

As an ecosystem of businesses and professionals, Enspiral has had several legal arrangements over time. The core of the legal model creatively employs the highly programmable New Zealand LLC structure.

In 2010, Enspiral's corporate structure was a freelancer group offering digital and web services under Enspiral Limited. Enspiral Limited was a simple LLC owned by the founder Joshua Vial, who operated the entity on behalf of the group's uses and needs[40]. This worked due to the group trusting Josh to be a benevolent owner, working in everyone's best interests.

In 2011, they had grown to around 12 people and established another entity called the Enspiral Foundation, also an LLC[41]. The Enspiral Foundation was set up as a non-profit company (LLC with a charitable purpose, but without charitable status), and each 'member' was a co-owner who had one voting share. Ownership shares were a right to decision-making, not financial upside[42]

---

40   Basterfield, S., & Cabraal, A. (2018). Better Work Together. Enspiral Foundation. https://betterworktogether.co/

41   ENSPIRAL FOUNDATION LIMITED (3415611) Registered. (n.d.). New Zealand Companies Office Register. Retrieved April 9, 2024, from hhttps://app.compa niesoffice.govt.nz/companies/app/ui/pages/companies/3415611

42   I. Alanna. (2019) Evolving Enspiral. In Basterfield, S., & Cabraal, A. Better Work Together (p. 44). Enspiral Foundation. https://betterworktogether.co/

In 2012, Alanna and Josh changed the name of Enspiral Ltd to Enspiral Services, which delineated the Foundation and the Services company. The Foundation was responsible for the commons, culture, brand, and shared services of Enspiral members, and governed by them, while the freelancer services business had its own entity and management system.

The network grew to hundreds of people and multi-millions in annual revenue, and businesses emerged or joined as separate legal entities. Rather than all the companies being 'Enspiral' there was a shift towards all teams having their own brands. The "Enspiral Ventures" system was developed for businesses to opt into the shared services as businesses, and their employees could decide if they wanted to be part of the Enspiral community or not on their own terms. Enspiral Services, previously the only services firm in Enspiral, became just one of the multiple companies that were considered Enspiral Ventures, such as a major enterprise software firm (Ackama[43]), an accounting company (Fairground Accounting[44]), a SaaS company focussed on decision-making products (Loomio[45]) and more. Small teams that were operating inside the services entity grew and spun out to make their own entities, such as a design firm (Bamboo[46]), a business operations firm (Optimi[47]), and multiple management consulting companies (GreaterThan[48] and The Hum[49]). After seven years, Enspiral Services closed in favor of the growth and development of new and specialized businesses.

---

43   Ackama. https://www.ackama.com/who-we-are/our-story/

44   Fairground. https://fairground.co.nz/about-us/

45   Loomio. https://www.loomio.com/about

46   Bamboo Creative. https://www.bamboocreative.nz/

47   Optimi. https://www.optimi.co.nz/

48   Greaterthan. https://www.greaterthan.works/

49   The Hum. https://www.thehum.org/

Financial Commons

Enspiral's legal infrastructure has allowed people to complete efficient financial transactions inside the protection of the LLCs. Being a member of Enspiral includes financial interdependence, granting access to a collaboratively managed financial commons.

Accounting, invoices and payouts

Money comes into a central bank account. Everyone in the network would invoice from the Enspiral entity to their client via standard accounting software so that all clients were paying 'Enspiral'. However, rather than incoming funds being communal and shared evenly, all funds were tagged as belonging to those who brought those funds in. Alanna Irving, previously a Director of the Enspiral Foundation, explained this to us during an interview in October 2023, "Because all the money was coming into one bank account, we built a virtual account software to show whose money it was, which business unit or person it belonged to"[50]. When people were paid, they were paid as employees or contractors of one of the Enspiral entities. The employment contracts were very simple and did not have minimum hours, specific job descriptions, or other requirements. This meant many people could be employees and just occasionally draw funds. Enspiral built a bespoke accounting tool on top of their bank account to show who held what within the pool. This virtual account software was built on a weekend and was called My.enspiral.

Virtual banking

My.enspiral had a login for every 'Enspiralite', where each person could see how much money from the wider pool was theirs, how much was held by the group, and all invoice histories. My.enspiral was synced with the company bank account, its payroll system, and its accounting software to stay up to date. Transfers between virtual accounts were free and pre-tax due to the money moving virtually. A small team of people worked directly for the Enspiral Foundation as staff who managed this system and other systems like it. Enspiral Accounting (now called Fairground) ran the

---

50   Alanna Irving, Personal Communication, October 10th 2023.

accounting systems for Enspiral internally as a shared service for all, much like the accounting department of any large business. Enspiral Services and Enspiral Foundation both paid taxes and paying company taxes was a shared cost for all involved. Membership dues covered the costs of basic shared administrative overhead and could be scaled up voluntarily to reinvest in network infrastructure.

Paying for shared services

In the early days, members could choose to contribute between 5-50% of their income to Enspiral itself to cover the cost of the accounting and legal work, or to invest in network systems. This could change from invoice to invoice; it wasn't a set rate that had to remain constant. Some freelancers or business owners got most of their business because they were part of Enspiral. If you gained more income due to being in the network, you likely contributed a higher percentage than if you got your clients without Enspiral's brand or support. Some people gave more to the Foundation when they were making a strong profit margin and wanted to give a generous pre-tax allocation toward the enhancement of Enspiral Foundation activities. In more recent years, Enspiral has adopted a subscription model. An annual fee structure allows the network's operating costs to be reliably covered and enables what they call a 'stable core'. At the time of writing, there are three tiers of contribution: Coffee, Beer, and Pizza[51]. After core costs are covered, voluntary contributions are additional. "It should feel more like an enabling platform that you can leverage to extend what you can do in the world." – Anthony Cabraal[52].

Investing in priorities using software

Funds available over and above the cost of shared services were allocated collectively. There have been a variety of approaches to this, such as monthly allocation rounds, and annual strategy processes to determine

---

51   Welcome to Enspiral. (n.d.). Enspiral. https://welcome.enspiral.com/

52   Cabraal, A. (2019). Coffee, beer ,and pizza. In Basterfield, S., & Cabraal, A. Better Work Together (p. 184). Enspiral Foundation. https://betterworktogether.co/

high-level budget priorities. CoBudget[53] was created to aid the allocation of funds, and Loomio specializes in collaborative decision-making. These two apps, combined with My.enspiral and Slack, allowed for fully transparent financial management to be achieved across hundreds of people and tens of companies without central authority. A 2020 article describes the priorities that were getting well funded internally: public relations, marketing, internal grant-making for new projects, impact reporting, and events[54].

Shared Services

Enspiral offered services to reduce overhead. In addition to the legal and accounting systems, Enspiral has previously offered services such as office space, facilitation, event management, and graphic design. Having the strength of a fully developed institution created a resilient container for creativity and community. Smaller services include email addresses, web hosting, the right to be marketed through Enspiral's communications channels, access to work opportunities, Google Suite, and more. Shared services have particularly high value for small and new businesses. "We're a year in. We have no legal structure. All of our money has come through Enspiral Foundation and is paid to us through Enspiral Services as contractors. It's given us this bubble that we live in" – CoBudget Team, September 2015.[55]

---

53   Cobudget. https://cobudget.com/

54   Pick, F. (2020, March 2). Sharing power by sharing money: the evolution of collaborative funding in Enspiral. Medium. https://medium.com/enspiral-tales/sharing-power-by-sharing-money-the-evolution-of-collaborative-funding-in-enspiral-a56643e9cd3

55   OSCE & Enspiral. (2015, September 29). Structure, Decentralization, Community & Consulting – A discussion with Enspiral. Open Source Circular Economy Days. https://community.oscedays.org/t/structure-decentralization-community-consulting-a-discussion-with-enspiral/4162

Membership Benefits and Participation Structure

"Enspiral doesn't have jobs, but we've got lots of opportunities, and we find that the right people tend to hire themselves."

– Joshua Vial, Founder of Enspiral.

People relate to Enspiral at different levels of commitment and buy-in, so there are different ways to join. The following outline represents how Enspiral has operated for most of its existence. At the time of writing, the network is undergoing new changes to enable a more scalable approach across continents.

- <u>Ventures:</u> A company part of the network, which is approved to associate itself with Enspiral, and contributes financially to the Foundation.

- <u>Members:</u> Voting members of Enspiral Foundation are shareholders, and after one year of membership graduate to becoming 'stewards' who, together, can rewrite the constitution[56]. Members also pay a subscription for access to the same community and software that contributors access. Members/Stewards have additional private governance groups that Contributors do not access.

- <u>Contributors:</u> Contributors pay an annual subscription to access Slack, Loomio, Cobudget, Google Suite & Email, and have access to the opportunities in the network. Individuals choose to pay for a 'coffee, beer or pizza'[57] level of subscription, reflective of the individual's ability to pay.

- <u>Friends:</u> Friends of Enspiral may be employees of an Enspiral venture who don't want to be more formally involved, or a partner organization, or a friend, colleague,

---

56   Enspiral. (n.d.-b). Foundation Stewards, Enspiral Handbook. https://handbook.enspiral.com/agreements/foundation-stewards

57   Welcome to Enspiral. (n.d.). Enspiral. https://welcome.enspiral.com/

or family member of someone more formally involved in Enspiral. Friends are welcome to attend events and receive newsletters.

- <u>Joining and leaving:</u> To discover Enspiral, people typically attend events online or offline and then join as a Contributor. Members vote on new members. Every six months there is an opt-out opportunity for anyone to leave the system.

Takeaways

Long-Term Relationships at the Center

" 'Always put the relationship before the deal' has served me well. When all parties in a negotiation are genuinely putting the relationship first, it becomes so much easier. Whether subcontracting, splitting equity, or allocating tasks, it makes the concept of exercising power over others seem odd. How can there be any quality of relationship if one person is using sticks and carrots to influence the other's behaviour?"

– Joshua Vial, Founder of Enspiral

Emphasis on relationships was strong from day one. The culture of inter-dependence originated from working together. Winning and delivering high-quality work with a variety of friends and colleagues required strong interpersonal skills and self-awareness. The financial commons enabled people to financially support each other when times were tough. Joshua's example is that "By creating a community with clear boundaries and norms, I could create a bubble where helping people unconditionally is normal. A high-trust, small-scale ecosystem takes a specific set of skills to manage, but I can't imagine working any other way." Alanna explained that "trust was important to maintaining this network. To unify the network, retreats were held twice a year to build rapport and trust and mutual awareness and relationships. These were intimate conferences of ideas and new ways to enhance the network."

Enlightened Self-Interest to Raise All Boats

Efficiency and competitive advantage are frequently seen as antithetical to other values like inclusiveness, transparency, and participation. Enspiral embodies the philosophy of enlightened self-interest[58] and a culture that integrates cooperative and competitive values systems. This explains behavior where a short-term gain may be sacrificed for the benefit of a long-term relationship that is expected to reap untold benefits. In Enspiral, the kinds of benefits and profits that motivate members are positive outcomes for the community, environment, and economic development. Collective benefit is seen as increasing personal benefit. People in Enspiral help each other make money doing good work and pitch into the group to experience the benefits of indirect reciprocity. This also creates a culture of personal development, where people invest in each other's growth for mutual benefit in the long-term.

A Feedback Loop Between Software and Culture

A notable feedback loop existed between Enspiral culture development and software creation. Cultural processes, designed by facilitators and administrators caught developers' attention, who could see ways to make those processes simple and repeatable with web tools. Software allowed processes to become sustainable and normative in the network and reduced the effort required to get members to use complex spreadsheets or long meetings to participate in decisions and allocations. Additionally, keeping these tools as simple as possible made them more successful. Rather than employing complementary currencies or web3 tools, the network served as an alpha tester for fast, inexpensive, minimum viable web2 apps. Loomio and Cobudget have gone on to become well-loved in the cooperative movement and participatory budgeting movement. Enspiral created these tools not just for internal use, but also to enable broader shifts towards transparency and collaboration in business culture globally. The tools are

---

58   Wikipedia contributors. (2024). Enlightened self-interest. https://en.wikipedia.org/wiki/Enlightened_self-interest

available for public use and are supplemented with detailed guidebooks and other information[59][60].

Operational & Risk Tolerant Leadership

Complex legal and financial projects, like Enspiral, require operational creativity and talented administrative leadership. Talented operations leaders pragmatically tackled intricate issues, rigorously handling matters like taxation and liquidity ratios to find win-wins between ideals and regulations. Creating alternative legal structures often necessitated individuals like founder Joshua Vial taking on legal liabilities by signing documents interfacing with the traditional economy, modeling generosity and trust through risk-buffering behavior.

In Enspiral's non-hierarchical environment, leadership manifested through action, convening, and organizing – a strong composition of leadership styles across the network allowed different strengths to benefit the whole system. There is a positive feedback loop between visionary and operational leadership which most traditional authorities squash by privileging compelling narratives over implementation and evidence. Enspiral developed sophisticated stances on leadership internally, to reduce the dichotomy between dreamers and doers[61].

Challenges with the Commons

Significant challenges emerged in the development of Enspiral's infrastructure. Here are a few worth noting:

- Brand commons: Managing a shared brand with multiple different kinds of businesses all operating under the same name increased the risk for all involved. If one client

---

59   Enspiral. (n.d.-a). Collaborative funding, Enspiral handbook. https://handbook. enspiral.com/money/collabfunding

60   CoBudget. (n.d.). How to run a kick-ass cobudget round. https://guide. collaborativefunding.org/

61   Irving, A. (2016, January 15). Full Circle Leadership. Medium. https://medium.com/enspiral-tales/ beyond-dreamers-vs-doers-full-circle-leadership-869557da1248

had a bad experience, it disproportionately affected other businesses.

- Legal structure implying centralization: People did not always find it easy to understand that it's not a corporation with central leadership even though there are central legal entities that govern common assets.

- Cultural and Personal Readiness: Some people were not ready to collaboratively govern. Collaboration and decision-making about shared finances requires a high level of comfort in talking about personal finances. These topics that have traditionally been private for many people, like discussing income levels or savings, were growth edges for many.

- Mission drift: As the founding group gave power away and diluted their decision-making power, there was less entrepreneurial leadership over time. In the almost 15 years of operating, Enspiral has become more oriented to mutual support and less about building new companies to add to the Ventures ecosystem.

- Services companies needing leadership: While internal shared services companies were essential, they were also understaffed and treated as an afterthought. "That issue—tragedy of the commons, essentially—is the same reason we never excelled at running our coworking office, Enspiral Space. Although good people did a lot of work to keep it going, no one was super passionate about it as their main venture. Enspiral Services and Enspiral Space provided critical functions in the network and benefited a lot of people, but they were no one's baby." – Alanna Irving

Recognizing the Privileged Context

New Zealand is a unique context to create collaborative business infrastructure. In New Zealand, 95% of companies are considered small to medium-sized businesses[62]. The business culture has a strong can-do attitude which is a source of pride, where business owners create innovative new solutions to hard problems continuously due to resource constraints[63]. New Zealand is also a bicultural nation: The founding document of the country is Te Tiriti o Waitangi / The Treaty of Waitangi, a treaty between indigenous Māori and the Crown of England[64]. This co-governance constitutional environment has allowed New Zealanders to integrate and learn from Māori approaches to community leadership.

New Zealand is ranked number 1 in the world for ease of doing business according to the World Bank due to streamlined systems[65]. New Zealand also has several major welfare programs such as universal accident coverage (ACC)[66] which make the country a far less litigious and risk-averse business environment, since the downside is often buffered by the government. Simply being a remote island has also engendered a strong culture of mutualism and interdependence.

During our interview, Alanna also pointed out that there is less VC capital circulating in New Zealand, so start-up culture itself is more frequently focused on bootstrapping and cooperation. She also pointed out that New Zealand has one of the highest rates of volunteering and charitable sector size in the world, indicating a general cultural leaning toward giving back and helping each other. These factors should be considered

---

62   Wikipedia contributors. (2024). Largest Firms. In List of Companies in New Zealand. https://en.wikipedia.org/wiki/List_of_companies_of_New_Zealand

63   Motovated. (n.d.). The genesis of Kiwi ingenuity. Retrieved April 7, 2024, from https://www.motovated.co.nz/genesis-kiwi-ingenuity/

64   The Treaty in brief. (2017, May 17). NZHistory. https://nzhistory.govt.nz/politics/treaty/the-treaty-in-brief

65   Wikipedia contributors. (2024). Ranking. In Ease of doing business index. https://en.wikipedia.org/wiki/Ease_of_doing_business_index#Ranking

66   Overview of the ACC Scheme. (n.d.). Community Law. Retrieved April 7, 2024, from https://communitylaw.org.nz/community-law-manual/chapter-19-accident-compensation-acc/overview-of-the-acc-scheme/

when evaluating the relevance and transferability of Enspiral's model into other contexts. "There is a much stronger social safety net here, compared to the U.S. where I grew up, which means more people can take risks as entrepreneurs. No one has to stay at their nine-to-five for health insurance, take out huge loans to get an education, or end up on the street if their startup doesn't work out." – Alanna Irving, Enspiral Member.

Goodworks Evergreen: A Rural Rollup

Jay Standish

Summary

The Goodworks Evergreen (GWE) initiative is a rural economic development approach that resembles a lumber products roll-up strategy.

GWE helps retain jobs and local independent businesses in rural Montana. It acquires small owner-operated businesses that would otherwise go out of business due to a lack of succession options. GWE helps their portfolio companies thrive by merging and professionalizing operations. The acquired companies each historically generated between $150-250k in annual revenue. By taking over these businesses, GWE saves a meaningful percentage of jobs in rural communities where the loss of even 10 jobs in a town of 200 people could amount to a 5% drop in the employment rate. Beyond retaining jobs, GWE raises wages, provides benefits, and contributes to the overall community resource base while providing necessary goods and services. Founded by an impact-driven family office that seeks to improve the lives of Montanans while doing good business, GWE has acquired 7 companies in 6 years.

> "Our only secret sauce is patient capital and people willing to roll up their sleeves"
>
> Kiah Hochstetler, COO Goodworks Evergreen

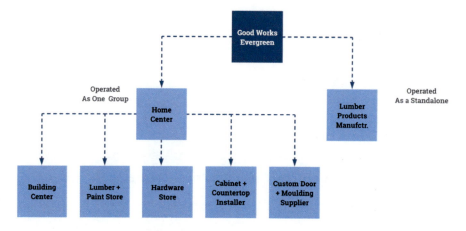

Ownership Structure of Goodworks Evergreen: A holding company holds majority equity and conducts asset management. Some subsidiaries also have minority equity investors. Six portfolio companies have been merged under one operation.

Context

Montana's economy is undergoing a major shift, transitioning away from traditional natural resource industries like ranching and logging towards new sectors such as tourism and technology. An ongoing wave of wealthier transplants is impacting housing, employment, and communities. With the retirement of baby boomers who owned small businesses across the state, there is a need to transition ownership and management of small businesses to retain local jobs and business services. In many rural towns of 200-2,000 people, the closure of a single small business has a noticeable impact on the community. Recognizing this challenge, a Montana physician named Mary Stranahan, who inherited substantial wealth, decided to use it for the greater good of the state. The Goodworks organizations were founded as a result of this vision.

Motivation

Goodworks Ventures was launched in 2007 by Mary Stranahan to create a place-based investment firm making investments in Montana companies acting as both a venture capital fund for new businesses and a steward of main street businesses. The fund has a portfolio of 35 early-stage companies across sustainability, technology, science, and food sectors. Mary Stranahan also established the High Stakes Foundation, a philanthropic partner, granting over $10 million to organizations across Montana.

In 2018, Goodworks Evergreen (GWE) was formed to acquire and operate local businesses in Montana that would otherwise close. GWE targets very small, independent businesses to preserve local community character and retain good jobs in these small towns. By acquiring multiple companies in one vertical, home improvement, GWE has taken a page from the private equity roll-up playbook and adapted it to save companies that lack buyers or family members to take them over.[67] Goodworks is also venturing into real estate development and partnering with municipalities to provide workforce housing in Missoula with plans to expand this strategy into more rural communities and teacher housing.

How it Works

Family Office Affiliation

The group functions as a family office with three components: an impact-driven venture fund, a 501c(3) foundation, and a small business acquisitions group. A small core staff of 5 is shared across all the projects.

Goodworks Ventures, while no longer making new investments, was very active in promoting the startup ecosystem in Missoula from 2007 to 2017. The High Stakes Foundation makes grants throughout Montana to a variety of causes. Goodworks Evergreen sponsors acquisitions of small businesses, leads hands-on integrations, and oversees long-term operations. It has one dedicated staff member as COO and shares 4 staff members with Goodworks Ventures and the High Stakes Foundation

---

67   Walzer, N., & Merrett, C. (2022). Rural areas in transition: meeting challenges & making opportunities. In Routledge & CRC Press (1st ed.). Routledge. https://www.routledge.com/Rural-Areas-in-Transition-Meeting-Challenges—Making-Opportunities/Walzer-Merrett/p/book/9781032249001

GWE Acquisitions History

Since 2018, GWE has acquired 7 businesses, primarily small, rural lumber and hardware supply stores with under 10 employees each. The initial acquisitions were funded by the family office, while later ones utilized cash flow from portfolio companies as well as outside capital. In the early years, the family office also supported the salaries of key staff that resourced the acquisition process. As of Q1 2024, cash flows from the portfolio sustain the GWE parent company salaries. Currently, 85% of the team's efforts are dedicated to supporting operations, with the remaining 15% focused on pursuing new acquisitions and investor relations.[68]

Portfolio

See below the Goodworks evergreen portfolio in chronological order of acquisition.

1) Home Center: Serves as platform and operating entity for hardware store roll-up

2) Lumber Products Manufacturer

3) Building Center: Rolled into Home Center #1 Operating Entity

4) Lumber and Paint Store: Rolled into Home Center #1 Operating Entity

5) Hardware Store: Rolled into Home Center #1 Operating Entity

6) Cabinet & Countertop Installer: Rolled into Home Center #1 Operating Entity

7) Custom Doors + Moulding Supplier:Rolled into Home Center #1 Operating Entity

Governance + Management

GWE owns 100% of its subsidiary portfolio companies; it is not employee-owned. Portfolio companies were typically run by the outgoing seller and did not have additional managers beyond the owner. GWE has brought

---

68   Kiah Hochstetler, Personal Communication, January 2024.

in new general managers for its acquisitions, either via internal promotion or recruiting from their networks. Post-acquisition transitions and integrations have been a hands-on endeavor, with GWE core staff involved in day-to-day operational improvements alongside general managers. GWE maintains governance control of its subsidiaries, and although there is not currently an employee ownership or governance component, the group is interested in these outcomes over the long-term, as well as sharing ownership with local community members.

Takeaways

Light Core Team

Despite having only one dedicated staff member and four additional team members shared between the philanthropic foundation and GWE (amounting to around two full-time equivalent employees), GWE has been able to acquire 7 companies in 6 years. By targeting small companies, the acquisition process for each deal was simpler compared to larger companies with more complex terms and financing requirements. This impressive result was made possible by the strategic guidance of CEO Dawn McGee, the backing of the family office, and the entrepreneurial practicality of Kiah Hochstetler, GWE's COO and sole full-time dedicated employee.

Heavy Operations Focus

The team focuses 85% of its efforts on operating and improving the companies in its portfolio. When an operating company only has 7 employees and one general manager, it requires additional support to improve systems and processes. This additional support comes from the GWE core team, which has worked to implement enterprise resource planning software, re-structure service offerings, improve worker compensation, and generally professionalize operations.

Tiny Companies Bought for Book Value

GWE has bought companies that previously made between $150-250k annually in cash flow. In most cases, the price was very close to the hard asset value of the real estate, equipment, and inventory on the balance sheet. Target companies usually had teams of less than 10, and the outgoing owner usually served as the only manager with most of the operational expertise. This tiny scale required the GWE team to roll up their sleeves and take a hands-on role in "rebooting" operations, but the low acquisition price meant that deals could be financially viable quickly if revenues remained similar to what they were pre-acquisition.

Geographic Roll-up

Six of the seven companies under GWE have been rolled up into a single operation run by a general manager. This further justifies the small acquisitions, because they are absorbed into a larger group, diluting fixed costs into a larger P+L. The five hardware stores have the same specific offering, but the other two companies are also generally in the home improvement and construction space. So, GWE has entirely focused on the home supply and home improvement industry. This is particularly strategic because in these rural towns, if the one hardware store in town goes out of business, residents might have to drive an hour each way to the next town for their hardware needs.

Elbow Grease For Local Needs

GWE shares a CEO with Goodworks Ventures who also is the President of the High Stakes Foundation, so the local needs and issues of Montana are very present. The family office previously made investments in startups which represent the "new Montana" but GWE is an effort to preserve the rural, independent character of Montana. In addition to the business-saving work, GWE is also venturing into real estate development. They are building an 89-unit community land trust workforce housing project in Missoula, which is arguably the city hardest hit by the influx of well-heeled transplants to the state. By putting capital to work to solve the real needs facing the state, GWE shows capital holders how real change can happen through long-term dedication and humble, hard work.

The Industrial Commons

Charity May

Summary

In the rural town of Morganton, North Carolina, stands an inspiring example of a networked enterprise. The Industrial Commons (TIC) is a multi-stakeholder cooperative ecosystem rooted in the unique texture of its town, people, and the textile industry. The Industrial Commons was established in 2015 as a 501(c)3 organization with the core purpose of creating economic opportunity for the people in the region. Its formation and ongoing development stand as a remarkable testament to the power of grassroots initiative and place-based design. From establishing a member-governed network of regionally based textile manufacturers to leading the successful conversion of other local businesses into worker-member cooperatives, The Industrial Commons has actualized so much of its vision in a relatively short period. Drawing from the learnings and models of Mondragon Cooperative Corporation and the Emilia-Romagna region in Italy, Morganton natives Molly Hemstreet and Sara Chester responded to the conditions of their community and began to form the groundwork for a capacity-building and capital-raising enterprise that would initiate this growing multi-stakeholder cooperative network.[69]

This case study sheds light on how The Industrial Commons came to be, its impact on regional economics, and the potential of public and private partnerships in fostering economic development strategies that are genuinely community-led. The story of TIC lays out a blueprint for rural communities aiming to reshape their regional economics in ways that honor the local culture, relationships, skills, and knowledge.

---

69 Hoover, M. (2023). Employee Ownership: a pathway to Economic resilience (L. Mayor, Ed.). Asset Funders Network. https://assetfunders.org/resource/employee-ownership-a-pathway-to-economic-resilience/

Fast Findings

The Industrial Commons multi-stakeholder cooperative ecosystem emerged as a resilient response to Morganton, North Carolina's economic challenges

TIC emphasizes the importance and tangible pathways of working from an embedded place of community, not just for it. This principle manifests itself in the active civic participation of worker-members and the development of impactful public-private partnerships such as The Innovation Campus and involvement in public service.

TIC leverages the regional heritage of textile manufacturing while innovating with circular economy principles and cooperative models. This approach illustrates the value of grounding innovation in place and local knowledge, recognizing the potential to revitalize and transform traditional industries through modern, sustainable practices.

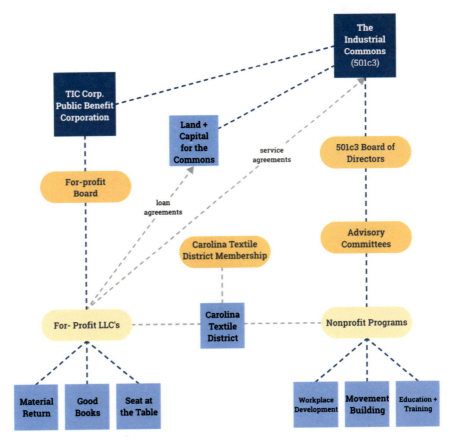

A Rural Multi-Stakeholder Cooperative Ecosystem: The Industrial Commons engages in the formation and development of enterprises that advance rural economic development through employee ownership. The non-profit embraces blended legal structures and democratic governance across the ecosystem to achieve this purpose. Original diagram provided by The Industrial Commons, reformatted by our team.

Context

The TIC cooperative ecosystem originated from the experiences of local community members, including the co-founders Molly Hemstreet and Sara Chester, and their efforts to respond to the changing conditions of their town's economy. Molly Hemstreet and Sara Chester were born and raised in Morganton. As young people, they witnessed the devastation that global trade agreements made on rural America, shuttering many local factories and jobs in the textile and furniture sectors in their region.

The Industrial Commons | 81

"There's a history of selling your community to the highest dollar so that folks can bring in whatever big box store or battery manufacturer to offer tons of discounts and incentives. At that moment, yes, labor rates increased. But just as quickly as they increased, they were also gone. Western North Carolina lived through this in 1992 and 1993. What was originally a town with 3-4% unemployment rates, with a large majority of people working in furniture and textile manufacturers, it was as if unemployment nearly tripled overnight."

– Aaron Dawson, Director of Workforce Development at TIC, describing what transpired during the 90s and the groundwork it laid to generate a regional appetite for employee ownership.[70]

Molly Hemstreet's community organizing in the 2000s led her to establish Opportunity Threads, a worker-cooperative, in 2008. Upon establishing this enterprise with a culture that prioritized employee ownership and engagement, it caught the attention of Sara Chester at the economic development agency Burke Development, Inc(BDI).

It was working. Worker-members actively participated as catalysts in both their workplace and community, resulting in a revitalization of the textile industry and the preservation of jobs within the region. Inspired by international and regional mavericks of cooperative economics, Sara and Molly joined efforts to expand the benefits of cooperatives in their region.

They formed the Carolina Textile District (CTD), a member-governed and member-driven network of values-aligned textile manufacturers in North and South Carolina. One distinctive point to make here is that while the Carolina Textile District, structured as an LLC, is housed under TIC and the worker-member cooperatives (such as Opportunity Threads and

---

70   Aaron Dawson, Director of Workforce Development at The Industrial Commons, personal communication, January 17, 2024. Also important to note that the impact of the 2008 recession hit the local economy hard, reaching 16% at one point and contributed to the growing motivation for Molly and Sara to engage in this work.

Material Return) are members of CTD, not all members participating in CTD are structured as cooperatives. CTD's open and voluntary structure allows cooperation with community assets without mandating the cooperative model, elevating the region's economic prospects.

Motivation

Cooperative Development for All

Opportunity Threads, Carolina Textile District, and The Industrial Commons sought out ways to develop the capacity of the enterprises, factories, and sectors established in the Western North Carolina region.

One of TIC's core capabilities is developing new cooperative enterprises based on the region's industrial needs. Two start-up cooperatives connected to TIC's network are Material Return, providing custom circularity services to turn waste into new products, and Good Books, a women and people of color-led cooperative offering bookkeeping services to regional enterprises.

TIC's cooperative enterprise development caught the curiosity of local small businesses. Retiring owners seeking technical support have reached out to TIC for succession planning support and to further consider transitioning ownership to employees. As of 2023, TIC has successfully transitioned two independent businesses from single-owner to worker-member enterprises with more conversions underway. This demonstrates TIC's desire to model the legacy of cooperative economics, which is to build out the cooperative economy beyond its organization. Businesses that transition to cooperative enterprises do not automatically join the network of TIC, but this presents a potential opportunity for further exploration.

Community Engagement & Active Citizenship

"We are doing this with the community, not to the community. Yes, we are certainly doing this work for the community because a majority of those within the ecosystem grew up here. But we aren't doing these programs and efforts to them, we're doing it with them. This is a really important component of cooperative ecosystem development."

– Aaron Dawson

The Industrial Commons' network of enterprises, as further described in the next section, is rooted in local people. The founders, most employees, and network partners are from Morganton. This hyperlocal nature acts as an accelerant to the networked advantage despite the complexities that come with cooperating among multiple enterprises and stakeholders as there is an intrinsic motivation to care for the place and people.

Many individuals within TIC's network are also civically engaged by serving on local boards, such as the Parks and Recreation Board, and councils, such as the Planning and Zoning Commission. When the motivation is not politically driven, these coordinated efforts to work across public and private spheres can create a vibrant win that transcends political divides.

One brilliant example of this public and private partnership can be found by looking at the capital campaign for The Innovation Campus. Anticipated to be a $40mm development project for the initial phase, the project attracted a land donation, an $8 million anchor investment, and bipartisan state support with a $5 million economic development investment. TIC's established relationships with community leaders facilitated local officials championing the state funding appropriation. Additionally, the project secured a $10 million federal grant from the Appalachian Regional Commission (ARC) in 2023, the largest single grant awarded by the ARC.[71][72]

---

71 North Carolina Department of Commerce. (2023, October 11). Textile Manufacturing Hub to receive "0 million Federal ARC grant to expand facility in Burke County [Press release]. NC Commerce. https://www.commerce. nc.gov/news/press-releases/2023/10/11/textile-manufacturing-hub-receive-10-million-federal-arc-grant-expand-facility-burke-county#:~:text=The%20 new%20facility%20will%20be,TIC)%20and%20throughout%20the%20textile

72 Aaron Dawson, Director of Workforce Development at The Industrial Commons, personal communication, January 17, 2024.

84 | Assets in Common

Major Initiatives

TIC members and allies work together to realize bigger projects for themselves and their community. Major priorities include developing The Innovation Campus hub for circular textile manufacturing, in collaboration with partners such as the Manufacturing Solutions Center. Additionally, efforts are underway to scale up textile recycling operations and secure more brand partnerships for material supply. These initiatives are possible due to the groundwork laid in establishing successful businesses with community buy-in and structural wealth democratization. Cooperation is advantageous to all, and co-investment in bigger projects is easier as a result. TIC shows us that cooperative businesses working together beyond the interests of their worker owners or members, for a greater community or regional vision, could be the future of the coop movement.

How it Works

Structure

As depicted in the visual above, The Industrial Commons operates as a multi-stakeholder network of enterprises connected through a myriad of ways like governance, economic interest, or market participation. Here we'll describe in detail the structure and how the enterprises interconnect.

Co-led by Molly Hemstreet and Sara Chester, TIC is the single-member owner of the for-profit Carolina Textile District LLC, which operates as a member-governed manufacturing network for the region. TIC, the non-profit, established a separate public benefit corporation of which it is a member-owner. The public benefit corporation operates as a governing body and the entity through which TIC holds founding shares in the standalone worker-member cooperative LLCs. Also within this ecosystem, TIC formed a community land trust – Land for the Commons – and a capital fund – Capital for the Commons. These entities serve the mission of the non-profit and operate within the network.

Economic Interest

At the worker-member cooperative enterprises, employees have the opportunity to purchase Membership Shares after two years of employment, granting them ownership voting rights and profit-sharing distributions.

As stated previously, The Industrial Commons Corp, a Delaware Public Benefit Corporation solely formed by TIC, holds a class of Founding Shares in these cooperatives. This class of shares gives TIC certain veto powers, such as preventing the sale of the company and allowing it to stay committed and involved in each cooperative's formation and strategic direction.

With TIC's established balance sheet and capacity to raise patient, philanthropic capital, the worker-member cooperatives benefit from sharing economic interests. TIC's balance sheet can be leveraged for capital in ways that the standalone worker-member cooperatives may struggle to access. For example, aligning with its local wealth-building mission, the non-profit can purchase major equipment and make it available for the cooperatives' use without burdening them with debt. This enables capital-intensive enterprises, like manufacturing, to launch with the necessary support.

Governance & Decision-Making

The Industrial Commons is governed by a board of directors. Operational management decisions of the worker-member cooperative LLCs within the network are held at each enterprise. However, strategic management decisions are influenced by TIC's founding shares in the worker-member cooperatives.

TIC is in the process of analyzing its current structure and may implement a governing council that provides oversight to the entire network without taking the form of a single corporation, similar to Mondragon's general assembly format. When describing the evolutionary journey, TIC is quick to offer that they have not yet figured it out. This position of curiosity, humility, and determination to work with iterations, to stay rooted in place and value, exemplify important characteristics necessary to build more shared economic futures.

Relationships

Many of the engaged members within the TIC network hail from Morganton, forming enduring relationships typical of small rural communities. This local connection not only nurtures deep bonds but also fosters sustainable solutions specific to the area.

Worker-members are directly engaged in the well-being of their enterprises and the town itself. This engagement in civic work has helped garner public support for employee ownership as a flagship model for workforce and economic development. This organic relationship and trust-building led to local representatives sponsoring the $5mm appropriation in the North Carolina state budget for the development of The Innovation Campus.

TIC also fosters integrated civic engagement through collaboration with local government agencies and mission-aligned organizations. Their partnership programs focus on developing a local youth workforce pipeline with Work in Burke Economic Development Center. TOSS, a local art studio, works with TIC to develop programming around creativity and innovation. Hometown Walkabout – an Australian Aboriginal concept – is a program that TIC promotes for ongoing place-based learning opportunities to engage in the town's local and historical context.

Member Benefits

As of 2024, the benefits available to cooperative enterprises that are members of the TIC public benefit corporation include the following:

- financial support from TIC through access to equipment that would otherwise burden the enterprises with excessive debt, and from Capital for the Commons, which funds initiatives directly related to TIC's cooperative development work;
- ongoing management, leadership, and cooperative development training through the robust programs provided; and,

- open flows between labor and production, as members, jobs, or roles may move throughout the network to support matching skills with market demands and needs as they evolve.

While there is currently no formal process for other regional cooperatives, whether converted or started outside of the TIC ecosystem, to join the TIC public corporation, this consideration may develop over time.

Takeaways

Evolutionary Growth

TIC has experienced remarkable growth since its inception, expanding from 2 to 29 staff members, and increasing its budget from $40,000 to over $3 million. It has successfully brought in combined grant and investment dollars of over $60mm to the region. Despite this rapid growth, the team is committed to uncovering sustainable pathways to stabilize their operations mission. Such measures include thinking deeply about proper support systems that prevent burnout among founders and other organizational leaders. Additionally, TIC has embarked on an exciting goal to develop a 27-acre brownfield in their community into The Innovation Campus that will further their work to lead regenerative textile innovation and advance cooperative development networked models.

Root Innovation in Place

TIC's ongoing growth, development, and sustainable success is driven by, in part, a two-fold innovation approach. The first approach was to recognize that disruption is not always the right tactic for innovation to develop from place. Opportunity Threads, TIC, and Carolina Textile District leaned into the regional heritage of textile manufacturing to foster pathways toward new processes such as the circular economy, which ultimately led to the development of new textile products. TIC took the development path of leveraging the existing and deep contextual knowledge and support systems of the community they are in.

The second approach was to reach out and learn from the legacy and foundation of cooperative developers who came before. While the networked ecosystem model does not mirror exactly Mondragon or Emilia Romagna, Western North Carolina learned from these models and adapted or innovated core principles to build the appropriate infrastructure for their region. This included heavy investment in training and education on management and leadership to support ongoing transitions to employee ownership.[73]

Grounded Leadership is Key

The methodical and intuitive formation of a regionally networked ecosystem centered on values alignment requires a certain type of leadership. Members of TIC note that entrepreneurial spirit is key and cultivating this spirit brings about the facilitation of these internetworked relationships and outcomes. In addition to strong community organizing and activism experience, understanding business and operations is key to the success of this highly relational and complex approach within a community.

Structure the Network to Serve the Purpose

TIC's formation as a nonprofit after Molly's experience of starting a for-profit cooperative and Sara's work in an economic development agency proved critical in activating this mission. The ability to interact between nonprofit and for-profit corporate entities promoted experimentation, greater risk-taking, and the ability to access diverse resources across financial, social, and political capital.

However, TIC members acknowledge that the ecosystem is alive and experimentation is necessary to figure out the best approach for the community. TIC's formation demonstrates the importance of being willing and ready to iterate. TIC members continue to ask, "How do we structure ourselves for the next phase?"

---

73   Lund, M. (2021). A learning journey through cooperative ecosystems. [White paper]. The Industrial Commons. https://static1.squarespace.com/static/57e91c7a9f7456dca3d73e10/t/6137d3d56176130f042fbec5/1631048665169/A+Learning+Journey+Through+Cooperative+Ecosystems+Research+Paper_HR_9-7-21.pdf

Organic Ecosystem Development

The region's formation into a multi-stakeholder cooperative interconnected ecosystem occurred organically, first responding to the needs of the sector as they arose. The initial need was for the redistribution of contract work that was coming to the region but getting lost due to limited capacity at Opportunity Threads. Organizers formed Carolina Textile District in 2013 as a member-governed and member-managed shared services company to aggregate and distribute contract work to other textile manufacturers in the region based on available capacity. CTD has since evolved to provide training programs for entrepreneurs on supply chain management and manufacturing processes, improving the pipeline of capable partners. This shared service was instrumental in keeping contracts within the region without requiring local small businesses to invest extensive capital for growth.[74]

In an interview conducted in 2023, Sara Chester made it clear why this approach is important. "We use a word with our partners in the Carolina Textile District, which is a membership network of textile companies: co-opetition. How do we both cooperate and compete? It's not about one person, or two people, making a large cut off of the business. The whole goal is really about stewardship, about [folks] being able to take care of that business and have dignity and voice every day, to show up with their whole selves and love what they're doing and do it [well]. And make a good living."[75]

These networked relationships opened pathways to catalyze more cooperative development, whether converting existing businesses to cooperative structures or supporting the launch of new necessary regional enterprises as cooperatives.

---

74   Carolina Textile District. https://www.carolinatextiledistrict.com/

75   Nguyen, F. (2023, May 9). An Appalachian Model for Regenerating Place-Based, Community Wealth. NextCity. https://nextcity.org/features/an-appalachian-model-for-regenerating-place-based-community-wealth

Mondragon Corporation

Charity May

Summary

Mondragon Corporation (Mondragon or Corporation) is an exemplary multi-stakeholder cooperative corporation serving an integrated network of autonomous cooperatives of various legal forms. A multi-stakeholder cooperative (MSC) varies from the more well-understood worker-member model of cooperatives in that an MSC gives ownership and governance rights to more than one membership class.[76]

Mondragon's structure strategically surpasses the limitations of single cooperative enterprises, enabling the collective to effectively compete with large corporations. Mondragon stands as a prime illustration of this model's touted success, demonstrating how a network of cooperatives can elevate a modest regional economy to a global playing field. Renowned within both the cooperative movement and complex corporate structures, Mondragon illustrates the dynamics of structuring interconnected multi-layered enterprises through a democratic process centralizing worker and cooperative agency in management decisions.

More importantly, Mondragon leans into the infrastructure of networked cooperatives to implement solidarity mechanisms between individuals and their cooperatives, and among the cooperative firms themselves. "Solidarity mechanisms" is the term used to describe the benefits shared among affiliated cooperatives, such as pooling profits, sharing labor, and designing services that meet the specific needs of the network.

In this case study, we're going back to the beginning to see how Mondragon grew into an MSC. We emphasize the relationships that form

---

76   Lund, M. (2011). Solidarity as a Business Model. Cooperative Development Center at Kent State University. https://resources.uwcc.wisc.edu/Multistakeholder/tool-oeoc-multistakeholder-coop.pdf

structure among cooperative firms. We'll highlight the inter-cooperative solidarity mechanisms this structure activates. Additionally, we'll examine the challenges cooperatives face when these inter-cooperative relationships are pressure-tested in a highly competitive and individual-focused global market and culture.

Fast Findings

Mondragon's evolution from a single vocational training school initiative to a global MSC highlights the importance of adaptability and innovation in scaling alternative economic models.

- The case of Mondragon underscores the necessity of continuous education and the cultivation of a cooperative mindset to navigate the challenges posed by competitive, neoliberal markets.

- The structure of Mondragon, with its emphasis on multi-layered democratic governance across its federated cooperatives, underlines the critical role and the challenges of active member participation in multi-faceted, complex, and sometimes messy decision-making processes.

- Mondragon's practice of sharing resources among its cooperatives strengthens both their financial foundation and their commitment to helping one another.

- A cautionary tale of balancing growth with adherence to cooperative values in a capitalist environment is illustrated by the rise and fall of Fagor Home Appliance within the Mondragon network.

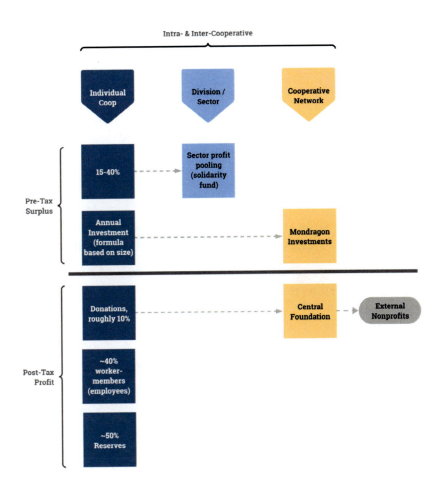

The Circulation of Surplus and Profits in Mondragon: The cooperative network of Mondragon employs multiple ways to aggregate and redistribute both pre-tax surplus and post-tax profits within and external from the firm cooperative members.

Context
The Emergence of Possibility

"As persons we are called to risk our initiative, responsibility, and our creative capacity starting from the most basic cell or creative working organism: the enterprise. In this manner we will be able to unleash a new attitude to transform the economy and to generate a new socioeconomic order, congruent with human dignity and the demands of human communities."

– Father Jose Arizmendiarrieta[77]

Mondragon's formation began in the small town of Mondragon, in the Basque Country of Spain in the 1940s and 1950s out of a response to the widespread destruction, repression, and region's distressed economy in post-Civil War Spain. Jose Maria Arizmendiarrieta, a Catholic Priest serving the region, responded to the dire social and economic needs of the community by forming an education and vocational training school. It was from this vocational training school that the first industrial cooperative – Fagor Electromdomesticos S Coop – opened. Five of his original students had gone on to receive engineering degrees and, together with some twenty local workers, they created the appliance cooperative enterprise in 1956.[78]

A Growing Intercorporate Ecosystem

As the industrial cooperative found its bearings, it became evident there was a need for business support services. In 1959, Father Arizmendiarrieta encouraged the first institutional collaboration among industrial worker cooperatives to organize a credit union, Caja Laboral (now branded as "Laboral Kutxa" after its 2012 merger with the agricultural cooperative credit union, Ipar Kutxa). This small group of industrial cooperatives combined their resources to establish Basque Country's first credit union, joining as user-members to ensure access to capital for ongoing investment. Coalescing around a financial institution was a monumental step in the formation of this multi-stakeholder cooperative ecosystem. However, Caja

---

77   Arizmendiarrieta, J. (2016). , As recalled in an internal letter to Mondragon. , https://static1.squarespace.com/static/58292a54cd0f681af51bccd1/t/586f0 c3f5016e17f5f528c57/1483672644724/Armi%CC%81n_Isa%CC%81sti-A_Ltr_ from_Mondragon.pdf.

78   Romeo, N. (2022, August 27). How Mondragon became the world's largest Co-Op. The New Yorker. https://www.newyorker.com/business/currency/ how-mondragon-became-the-worlds-largest-co-op

Laboral's central financial services expanded further. At the time, worker-owners of cooperatives lacked recognition by the national social security system. Thus, Caja Laboral members formed their own service extension, which by 1967 spun out into Lagun Aro, an independent multi-stakeholder cooperative with worker members as individuals and user-member cooperative firms involved in governance and ownership.[79] [80] [81]

A New Era

Through the mid-1980s, Mondragon continued to grow affiliation among cooperatives, primarily through banking interactions. By this time, the cooperatives felt it was time to restructure its governance form. In 1984, they created the Mondragon Cooperative Congress – a new governing body that agreed to reorganize corporate relationships from the regional subgroups they were associated with at the time. In 1991, the Congress voted to establish the Mondragon Corporation, organizing the affiliation of member cooperatives in four business divisions – financial, industrial, retail, and knowledge. Each of these sectors operates as a division within the Corporation to facilitate the sharing and distribution of resources and information among the cooperatives organized under each sector.[82]

As of 2024 reporting on Mondragon's website, the Corporation consists of 81 cooperative companies and over 130 affiliates and subsidiaries on four continents, with a total workforce of nearly 70,000. In 2023, it was reported that about 25% of the individual cooperatives are

---

79   Imaz, O., Freundlich, F., & Kanpandegi, A. (2023). The Governance of Multistakeholder Cooperatives in Mondragon: The Evolving Relationship among Purpose, Structure and Process. In Humanistic Governance in Democratic Organizations (pp. 285–330). Palgrave Macmillan. https://doi.org/10.1007/978-3-031-17403-2_10

80   Flecha, R., & Santa Cruz, I. (2011). Cooperation for Economic Success: the Mondragon case. In Lucius & Lucius, Analyse & Kritik (Vol. 01, Issue 2011, pp. 157–170). https://www.analyse-und-kritik.net/Dateien/5696575a8cb2e_ak_flecha_santa-cruz_2011.pdf

81   Ibid

82   Ibid

multi-stakeholder cooperatives, while the rest take on a myriad of legal cooperative forms (discussed in detail in the How it Works section below).[83] [84]

Motivation

By adopting a multi-stakeholder cooperative model, Mondragon aimed to achieve a scale that would allow it to compete effectively on a global scale while also adhering to its values and principles of collective well-being for workers and place. This model enables a network of cooperatives to pool resources, share knowledge, and collaborate on strategic initiatives, thereby enhancing their collective competitiveness and market reach.

The networked multi-stakeholder model also supports Mondragon's goal of maintaining democratic governance and active participation by all members in various layers of decision-making processes. This approach reinforces the mutualistic and democratic ideals at the heart of Mondragon's philosophy.

How it Works

Structure[85]

The Mondragon Corporation is structured as an integrated network of cooperatives, where each entity maintains its autonomy while adhering to Mondragon's corporate terms of affiliation. These terms, which we'll explore in more detail later, outline the mutual responsibilities and benefits of association with Mondragon. Importantly, each cooperative, as a standalone entity, legally retains the right to elect its governing body

---

83   Ibid

84   Mondragon Corporation. https://www.mondragon-corporation.com/en/about-us/

85   Imaz, O., Freundlich, F., & Kanpandegi, A. (2023). The Governance of Multistakeholder Cooperatives in Mondragon: The Evolving Relationship among Purpose, Structure and Process. In Humanistic Governance in Democratic Organizations (pp. 285–330). Palgrave Macmillan. https://doi.org/10.1007/978-3-031-17403-2_10

and has the flexibility to join or leave the Mondragon network at any time. The corporation is organized into four main business sectors —finance, industrial, knowledge, and retail—each consisting of cooperatives grouped into these divisions. This structure facilitates collaboration and information exchange within and across sectors. A corporate center offers common services to all members, spearheading strategic reflection as well as new strategic initiatives, enhancing the network's coherence and efficiency. Moreover, cooperative law in the Basque region is highly developed, allowing Mondragon's structure to accommodate a variety of legal forms tailored to the specific types of its member cooperatives.[86]

Mondragon's initial journey to achieving legal cooperative status in 1959 marked a deliberate departure from the fascist ideologies embedded in the Act of 1942 (the governing cooperative law at that time). Bylaws were drafted to reflect a vision of subordinating capital to labor. It took four years to achieve legal status through the approval of the bylaws by the Basque Labor Ministry. The attempt was to structure a governance and ownership model whereby private property and individual initiative could coexist with social service and just economic distribution among its members.[87]

As such, the networked effect of Mondragon's corporate structure allows for a diversity of legal forms based on the type of members. The member type typically falls within a few categories, summarized in the table below:

---

86   Flecha, R., & Santa Cruz, I. (2011). Cooperation for Economic Success: the Mondragon case. In Lucius & Lucius, Analyse & Kritik (Vol. 01, Issue 2011, pp. 157–170). https://www.analyse-und-kritik.net/Dateien/5696575a8cb2e_ak_ flecha_santa-cruz_2011.pdf

87   Molina, F. (2011). The Spirituality of Economics: Historical Roots of Mondragon, 1940–1974. In Bakaikoa, B., & Albizu, E. Basque Cooperativism. Center for Basque Studies Press. https://scholarworks.unr.edu/ bitstream/handle/11714/5063/CR6_Basque%20Cooperativism_acc. pdf?sequence=1&isAllowed=y .

Member Class	Description
Worker members	People who work in the cooperative and earn membership status from their peers. This membership class holds primacy in many ways. All co-ops in the Mondragon network have this class. About 60 of the 81 co-ops in the group are structured as worker co-ops.
Collaborating members	Organizations with an interest in supporting the multi-stakeholder cooperative's activities, though are not often direct and continuous users. An example of a collaborating member might be a public institution or a local business.
User members	User members are typically other cooperative enterprises, not individual persons, who do make use of the co-op's services.[88] Many Mondragon co-ops are user members of the purchasing portal co-op, Ategi, along with most of its workers.

In a category of their own are investors. While external investors may play a role in the ownership of certain cooperatives, they are largely a class used to describe the investment arm of Mondragon – Mondragon Investments – within the context of the Mondragon cooperative ecosystem. The role of investors is largely constricted to providing capital, with only a few cooperatives including Mondragon Investments in its ownership structure.

The table below summarizes the multiplicity of legal forms that exist among the 81 cooperatives affiliated with Mondragon.

---

88   One exception is the co-op supermarket chain

Legal Forms of Member Cooperatives

Worker cooperatives	Education cooperatives	Mixed cooperatives	Second-degree cooperatives
People who work in the firm are members	Workers, users, and collaborators are integrated into the owner-ship structure	Allows for the participation of a minority of inves-tor members holding limited governance rights	Composed of other coopera-tives of any kind and are a type of multi-stakeholder cooperative
Consumer cooperatives	Credit cooperatives	Service Cooperatives	Multi-stakeholder Cooperatives
Users are members	Users are members	A cooperative constituted to facilitate, guaran-tee or complete the business or professional functions, activity or operational results of its members who may be pro-fessionals or enterprises	Workers, users and collabora-tors represent the diversity of stakeholders involved at all levels of gov-ernance and operations. About 25% of the cooperatives in the Mondragon integrated network are multi-stakeholder cooperatives.

Governance & Decision-Making[89]

As a complex ecosystem of relationships, decision-making, and operations, Mondragon navigates through it all through overlapping levels of democratic governance – direct democracy at the base and then several levels of representative democracy from the individual co-op up to the full Mondragon network (corporation level).

Corporate Governance

At the corporate level is the Mondragon Cooperative Congress, consisting of 650 representatives from all the cooperatives within the network. The number of representatives for each cooperative is indirectly based on the number of employees they represent. This is to ensure that the largest co-ops cannot dominate decision-making, with no more than two representatives per member. This body is the 'highest' authority and convenes to make significant decisions and set the strategic course for the entire corporation. When the Congress is not in session, its President and a Standing Committee assume the highest governing authority. The Standing Committee is composed of members from the governing councils of individual cooperatives across various business sectors and regional subgroups and is responsible for appointing the President of a strategic management body, the General Councils, and ensuring continuity in governance and strategic alignment. Additionally, the General Council provides general strategic orientation. It is made up of the President, Vice Presidents, Directors of the various sectors and regional subgroups, and key staff from different departments. Notably, the General Council does not oversee the day-to-day operations of the cooperative firms but focuses on broader strategic guidance, coordination, and services. This governance structure emphasizes participation, collaboration, and shared leadership

---

89   Imaz, O., Freundlich, F., & Kanpandegi, A. (2023). The Governance of Multistakeholder Cooperatives in Mondragon: The Evolving Relationship among Purpose, Structure and Process. In Humanistic Governance in Democratic Organizations (pp. 285–330). Palgrave Macmillan. https://doi.org/10.1007/978-3-031-17403-2_10

across the network, aligning with Mondragon's cooperative principles and its commitment to democratic practices.

Local Governance

At each cooperative, business operational management is separated from governance. Day-to-day operations are managed by the senior management put in place by the governing body. Members participating in democratic governance are elected to make or modify their co-op's basic rules and policy, make a series of key decisions (e.g. hiring new members), and provide oversight to the management of the company. There are several governing bodies in place that fulfill different, yet equally important functions:

- General Assembly – the general assembly is considered the highest level of authority and is composed of all active members of the cooperative.

- Governing Council – the general assembly elects a governing council from among its members, whose responsibility is akin to a board of directors of a conventional corporation. The governing council appoints the firm's senior manager who directs the co-op's management council and approves the senior manager's choices for other members of the management council.

- Management Council – Along with the senior manager, the management council consists of the managers responsible for overseeing the day-to-day operations of the enterprise.

- Social Council – this optional representative body provides consultation to the other bodies on issues pertaining to the members and their ability to hold multi-directional communication between members and the governing bodies. Each work area in the cooperative nominates representatives to serve on the social council.

- Audit Committee – the audit committee is an oversight function required by law for cooperatives with a membership greater than 100. When in place, the general assembly will elect three members to serve on the audit committee.

Economic Interest

Instead of using equity shares to reflect ownership, Mondragon utilizes economic stakeholding reflected through paid-in capital accounts for each member, funded by worker-member salaries over time. These accounts earn an annual interest of up to 7.5%, decided by the Governing Council based on the cooperative's performance. Members can access the balance when leaving or retiring.[90]

Cooperative enterprise members share economic interests through pooling at two levels – post-tax and pre-tax. The first level is at each cooperative and its post-tax profit distributions. For post-tax profits, Basque law allows a maximum of 70% distributed to worker-members, 20% held in reserves, and 10% donated to nonprofits. Mondragon cooperatives typically split this as 40-50-10% respectively, determined by each cooperative's general council. At the pre-tax level, typically, 15-40% of profits are pooled within each of Mondragon's four business divisions (finance, industrial, knowledge, and retail) as decided by the Cooperative Congress.[91]

---

90   Fred Freundlich, Mondragon University Professor, personal communication, October 30, 2023.

91   Arando, S., Freundlich, F., Gago, M., Jones, D. C., Kato, T.,(2010). Assessing Mondragon: Stability & Managed Change in the face of Globalization. William Davidson Institute Working Paper Number 1003. https://deepblue.lib.umich.edu/bitstream/handle/2027.42/133017/wp1003.pdf

Divisional profit pooling and post-tax contributions can also be described as mutual aid inter-cooperative funds. These funds are briefly described below:[92] [93]

- Mondragon Investments: each cooperative contributes an initial investment and annual contributions to Mondragon Investments, which acts as the network's venture capital arm, supporting strategic projects that may extend beyond the risk capacity of individual cooperatives or divisions.

- Central Foundation (an inter-cooperative education and promotion fund): each cooperative enterprise member makes post-tax donations to the central foundation, which funds training, education, and research and development among members, as well as donations to external non-profits.

- The Inter-Cooperative Solidarity Fund: the divisional profit pools act as solidarity funds that are available for redistribution to meet the needs of the sector cooperatives. This function primarily serves the Industrial business division.

Relationships

The general assembly of an individual cooperative applies to join the Mondragon Corporation. In exchange for membership, which enables collaboration among other cooperatives and access to group-level funds, the cooperative agrees to the rules, regulations, and principles of the corporation. If a cooperative decides that it no longer wants to abide by these

---

92   Arando, S., & Bengoa, I. A. (2018). Inter-Cooperation mechanisms in Mondragon: Managing the crisis of Fagor ElectrodomÉsticos. In Employee Ownership and Employee Involvement at Work: Case Studies (Advances in the Economic Analysis of Participatory & Labor-Managed Firms, Vol. 18) (pp. 7–35). Emerald Publishing Limited. https://doi.org/10.1108/s0885-333920180000018008

93   Flecha, R., & Santa Cruz, I. (2011). Cooperation for Economic Success: the Mondragon case. In Lucius & Lucius, Analyse & Kritik (Vol. 01, Issue 2011, pp. 157–170). https://www.analyse-und-kritik.net/Dateien/5696575a8cb2e_ak_flecha_santa-cruz_2011.pdf

regulations and principles, or falls out of alignment for other purposes, its general assembly votes to leave. This happened most recently, with the ULMA Group and Orona co-ops in December 2022.

Fostering a culture of cooperative autonomy and mutuality is key for individual cooperatives. There is a probationary period before new employees become member-owners, though this period may vary based on the rules set by each cooperative (within the legal requirement of six months). Ongoing education and training through Mondragon University is also key for strengthening relationships between cooperatives, employees, and the corporation. As culture shifts and markets change, such initiatives are becoming crucial for promoting participation and continuing the revitalization of a cooperative identity throughout the network.

Evidence suggests that turnover among frontline workers is quite low, due, in part, to high unemployment within their regions and strong community ties. This is less the case as members advance or take on managerial roles within the cooperative. Managers face more options given the pay disparities with conventional firms, particularly for mid-to-higher-level engineering and management positions. However, the labor market operates quite differently in a region rich in cooperatives compared to the labor market in the U.S. This anecdotal consideration also highlights that membership is more stable, signaling stronger relationships between worker-members and firms, firms, and the corporation within the Mondragon network.[94]

---

94   Fred Freundlich, Mondragon University Professor, personal communication, October 30, 2023.

Member Benefits[95]

While general parameters related to membership requirements are set by Basque law, most detailed requirements are dictated by the cooperatives themselves.

Between Worker-Members and Cooperatives

Membership is open and extended to all membership classes. Being a worker-member of a cooperative allows for several benefits, some defined below:

- controlled gap between wages and salaries – top executive salary does not exceed six times that of the lowest paid individual in most co-ops.[96]
- jobs can be passed on to family members in certain co-op groups for unskilled positions
- extensive training is provided
- employees share in the distribution and reinvestment of economic surplus
- voices are represented through democratic governance structures
- employment opportunities immediately expand beyond the individual cooperative enterprise.

Between Cooperatives and The Corporation

Mondragon offers various 'solidarity mechanisms' that reinforce membership value and association across the enterprises. Notable examples

---

95   Arando, S., & Bengoa, I. A. (2018). Inter-Cooperation mechanisms in Mondragon: Managing the crisis of Fagor ElectrodomÉsticos. In Employee Ownership and Employee Involvement at Work: Case Studies (Advances in the Economic Analysis of Participatory & Labor-Managed Firms, Vol. 18) (pp. 7–35). Emerald Publishing Limited. https://doi.org/10.1108/s0885-333920180000018008

96   In the largest cooperatives, the wage gap can be closer to seven times, and for the President of the General Council of Mondragon, it is approximately eight times the lowest paid individual.

include profit pooling, sharing knowledge, technology, and innovation, and providing diversified 'employment aid'.

Through equitable contributions from each member cooperative, Mondragon Corporation is able to extend its balance sheet in a myriad of ways to support struggling cooperatives, strategic investments, and start-up cooperatives. The Corporation's head office is responsible for redistributing pooled pre and post-tax funds, according to its distribution and reserve policies. With transparent insight into the profit and loss statements of each member cooperative through reporting arrangements, Mondragon's head office is equipped with the ability to adjust distributions and tap into reserves in response to the needs of its members.[97]

Shared knowledge and innovation across sector divisions allow cooperatives to benefit from collective R&D and education initiatives. Mondragon is also able to keep its exposure to the broader labor market limited by managing the flow of labor within the cooperative network. The social security cooperative offering health and related insurance pensions, Lagun Aro, is the primary administrator of employment aid through three core mechanisms.

a) Facilitating a demand-based work calendar whereby employees can adjust the number of hours they work based on the demand of production;

b) Facilitating an online matching system to identify jobs at other cooperatives for relocation, periods of unemployment, and when talent needs call for redistribution; and,

---

97   Arando, S., & Bengoa, I. A. (2018). Inter-Cooperation mechanisms in Mondragon: Managing the crisis of Fagor ElectrodomÉsticos. In Employee Ownership and Employee Involvement at Work: Case Studies (Advances in the Economic Analysis of Participatory & Labor-Managed Firms, Vol. 18) (pp. 7–35). Emerald Publishing Limited. https://doi.org/10.1108/s0885-333920180000018008

c) Administering pre-retirement for worker-members at 58 years old, or severance compensation when broader market conditions require adaptive measures.

These mechanisms help to stabilize the labor market, as the movements are considered lateral for the Corporation, worker-members benefit from higher employment security.[98]

Takeaways

The Mutual Mindset Must be Cultivated

To ensure the success of large-scale cooperative businesses, it's essential to cultivate a widely shared mutual mindset that diverges significantly from the competitive, individualistic ethos dominating today's neoliberal markets. This requires dedicated cooperative education where worker-members at all levels reflect on cooperative principles, adjust and re-invent them in the context of business, and design concrete ways to put them into practice. Mondragon University and the Management and Social Affairs office play a vital role in cultivating this cooperative psychology of ownership and social cohesion to guide the enterprises.

The shift toward a cooperative commonwealth—a society grounded in cooperative principles rather than competitive individualism—demands that we reevaluate and transform the prevailing market-driven attitudes. In the conventional business world, market pressures, and dominant cultural norms can push co-op managers and employees towards traditional, hierarchical modes of thinking, leading to an "us vs. them" mentality that fundamentally opposes the essence of cooperation.

One such example of the ongoing balancing act of holding individual interests and rights alongside collective rights and responsibilities is the recent voluntary departure of two cooperative members from the Mondragon Network. In 2023, Ulma (a collective of nine cooperatives) and Orona separately voted to exit the Corporation. Combined, these core industrial cooperatives single-handedly removed 11,000 of the 80,000

---

98   Ibid

workers and 15% of sales from Mondragon These individual cooperatives publicly express that one of the main reasons for the departure is their general council's belief that their voices will be better expressed through an arm's length relationship with Mondragon Corporation. Yet, the exit also reinforces the cooperative principle of open and voluntary membership. The decision to exit was reached democratically and is being observed with respect.[99] [100]

The cooperative movement emphasizes developing a balanced mindset recognizing individual agency while collaborating for community benefit and sustainability, not maximizing profits. This approach is inherently antithetical to the competitive individualistic markets that define neoliberalism today, marking a radical departure towards a more equitable and inclusive economic model.

Degeneration Dynamics

As we've noted in the case study above, it is extremely difficult, and thus rare, for a corporation to not only promote the involvement of workers in the management and governance of the corporation but also to embed this stance and process into the very structure of the corporation itself. Cooperatives of any form face this tension – whether to maintain a small size to preserve democratic governance, or expand at the risk of degenerating that democratic nature. As more divergent voices (different membership classes) are represented in the collective body and, as co-ops

---

99   Fred Freundlich, Mondragon University Professor, personal communication, October 30, 2023.

100   Hadfield, M. (2023, February 1). New trouble for Mondragon as two industrial co-ops leave the fold. Co-operative News. https://www.thenews.coop/167739/sector/worker-coops/new-trouble-for-mondragon-as-two-industrial-co-ops-leave-the-fold/

grow, the workforce's attitudes will tend to be closer to those in the broader society.[101]

Degenerative dynamics within cooperatives reveal a complex set of challenges that can erode the foundational cooperative principles over time. These dynamics are not always straightforward and can manifest in various aspects of a cooperative's operations and ethos. Here's a closer exploration based on insights from academic observations:[102]

- Prioritization of Financial Gain Over Human Well-being: A key indicator of degeneration is when a cooperative begins to prioritize financial gain at the expense of the well-being of its members mirroring conventional corporate behavior.

- Decreased Participation in Decision-making: As cooperatives grow, there's a risk that member participation in crucial decision-making processes diminishes. This reduction in participatory governance can lead to decisions that favor hierarchical structures over the collective input of all members, undermining the democratic foundation of cooperatives.

- Changes in Work Relations, Authority, and Hierarchy: An increase in hierarchical structures and authority gradients within a cooperative can signify a move towards conventional corporate models. This shift often accompanies a decrease in transparency and an increase in pay differentials, further distancing the cooperative from its original egalitarian and democratic principles.

---

101   Basterretxea, I., Cornforth, C., & Heras-Saizarbitoria, I. (2020). Corporate governance as a key aspect in the failure of worker cooperatives. Economic and Industrial Democracy, 43(1), 362–387. https://doi.org/10.1177/0143831×19899474

102   Fred Freundlich, Mondragon University Professor, personal communication, February 28, 2024.

- External Relationships and Community Contribution: Degeneration can also affect how a cooperative interacts with its local and broader communities. A focus on internal gains over external contributions can diminish the cooperative's role in community development and societal well-being.

- Concerns Over Scale: The departure of groups like ULMA from the Mondragon network highlights a critical debate within cooperatives regarding scale. The question of "how big is too big" for effective inter-cooperation and representation of all voices and interests reflects concerns that growth can dilute cooperative principles and member engagement.

- Lack of Shared Ownership in Overseas Subsidiaries: The challenge of extending cooperative principles, including shared ownership, to overseas subsidiaries is a complex issue reflecting potential degenerative trends. Despite examples of successful shared ownership models in worker-owned companies, the interest in pursuing this within Mondragon has been variable, indicating a need for renewed focus and commitment to cooperative values globally.

When Shortfalls Arise[103] [104] [105]

Mondragon's success served as a beacon of hope for the global cooperative movement. Not only does Mondragon promote the development of more cooperatives through its model and open association policy. They are also among the few to demonstrate a cooperative can in fact compete at a global scale with multinational corporations. However, the 2013 shuttering of Fagor Electrodomesticos, Mondragon's original founding enterprise, raised questions about potential sacrifices to core cooperative principles amid growth.

Fagor grew into a large residential appliance manufacturer through overseas joint ventures and acquisitions of non-cooperative enterprises. By 2007, they had over 11,000 workers, 18 production plants, and 1.8 billion euros in sales.

However, in 2008, the Great Recession initiated a cascade of events that led to Fagor's demise. Sales were hit hard during the Great Recession. Poor macroeconomic conditions, excessive dependence on one market, underutilization of production facilities, and an outsized debt-to-assets ratio of 300% brought Fagor through a series of fits and lifelines provided by Mondragon Corporation, the Spanish government, private investors, and other banks. When Mondragon's Standing Committee and General Council

---

103   Basterretxea, I., Cornforth, C., & Saizarbitoria, I. H. (2020). Corporate governance as a key aspect in the failure of worker cooperatives. Economic and Industrial Democracy, 43(1), 362–387. https://doi.org/10.1177/0143831×19899474

104   Errasti, A., Bretos, I., & Nuñez, A. (2017). The viability of cooperatives: The fall of the Mondragon Cooperative Fagor. Review of Radical Political Economics, 49(2), 181–197. https://doi.org/10.1177/0486613416666533

105   Arando, S., & Bengoa, I. A. (2018). Inter-Cooperation mechanisms in Mondragon: Managing the crisis of Fagor ElectrodomÉsticos. In Employee Ownership and Employee Involvement at Work: Case Studies (Advances in the Economic Analysis of Participatory & Labor-Managed Firms, Vol. 18) (pp. 7–35). Emerald Publishing Limited. https://doi.org/10.1108/s0885-333920180000018008

voted to cease sending aid to Fagor and surrender the firm to bankruptcy, it did not signal the end or refusal to enact the solidarity mechanisms that are characteristic of cooperatives. Mondragon invested heavily in relocating to other co-ops the worker-members impacted by the Fagor bankruptcy. The overall Mondragon Cooperative Congress voted in favor to continue issuing lifelines of capital and absorbing workers in other co-ops when management decisions suggested layoffs or factories shutting down.[106]

While macroeconomic factors were central, some observers noted degenerative cultural shifts as Fagor expanded, with claims of entitlement and the "us vs. them" mentality hindering workforce integration across geographies and values. Mondragon University Professor, Fred Freundlich notes that Fagor illustrated an example of a common dilemma facing scaling cooperatives. "There's a dilemma that successful co-ops will always face in trying to operate as a cooperative enterprise with a cooperative culture in a ferociously capitalist environment. It's very difficult... I would rather have us, as a co-op, discuss and debate how to act, how to behave in the face of these dilemmas than to surrender."

The story of Mondragon, especially through the lens of Fagor Home Appliances S Coop's rise and fall, underscores the delicate balance between unfettered expansion and pragmatic implementation of the cooperative principles embedded in the operations and governance model of Mondragon. The corporation's experience highlights the inherent tensions cooperatives face in scaling up and operating within an individualistic market framework.

---

106   Errasti, A., Bretos, I., & Nuñez, A. (2017). The viability of cooperatives: The fall of the Mondragon Cooperative Fagor. Review of Radical Political Economics, 49(2), 181–197. https://doi.org/10.1177/0486613416666533

Obran: A Cooperative Holding Company

Jay Standish

Summary

Imagine if a private equity firm and a worker cooperative fell in love and had a baby. Obran Cooperative would be their child – equal parts ambitious pragmatism and earnest idealism.

Obran is a worker-owned cooperative holding company rooted in the values of social justice and equity. It prioritizes the economic advancement of its worker-owners and has championed marginalized groups as core stakeholders since its founding in 2018. Expanding through both acquisitions and startups, Obran has a portfolio of four companies operating in three focus areas: healthcare, employment services, and logistics. However, Obran's driving mission extends beyond business growth alone – it aims to become the world's largest worker-owned cooperative.[107]

---

107   Kerr, C. (2022). Obran Cooperative, LCA. In Case Studies of Worker Cooperatives in Health. CLEO, Rutgers. https://cleo.rutgers.edu/wp-content/uploads/2023/01/CASE-STUDY-OBRAN.pdf

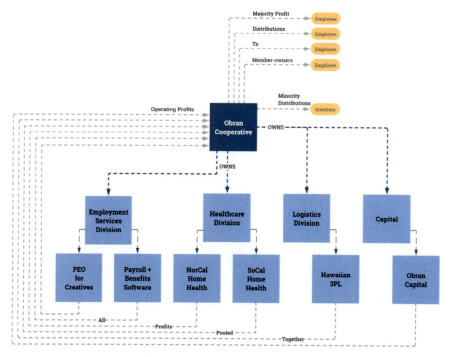

Ownership and Profit Distributions of Obran Cooperative: The top-level holding company holds at least 51% equity in all subsidiaries, which are grouped by functional divisions. Worker-owners hold a stake in the top-level cooperative, and receive ownership distributions based on the performance of the group.

Context

Obran was born in Baltimore through two worker cooperatives founded by Joseph Cureton; Core Staffing, a staffing agency focused on serving the formerly incarcerated, and TribeWorks, a Black-owned technology agency. The two groups decided to merge and build a larger platform – Obran – focused on growing by adding more companies to the group.[108] By balancing visionary ambition with no-nonsense practicality, Obran has been deliberately built for scale and subsidiarity.

---

108   Perry Abello, O. (2020, June 11). Worker-Owned industrial conglomerate makes first acquisition. Next City. https://nextcity.org/urbanist-news/worker-owned-industrial-conglomerate-makes-first-acquisition

Motivation

In the United States, there are a host of socioeconomic challenges for working and middle-class individuals. These challenges are particularly acute for certain groups such as people of color and formerly incarcerated individuals. Worker cooperatives present a hopeful opportunity for workers to band together in mutual support and take control of their economic destiny. But most are small, with a median revenue of $282,000 and 10 employees.[109] There is an opportunity to approach worker cooperatives at a larger scale to provide more jobs at larger, more stable companies.

Obran is an effort to create a worker cooperative that benefits from the same economies of scale enjoyed by large corporations but for the benefit of working-class employees. Doing so is fairly uncharted territory, and as trailblazers, Obran is likely to get some thorns and scratches along the way. It's unclear whether employees share this vision of scale as an enduring purpose and central cause. Over the past few years, Obran has been establishing structures and strategies for growth. As of 2024, it is poised to build upon this foundation to achieve its large-scale worker cooperative model.

How it Works

Organizational Structure

Obran's portfolio is grouped into three divisions, each with an industry-focused "sub-HoldCo" and directors who support each group. There are shared services groups within each division and across the whole cooperative. These shared services units provide back-office functions like accounting and payroll and also manage their investment fund. The organizational structure has three layers: underlying Operating Companies, Industry Groups, and the Obran "head office" comprising Core and Shared Services teams.

---

109   Democracy at Work Institute. (2021). 2021 State of the Sector: Worker Cooperatives in the U.S. Democracy at Work Institute at the US Federation of Worker Cooperatives. https://democracy.institute.coop/2021-worker-cooperative-state-sector-report t

One of the oldest companies in their portfolio, TribeWorks, is essentially a back-office service for independent artists and creatives. This has given Obran expertise in building and running professional and administrative operations.

Ownership Structure

Obran is structured as a Colorado Limited Cooperative Association at the top HoldCo level. This legal structure is better for taking on outside investors than a traditional worker coop, but it still allows governance control to remain with workers.[110]

The underlying portfolio companies are subsidiaries of Colorado Cooperative and are either LLCs or traditional corporations. We'll be calling these "operating companies" or "OpCo's." Employees in these OpCo's have membership and ownership rights in the entire umbrella cooperative rather than just the OpCo where they work. That means that employees benefit from the diversification and scale of the overall Obran portfolio.

Financial investors can gain ownership at both the subsidiary level and the umbrella level, but Obran Cooperative must retain a 51% controlling stake in each entity. This controlling stake means that Obran is an active owner-operator of the companies rather than a passive minority investor in independent firms.

Governance Structure

Workers at operating companies can elect board members at their individual OpCo level as well as the parent HoldCo level. The HoldCo board is democratically elected by the individual members, with each member having equal voting power. Individual worker-members are eligible to run for the board.

To ensure workers retain majority control, there are limitations on the number of financial investor board seats. The ownership and governance

---

110   B. Dean, J., & Earl Geu, T. (2008). The Uniform Limited Cooperative Association Act: An Introduction. Drake Journal of Agricultural Law, 13, 63–81. https://aglawjournal.wp.drake.edu/wp-content/uploads/sites/66/2016/09/agVol13No1-Dean.pdf

structure has been designed so that Obran maintains a controlling ownership stake, and employees always have board control. This means the employees of Obran, collectively, have full governance control of all the companies in the group.

Acquisitions Strategy

A major way Obran intends to drive growth is through acquiring existing companies in three industry groups: Healthcare, Employment Services, and Logistics. It finances these acquisitions through a fairly standard capital stack comprised of senior debt, seller financing, and equity. The cooperative has an internal Acquisition Fund contributing $700k – $2M equity per deal. Directors have meaningful financial incentives tied to the growth in enterprise value of their groups, seeing as much as 20% of the uplift in the value of the companies in their group. However, this performance-based compensation is also contingent on dollars going to worker-owners, which is determined by an increase in the disposable income of workers in the group. In essence, directors can earn a healthy cut, but only once employees see real financial gain first.

Portfolio

Apollo – Home Health Care in Northern California – HEALTHCARE

Acquired by Obran in 2022 and thus converted to employee ownership.

Apollo offers various in-home healthcare services where nurses and other skilled healthcare workers come to patient's homes to provide care.

Physicians Choice – Home Health Care in Southern California – HEALTHCARE

Acquired by Obran in 2022 and thus converted to employee ownership.

Physicians Choice has largely the same service offering as Apollo.

Tribeworks – Solidarity PEO for Independent Creatives – EMPLOYMENT SERVICES

Started by Obran founders in 2018. "Seed company" to later become Obran.

As a Professional Employment Organization (PEO) TribeWorks acts as an "Employer of Record" so that freelancers and small groups can access health benefits, and get coaching and support with financial planning and other administrative needs. TribeWorks is also a community network of mutual support for artists and creatives.

8×5 – Payroll + Benefits Software for Freelancers – EMPLOYMENT SERVICES

Started by Obran directly, the company provides back-office finance, HR software for freelancers. The software allows independent contractors to invoice and receive payments from clients, make payments to subcontractors, and access health benefits.

Courier Corporation of Hawaii – 3PL + Delivery Service – LOGISTICS

Acquired by Obran in 2022 via Kaiser Permanente EO partnership

With over 150 employees, CCH provides package shipping and door-to-door courier service to the Hawaiian islands. CCH was identified as a potential acquisition target through a partnership the the healthcare HMO Kaiser Permanente whereby Kaiser connects Obran with vendors in the Kaiser network that could be ripe for conversion to employee ownership.[111]

Obran Capital Advisors – CAPITAL

Obran Capital Advisors is a financial planning firm that specializes in helping clients align their investments with their social justice values. The company works with a network of tax accountants, attorneys, and investment

---

111   Kaiser Permanente. (2022, April 26). Employee-Owned businesses foster healthier local economies. https://about.kaiserpermanente. org/commitments-and-impact/healthy-communities/news/ employee-owned-businesses-foster-healthier-local-economies.

professionals to develop customized financial and giving plans for their clients. These plans often include strategies for socially responsible investing, wealth redistribution, and tax planning.

Takeaways

Seeding a HoldCo

A "seed company" is a powerful strategic start for a HoldCo. For Obran, they started by creating a staffing firm and then formed another cooperative and merged them to become a HoldCo. Alternatively, an existing cash-flowing company can serve as the seed through an acquisition buyout. By skipping the risky "startup" phase, this seed company can serve as an economic foundation to fund additional acquisitions, and to grow organically. This can accelerate the path to viability and scale, and there are examples of groups that have bought one small company per year for a few years to assemble a healthy shared balance sheet.

Agility, Practicality, and Portfolio Strategy

Obran has taken a very pragmatic approach to starting and acquiring companies. Although they began by starting their staffing agencies, Obran didn't continue with a myopic focus in that space. They expanded their horizons, both in terms of industry and enterprise model, through acquiring companies in the home healthcare industry rather than starting from scratch. By choosing three industry sub-groups, Obran maximizes the advantages of specialized industry knowledge. Instead of charting unfamiliar waters and buying companies in entirely new industries, they are acquiring similar companies in familiar domains. This quasi-rollup means they will be better at assessing value, knowing where they can add value, and benefiting from economies of scale via shared services and repeatable playbooks.[112]

Scale, Ambition + Executive Incentives

The publicly stated goal of Obran is to be the world's largest worker-owned cooperative. To achieve this, they are incentivizing entrepreneurial

---

112   Camille Kerr, personal communication, November 22, 2023.

gumption in their division directors. These directors may be in a position in their career where they could start or buy their own company, raise a fund, or successfully climb the corporate ladder. Instead of asking them to take a pay cut "for the cause" Obran is offering them meaningful stakes of up to 20% in the performance of their portfolios. However, these bonuses are contingent upon corresponding increases in the disposable income of workers in the portfolio.

Assuming Obran can grow significantly over the next 10 years, it will be interesting to see how culture and governance play out and how much positive employee impact results are created. Perhaps the larger scale will generate multiplier effects that greatly benefit employees. For any organization to scale quickly, there will be growing pains, and many questions arise with respect to the impacts of scaling. Will employees be enthusiastic about ambitious growth, and be motivated to help drive growth year after year? If growth happens mostly via new company acquisition, will it impact the day-to-day experience of teams at the other companies? If major amounts of outside capital are required to finance acquisitions, what will Obran's balance sheet look like? Is unlimited growth only bad when it centralizes wealth and power, and somehow good when it benefits more stakeholders?

A Unique Leadership Blend

A different style of leadership is needed for an organization that casts everyday workers as the lead of the story. The organization's primary metrics for success are based on employee outcomes, not shareholder value. Obran leadership has put careful effort into designing the organization with both hard-nosed business rigor and deeply-seated human values. It takes a skillful blend of entrepreneurial boldness and social intelligence to strike this balance. Boldness is a common attribute in American business culture, but social cohesion and democratic decision-making are much more rare. Obran's culture seems to enable the rare ability to listen, facilitate genuine group discussion, and, defer decision-making to the collective, while at the same time not getting bogged down in the pitfalls of a consensus process.

Evolving the Culture of Worker Cooperatives

Obran is almost a hybrid of a private equity firm and a worker cooperative, which produces creative tensions where others might fall into discord. It ditches notions of martyrdom that are endemic to much of the solidarity economy. Instead, it powerfully repurposes the tools of capitalism to benefit workers. By using a private equity playbook for the people, Obran is pushing the worker cooperative movement out of its comfort zone.

Rotating Savings and Credit Associations

Charity May

Summary

At the heart of many communities in the Global South, and quietly tucked away among immigrant communities in the Global North, lies a vibrant, self-organizing banking system known as Rotating Savings and Credit Associations (ROSCAs). ROSCAs are informal community-led money collectives between a small group of individuals who agree to contribute after-tax funds to a pool, rotating the distribution of funds to each member. These informal financial systems are deeply embedded in solidarity relationships, empowering the flow of capital and financial support to those who have been ostracized by conventional and institutional systems of banking and philanthropic capital.

ROSCAs exemplify one of the longest-standing mechanisms for pooling financial and social resources, rich in both history and misconceptions among Western economies. They stand as a testament to the sustaining power of community-driven financial technology, where mutual aid is aggregated and distributed without interference from external agents.

In this case study we'll describe the global context of ROSCAs, its powerful influence in community-led initiatives, and highlight one example rooted among immigrant communities in Canada.

Fast Findings

- ROSCAs are a mutual aid tool that creates access to capital, agency, and social connections.
- ROSCAs operate based on mutual social agreements, emphasizing the importance of self-organization, flexibility, and informal governance structures.

- Despite their benefits, ROSCAs face societal and regulatory misconceptions in Western economies, including racial profiling and civil asset forfeiture.
- Cooperative initiatives can engage in movement-building work and partner with traditional financial institutions for mutual benefits, as demonstrated by the Banker Ladies Council's partnership with Meridian Credit Union.

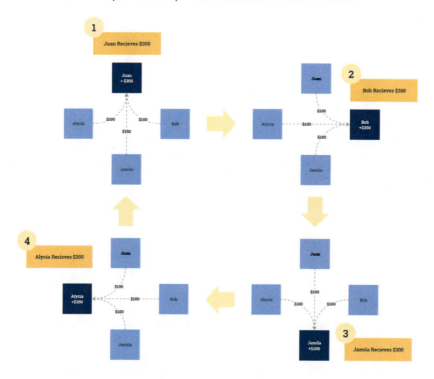

How a ROSCA group works: Each participant contributes the same sum of money each month. The total amount contributed is distributed to a different member each period until everyone has benefited from the round.

Context

A Rich Genealogy of Community Banking

ROSCAs can be traced as far back as the 1500s. Around the world, the financial technology of sharing savings among a small kinship group is recognized as the indigenous name of the community it serves. In Ghana, they are called susu, and in Ethiopia, equub. In Japan, resource pools are known as kou, and in India, chits. In Jamaica they are called partners, and in Mexico, tanda. ROSCAs flourish as a common banking practice across Africa, Asia, and the Americas regardless of being less known among conventional banking systems or considered informal finance. The evolution of microfinance and decentralized banking can find roots in the place-based and grassroots efforts of communities.[113]

ROSCAs are known to be a mutual aid system, often initiated by women, that creates agency, access to capital, and social connection through solidarity. In Dr. Caroline Hossein and Christabell P.J.'s analysis of over 400 interviews with ROSCA participants, they note that "women who make the effort to form community-focused money groups blur the lines between business, community and daily living." ROSCAs provide short-term, interest-free financing for members to use for a myriad of purposes such as investing in education, contributing to a down payment, capitalizing a new business, or funding a family vacation[114]

The roots run deep and travel wide with these communities as they immigrate to Western economies, where the values of trust, mutuality, solidarity, and care are not core tenets of the conventional financial system.

Motivation

Self Organizing Mutual Capital Flows

ROSCAs are an ancient financial technology that continues to thrive and support the cooperative commonwealth in the holding, caring, and

---

113   Hossein, C. S. (2015). Black women as co-operators: Rotating Savings and Credit Associations (ROSCAs) in the Caribbean and Canada. Journal of Co-operative Studies, 48(3), 7–18. https://hubble-live-assets.s3.eu-west-1.amazonaws.com/uk-society-for-co-operative-studies/file_asset/file/235/2015_JCS_48_3__Hossein-145.pdf

114   Hossein, C. S., & Christabell, P. J. (2022). An introduction: ROSCAs as living proof of diverse community economies. In Community Economies in the Global South: Case Studies of Rotating Savings and Credit Associations and Economic Cooperation (pp. 1–26). Oxford Academic. https://doi.org/10.1093/oso/9780198865629.003.0001 .

distribution of community resources. Such a system significantly lowers the barriers to financial access for members, who may not meet the stringent requirements of traditional banking institutions or who are often overlooked by conventional philanthropic efforts. By providing a platform where members can save, borrow, and invest with minimal formalities and zero interest, ROSCAs empower individuals with the means to manage their finances, support one another in times of need, and encourage economic self-sufficiency. This grassroots approach to capital flow ensures that resources are directly channeled to those who are most in need, thereby enhancing financial literacy and confidence among participants.

Fostering a Sense of Community

Beyond the financial benefits, ROSCAs inherently foster a strong sense of community among its members. The success of these associations is deeply rooted in the trust, solidarity, and mutual respect shared by its participants. In the context of ROSCAs among immigrant women in Canada, this sense of community is exemplified by the women who, despite possibly working low-wage jobs, are actively engaged in community development. These women demonstrate not only financial acumen in managing the collective funds but also a commitment to uplifting each member's dignity and integrity. This communal aspect of ROSCAs is a testament to their role in not just facilitating financial inclusion but also in building cohesive and empowered communities where traditional support systems may fall short.[115]

How it Works

Structure

The basic principle behind ROSCAs is a mutual social agreement among a group of self-selected members to regularly contribute a fixed amount of money into a common pool/fund. The total sum is then given to one member of the group on a rotating basis, either through a lottery system or auction.

---

115   Dr. Caroline Hossein, University of Toronto Professor, personal communication, November 26 2023.

This cycle continues until every member has received the lump sum once. At that time, the members can collectively agree to renew the rotation or disband. Membership can range from 5 to 20 and, as is the case in immigrant communities, can also span geographic regions when supported with financial technology to administer fund transfers.

With no legal institution to back their operations, the form and structure are held together largely by the social cohesion that is formed among the participating members. Such social contracts are not documented in a legal agreement. The word and action commitments of each member carry each ROSCA forward. Given the informality of its structure, the ROSCAs can easily be created or disbanded within communities, generating ease of access for participating.

Governance & Decision-making

Each member of the ROSCA has a voice in the formation of the group. While operating as a self-organizing body, each group will select or agree upon a key administrator, or 'banker lady'. The Administrator's role is to organize the social gatherings during which collections will be made, and track and administer contributions and distributions. Some groups may elect to contribute a small amount to pay an 'administrative fee' to the administrator, but in many cases, this role is voluntary. Some groups may choose to include parameters for what the funds can be used for, but fund usage is largely left up to the recipient during their rotation.

Relationships

The trust-building and power of 'peer pressure' as the inherent regulatory measures necessary to maintain the effectiveness of the ROSCA. Focus groups conducted among ROSCAs within immigrant communities have highlighted that participants enjoy and prefer participating with cash and having face-to-face interactions relative to leveraging digital tools for organizing and administering contributions and distributions.[116] "We show we can do it [business] ourselves and also... is a social thing... we drink tea and talk." – Fardowsa, a ROSCA member in Canada[117]

Member Benefits

Members participating in ROSCAs note a wide variety of benefits from this financial technology. Immediate comradery and community are some of the strongest benefits expressed by members. Other benefits include the activation of mutual savings and support and the ability to access funds in a manner that honors dignity and values. Little to no paperwork is required to participate, and anyone can initiate the formation of a ROSCA among a small group of trusted friends or family.

Takeaways

Navigating the Shadows of Informal Banking

Despite their widespread use and importance, these self-managed money collectives often operate under the radar in Western economies due to societal and regulatory misconceptions. While the pool of funds is generated with after-tax dollars, immigrant communities with pools of cash in both the United States and Canada have faced racial profiling from financial institutions and civil asset forfeiture, where authorities confiscate suspicious concentrations of cash without any evidence of a crime being committed. Such laws paired with implicit biases can create a more hostile

---

116   Hossein, C. S., & Christabell, P. J. (2022). An introduction: ROSCAs as living proof of diverse community economies. In Community Economies in the Global South: Case Studies of Rotating Savings and Credit Associations and Economic Cooperation (pp. 1–26). Oxford Academic. https://doi.org/10.1093/oso/9780198865629.003.0001 .

117   Hossein, C. S. (2015). Black women as co-operators: Rotating Savings and Credit Associations (ROSCAs) in the Caribbean and Canada. Journal of Co-operative Studies, 48(3), 7–18. https://hubble-live-assets.s3.eu-west-1.amazonaws.com/uk-society-for-co-operative-studies/file_asset/file/235/2015_JCS_48_3__Hossein-145.pdf

environment for these communities that further drives them away from established financial systems and technology.[118]

What greatly contributes to the unfriendly environment towards ROSCAs in the U.S. and Canada is the lack of awareness of the nature and heritage of these groups and their essential role in community development and mutual aid. Formal financial regulations often do not cover ROSCAs, which leads to potential legal ambiguities and limited protection for participants. However, the Global South demonstrates leadership for the Global North to follow in acknowledging the economic benefits of ROSCAs and community leadership demonstrated by the organizers of ROSCAs.[119]

One example is evidenced in India. State governments in India acknowledged that chits were fulfilling a key role in the economy, providing access to capital for the underbanked and unbanked. They instated a registration process for chit-fund participants to register their chit-fund for state regulation. When and if bad actors are operating in a chit-fund circle, the participants can lean on the state to enforce default measures. With regulation comes the acknowledgment of chits as alternative financial lenders that coexist alongside conventional banking and finance.[120] [121]

However, the women interviewed by Hossein and the leading ROSCAs in Canada are not sure that state regulation is the way they want to go to raise awareness and acceptance. The views about formality are

---

118 Civil forfeiture. (n.d.). In Legal Information Institute, Cornell Law School. https://www.law.cornell.edu/wex/civil_forfeiture

119 Hossein, C. S., & Christabell, P. J. (2022). An introduction: ROSCAs as living proof of diverse community economies. In Community Economies in the Global South: Case Studies of Rotating Savings and Credit Associations and Economic Cooperation (pp. 1–26). Oxford Academic. https://doi.org/10.1093/oso/9780198865629.003.0001

120 The Chit Funds Act,1982. India. (1982)., www.indiacode.nic.in/bitstream/123456789/15355/1/the_chit_funds_act%2C_1982.pdf

121 "Chit funds in India. (n.d.). Business Maps of India. https://business.mapsofindia.com/investment-industry/chit-funds.html

mixed. What they do know for certain is that the "oppression, surveillance, the confiscation [through civil asset forfeiture] and all kinds of negative stereotypes to stop."[122]

The Banker Ladies of Canada[123] [124]

National initiatives of movement-building work are underway to shift the narrative and raise awareness beyond practicing immigrant communities. The Banker Ladies Council in Canada, established in 2020, focuses on educating the public about their cooperative rights, enhancing the capacity of informal sectors, and advocating for ROSCAs within Canada's financial industry. Led by Director Andria Barrett, the Council comprises 12 women of the African Diaspora who hold Banker Lady positions in their ROSCAs or are active participants in one. Most of these women have been involved in ROSCAs their entire lives and remember the ROSCAs of prior generations.

The Banker Ladies Council is an initiative under the Black Social Economy Project formed by Dr. Caroline Hossein, which seeks to combat injustices and promote the Black Social Economy's role in creating a more equitable economic landscape.[125] The Council aims to foster cooperative economics and address the challenges ROSCA participants face nation-wide, including efforts to form a ROSCA federation for broader educational outreach to government, law enforcement, and traditional finance institutions. The advocacy efforts are opening doors to partner with traditional banking systems. In a historic effort to acknowledge this community work,

---

122 Dr. Caroline Hossein, University of Toronto Professor, personal communication, November 26, 2023.

123 Diverse Solidarity Economies Collective. (2021). The banker ladies. In Films For Action. https://www.filmsforaction.org/watch/the-banker-ladies/

124 Collective Diaspora. (2023, September). The Banker Ladies Council: Demanding respect for African Cooperative finance [Video]. Youtube. https://geo.coop/articles/banker-ladies-council

125 Holmes, N. (2022, March 30). ROSCAS: a model for Sustainable Economic development. Medium. https://medium.com/postgrowth/roscas-a-model-for-sustainable-economic-development-2ccac335f542

in 2023, Meridian Credit Union of Ontario (one of the largest credit unions in Canada) became one of the first banks to recognize the work of the Banker Ladies and put institutional resources behind this verbal support. A 5-year commitment that includes $100,000 of grant capital, unlimited technical assistance, access to buildings and infrastructure, and other support as needed. Through these resources, the Banker Ladies Council will be able to continue its advocacy and community education work. This commitment is a kickstarter for the Banker Ladies Council, as ongoing support and acknowledgment are still needed.[126]

Resource Sharing is for Everyone

A low barrier to entry activates resource sharing and distribution. Individuals can start with what savings they have to contribute. Small business owners can pool funds to support working capital needs or initiate a rainy day fund. While the informal practice of ROSCAs does not include formal agreements, each sharing circle can establish protocols and procedures that provide the security and sense of trust desired by the members.

---

126   Ontario Co-operative Association. (2023, October 19). Ground-breaking collaboration to focus on raising the profile of rotating savings and credit associations in Ontario [Press release]. https://ontario.coop/raising-profile-roscas-ontario

Sardex: A Complementary Currency

Charity May

Summary

In this case study, we look at Sardex – one of the most successful mutual credit and complementary currency financial technologies in the modern era. Sardex is a digital platform that facilitates the trading of production goods and services among small and medium enterprises (SMEs) within a defined geographic region. The platform issues credits in digital Sardex units, the complementary currency pegged to the Euro, to jumpstart purchases when businesses join as members. Members buy and sell goods and services from each other without the need for cash. Each transaction operates as a closed circuit, whereby a purchase and sale must match to bring the account's credit balance to zero. The circuit promotes the circulation of the Sardex units, enabling local businesses to access liquidity through the trading of excess goods and services in Sardex units.

> "Sardex is thus a technology that is symbolic and material, virtual and real, individual and social, old and new, effective and rational, capitalist and commons-based."[127]

This case study explores Sardex's development from one founder's perspective. We highlight the successes and obstacles and identify the groundwork laid for future digital platforms that empower geographically rooted communities to forge a more sovereign economic narrative. Sardex demonstrates that the concept of money can be formed to serve a community and to empower mutual benefit in the sharing and redistribution of resources.

---

127 Motta, W., Dini, P., & Sartori, L. (2017). Self-Funded Social Impact Investment: An interdisciplinary analysis of the Sardex Mutual Credit System. Journal of Social Entrepreneurship, 8(2), 149–164. https://doi.org/10.1080/19420676.2017.1321576

Fast Findings

- Mutual credit systems and complementary currencies are financial technologies that can thrive in a regional and commercial context.

- Money as a commodity gives way to incentives for accumulation and speculation, which are the antithesis of financial tools designed for mutual aid and circulation of capital.

- Sardex's intentionality in the design of the fintech platform gave way to a successful model that evoked community buy-in to reach high transaction volumes and expand the use of Sardex units from the business sector to the government sector.

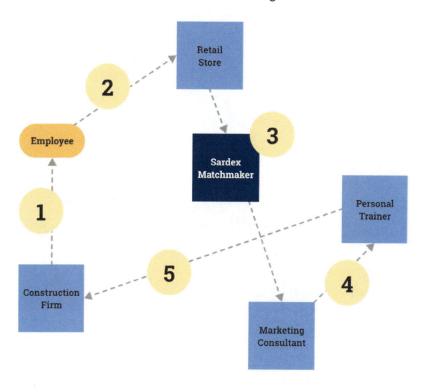

A Simplified Sardex Unit Circuit Illustration: Each participating business begins with credit in Sardex units. These credits are designed to flow in between the businesses, and typically flow through different business sectors at varying velocity. Matches are also facilitated by a broker acting as the Sardex Matchmaker. The circuit is complete when the business trade balance returns to zero.

134 | Assets in Common

Context

The Seedbed of Innovation during Economic Catastrophes[128]

In the wake of the global financial crisis of 2008, five friends with zero history in the financial sector, found themselves back home on the island of Sardinia, Italy, facing a local catastrophic economy. The prospects of job security, opportunity, and promise were grim. With nothing to lose, these friends began a quest to understand what methods have existed in history that improved resiliency to global market collapse among regional communities. In their searches, they discovered the WIR (Wirtschaftsring-Genossenschaft)[129], also known as the Swiss Economic Circle.

During the Great Depression, currency shortages were a part of the financial instability worldwide. WIR was developed as a response to the failure of centralized currencies to keep capital and goods moving. The WIR acted as a complementary currency system that did not replace the central currency but rather introduced a private currency that allowed dual-currency transactions.[130]

Facing a similar global financial collapse, the founders of Sardex sought out to activate a complementary currency based on mutual credit for the local businesses of Sardinia. They were interested in testing out whether SMEs would trust each other enough to use a trading mechanism that wasn't the Euro.

---

128   Littera, G., Sartori, L., Dini, P., & Antoniadis, P. (2017). From an idea to a scalable working model: merging economic benefits with social values in Sardex. International Journal of Community Currency Research 21, 21, 6–21. https://doi.org/10.15133/j.ijccr.2017.002

129   WIR (German: Wirtschaftsring-Genossenschaft) is an independent complementary currency system developed in 1934.

130   Studer, T. (1998). WIR and the Swiss national economy (P. H. Beard, Trans.) [Report]. WIR Bank, Basel. https://base.socioeco.org/docs/wir_and_the_swiss_national_economy.pdf

A Complementary Currency for the Island

The Sardex platform allows businesses across various industries within Sardinia to trade goods and services instead of fiat money. Each transaction is still subject to VAT paid in Euros. Each member business is granted Sardex credit (the mutual credit system), which is equivalent to the Euro value, though Sardex cannot be exchanged for Euros (more on this later). Over thirteen years, the platform has grown to host over 7,000 active professionals, traders, and SMEs with more than 600 million transactions. Transaction volume illustrates that the average number a Sardex credit changes hands in 12 months is 4.8 times, compared to 1.0 times for the Euro, and 1.5 times for USD. Businesses can also use Sardex to provide goods/services to employees (like corporate welfare) and consumers (generating cashback in Sardex credits). Sardex also facilitates the implementation of commercial credit circuits in 12 other regions in Italy, through partnerships with local governments.

One of the founders, Guiseppe Littera, anchors the foundational purpose from which Sardex began. "Our idea from the start was to create something that would outlive us. We didn't want to 'rule' the platform and become techno-feudalistic, which is commonplace in the tech startup world."[131]

This intention was made clear when Sardex was under development, they searched for the appropriate structure and capital to build this mutual aid technology for sustainability and scale. They desired to adopt cooperative economics where possible, and eventually see the membership community share in ownership and governance of the enterprise.

"Sardex plays a role similar to the state, as provider of a robust social structure that supports a stable socially embedded world (the network of

---

131   Giuseppe Littera, one of the original founders of Sardex, personal communication, December 1, 2023.

exchange) where economic actors can engage with each other, trust each other, and trade."[132]

Aligning Capital to Build Social Infrastructure

Before Sardex could attain the goal of shared ownership, it needed outside capital to develop the platform and team. They sought investors with a more patient and collective investment strategy, aligned with building a digital platform company as a public service across the region. Sardex founders were faced with negotiating the term sheets among conventional venture capital. With a directive to scale towards an initial public offering, the pace of fundraising began to move past the pace Sardex needed to build the platform more aligned with cooperative economics.

After the initial investors provided seed capital, Sardex conducted two fundraising rounds, one in 2016 and another in 2020, raising a total of ~$10 million. This was followed with the last attempt at democratizing participation by conducting an equity crowdfunding campaign in 2021, raising another $1.6 million, over 2x the initial ask.[133] [134]

---

132 Sartori, L., & Dini, P. (2016). From Complementary Currency to Institution: A micro-macro study of the Sardex Mutual Credit System. Stato E Mercato: Quadrimestrale Di Analisi Dei Meccanismi E Delle Istituzioni Sociali, Politiche Ed Economiche, 107(2), 273–304. https://doi.org/10.1425/84070.

133 Angelou, L. M. (2020, July 26). The Italian fintech company Sardex collects €5.8 million in a financing round. Born2Invest. http://www.born2invest.com/articles/italian-fintech-company-sardex-e5-8-million-financing-round/.

134 Atwood, I. (2021, April 26). SardexPay launches a crowdfunding campaign on BacktoWork24. Born2Invest. https://born2invest.com/articles/sardexpay-virtual-currency-fintech-opens-up-to-crowdfunding-investors/.

Motivation

"What works in business is to tie oneself to the territory and the identity of the place, instead of shaping ideas from abroad that have little to do with Italian culture. Technology must never be an end in itself, but it must be put at the service of the territory."

— Marco De Guzzis, Sardex CEO[135]

The development of this complementary currency is grounded deeply in the place and cultural history of Sardinia and its position relative to the broader economy. Sardex took root in a distraught economy, exemplifying how complementary currencies are counter-cyclical.

Complementary Currencies as a Solidarity Measure

In the case of Sardex units, the "capital" is actual products, services, and goods that are traded on the exchange. As a complementary currency, it cannot be traded for Euros. This prevents speculation and commodification of Sardex credits, which are simply created and extinguished to facilitate trades.

Since there is zero interest on Sardex credits and no possibility of arbitrage and speculation it stimulates the circulation of goods and services instead. This provides liquidity by allowing SMEs to trade their surplus inventory and excess capacity on the exchange.

Match-Making for Trading Surplus[136]

Participating businesses that sign up to become members are given Sardex credit to begin trading. However, the platform has built circulation and trading incentives into the platform to dissuade any party from accumulating

---

135   Ibid.

136   Sartori, L., & Dini, P. (2016). From Complementary Currency to Institution: A micro-macro study of the Sardex Mutual Credit System. Stato E Mercato: Quadrimestrale Di Analisi Dei Meccanismi E Delle Istituzioni Sociali, Politiche Ed Economiche, 107(2), 273–304. https://doi.org/10.1425/84070.

Sardex units. The other component that promotes circulation is the certainty of finding a match or someone to trade with. This is where the nuances of the regional economy of Sardinia play a large role. Sardex has to be quite hands-on in managing membership because the businesses that participate correlate to the types of goods and services that will be traded on the platform.

Sardex goes through a robust process to review applications and properly vet the companies that express interest in participating in the mutual credit network. Because of the hyper-locality of the trading, the diversification of the membership needs to be balanced. For example, if there are too many of one company type, the circuit of exchange could break or cause an accumulation of Sardex balances.

How it Works

Structure

Sardex S.p.A. is a joint stock company operating a subscription-based digital services platform that provides private credit-clearing services for SMEs. SMEs interacting with the service trade Sardex units within a circuit, defined as an informal, economic circle between members. Businesses become members through an application and vetting process, where they enter a subscription and membership agreement to pay a subscription fee for access to the platform.

Each member is extended a line of Sardex credit, which enables them to immediately buy from other businesses within the network without any cash. When they make an equivalent sale on credit, it brings their account balance back to zero. Each transaction has up to 12 months to rebalance to zero. All exchanges are recorded on a digital ledger, ensuring transparency and accountability. Sardex units exist solely within the platform – they cannot be earned or spent outside the Sardex network, preventing external trading.

Governance & Decision-making

The design and operations of the platform are governed as a joint-stock company with a board of directors consisting of designations made by founders, lead investors, and other shareholders.

One of the most interesting design features of the mutual credit system is the self-governance built into the rules for members. The extensive application process and clear membership agreement promote self-regulation and social norms to keep platform activity aligned with circulating the complementary currency as intended. The membership agreement signed by all active members specifies conditions and parameters related to behavior on the platform, structured effectively in a manner to promote self-governance among the members via the digital platform. A thorough vetting process is conducted once a business applies to join. The membership agreement limits transaction volume conducted in Sardex to a negotiated level proportionate to each business type and expected volume. In addition, there is a maximum amount of credit permitted based on certain indicators such as the enterprise's history and turnover rate.[137]

As a mutual credit system, there still remains the risk of default. In the cases that negative balances on the platform cannot be recovered for any reason, a credit recovery company is hired.

Economic Interest

Economic interest among Sardex stakeholders varies. Through multiple funding rounds, Sardex issued different share classes, ranging from Class A for founders to Class E for later-stage investors. The equity crowdfunding campaign conducted in 2021 resulted in the issuance of Class CF shares for those participants. While founders originally sought out user ownership, Sardex SME members do not actually hold equity in the company. The use

---

137   Fleischman, T., Dini, P., & Littera, G. (2020). Liquidity-Saving through Obligation-Clearing and Mutual Credit: An Effective Monetary Innovation for SMEs in Times of Crisis. Journal of Risk and Financial Management, 13(12), 295. https://doi.org/10.3390/jrfm13120295

of venture capital investment leads to its ownership and governance model staying largely intact.[138]

SME members pay a subscription fee to operate on the platform but do not benefit from profit sharing or get incentives for higher transaction volume. In the early stages of development, Sardex experimented with transaction fees, however, the founders quickly determined that the model misaligned incentives, so they adopted a subscription-based model instead.

One risk that remains when forming any trading service platform is regulatory risk. Sardex successfully aligned the interests of its local government by ensuring that VAT is paid separately in euros rather than Sardex credits.

Relationships

Members on the Sardex platform come from diverse regional sectors like construction, wholesale, professional services, retail, hospitality, and manufacturing. Sardex facilitates exchanges primarily between businesses within a specific geographic region. However, in its growth and iteration, the platform expanded capabilities to allow businesses to pay employee salaries with Sardex units, giving employees the ability to participate in the marketplace. Another initiative is DigiPay4Growth, a 'time-delayed' credit for payments of public sector suppliers. This allows regional governments to pay suppliers in Sardex units, generating credits the suppliers can use.

A circuit's success depends on members' intrinsic trust in the platform and each trade. Members understand that to access the benefits, they must reciprocate by offering similar benefits to other members. While members can set the price for the goods and services they are trading, they are motivated to set a price that is comparable to the off-platform value of the good or service.

---

138   Sardex. (2021). Sardex S.P.A. Shareholders' Agreement. In Sardexpay. https://www.sardexpay.net/app/uploads/2021/11/03-SARDEX-Crowdfunding-Round-Shareholders-Agreement-EXE-v-3_Omissis.pdf

Little room is left in the functional design of Sardex to benefit members who may attempt to stock up on credits or create arbitrage in the value set for the trade. Such activities break the digital circuit, as well as the circuit of trust among members. Such measures illustrate that social agreement, even in the operations of a digital platform, can provide a regulatory function among a community. This suggests less of a need for a third party or governmental regulatory function when the relational contracts are intact.

Sardex also extends the use of its platform to other regions across mainland Italy, allowing for exclusive membership and transactions within a hyperlocal context. These affiliated networks leverage the technology platform of Sardex with the support of local partner organizations to self-operate.

Member Benefits

"The online credit circuit platform itself is only one element for building a successful mutual credit network. Going out and recruiting new members face-to-face, teaching them how to use the platform effectively, providing effective deal-brokerage services – these are essential too."

– Paolo Dini[139]

A core operating function of the trading platform is the brokers, or 'match-makers'. Brokers disseminate information about participating members, supporting the efforts to find matches among goods and services offered on the platform. With their focus on distributing information and bringing buyers and sellers together, trade efficiency grows, as well as the speed at which member credit balances return to zero, squashing

---

139   Zimmermann, N. (2018, September 5). B2B cashless currency set to take on the world. dw.com. http://www.dw.com/en/ italys-b2b-cashless-sardex-currency-set-to-take-on-the-world/a-45300395

accumulation. There are no transaction fees, as is the case in other small business trading platforms that use brokers.[140]

Takeaways

A Quest to Redesign Money by the People[141]

The development of Sardex as a mutual credit system deliberately breaks the logic of neoliberal capitalism by recognizing that money is not neutral, and the medium of exchange can be redesigned. To fully understand how Sardex works as a complementary currency, and why its intentional design was a success, we revisit the textbook definition of what money is.

To account as money, these four characteristics are present:

- a unit of account,
- a medium of exchange,
- a store of value, and
- a means of payment.

During the design phase of Sardex, the founders were deliberate in tweaking two core functions of how money works: (a) removing any incentive to accumulate the units and (b) removing any possibility of speculation and arbitrage. While Sardex provides a unit of account, it is pegged to the Euro. Sardex also offers a medium of exchange to facilitate trading. However, Sardex units cannot be exchanged for Euros. This contrasts with other digital currencies, such as Bitcoin, which can be traded for fiat money.

For Sardex, the value is stored in the production of goods and services which are valued at a certain number of Sardex units, relative to

---

140   Littera, G., Sartori, L., Dini, P., & Antoniadis, P. (2017). From an idea to a scalable working model: merging economic benefits with social values in Sardex. International Journal of Community Currency Research 21, 21, 6–21. https://doi.org/10.15133/j.ijccr.2017.002

141   Motta, W., Dini, P., & Sartori, L. (2017). Self-Funded Social Impact Investment: An interdisciplinary analysis of the Sardex Mutual Credit System. Journal of Social Entrepreneurship, 8(2), 149–164. https://doi.org/10.1080/19420676.2017.1321576

their Euro value. Sardex does not allow for any interest to be charged or accumulated through the exchange. This is contrary to the ordinary money systems, whereby the "medium of exchange is itself a commodity, whose price is the rate of interest".[142]

By redefining the foundational dynamics of money—eschewing accumulation and speculation while firmly anchoring its value in tangible goods and services—Sardex pioneers a transformative approach to economic exchange. This recalibration not only distinguishes complementary currencies from the volatile domain of cryptocurrencies but also sets the stage for exploring how such innovations can foster more resilient and equitable community economies moving forward.

Aligning Capital Investments with Public Goods

In the formation of Sardex, aligning capital investments with the development of public goods revealed a nuanced challenge. The endeavor to secure the necessary funding for technological development and operational growth initially aligned with investor interests in scalability. In reflections with Littera on the role that resourcing capital played in the formation of Sardex, he laments the lack of values-aligned capital structures.

The potential for Sardex, and similar platforms, to catalyze local economic empowerment extends beyond traditional venture capital investment metrics. This suggests an opportunity for public finance mechanisms to directly support service platforms dedicated to activating hyperlocal economic development. There is untapped potential in combining public finance mechanisms with community-centric fintech to explore to achieve broader socio-economic goals within a region.

The Road to Interoperable Sovereignty

Sardex partnered extensively with the public sector to design, test, and promote the idea of commercial credit circuits as complementary currencies. These efforts included publishing research on the foundation of

---

142   Amato, M., & Fantacci, L. (2016). Failures on the market and market failures: a complementary currency for bankruptcy procedures. Cambridge Journal of Economics, 40(5), 1377–1395. http://www.jstor.org/stable/24915645

Sardex as a mutual credit system and complementary currency, as well as on the formation of Sardex as a socio-political enterprise. As Sardex evolved its platform, the company worked with the local governments of other regions to instate commercial credit circuits. As of 2024, Sardex is powering regional circuits across 15 regions in Italy.

Interoperability, in the context of digital platforms and community currencies, refers to the capacity of diverse systems and organizations to work seamlessly together, enabling the exchange of information and value across different networks without barriers. Littera believes this concept is crucial for communities seeking to leverage digital platforms for economic and social empowerment, as it ensures that their systems can connect and communicate with broader networks, thus expanding their reach and impact.

"The problem with 95% of community currencies is that if they reach a stable point, they fail because they do not build interoperability into the foundational infrastructure." – Giuseppe Littera

For communities utilizing complementary currencies and mutual credit systems like Sardex, interoperability is not just a technical feature, it extends the pathway to community sovereignty, though, in the current form of Sardex, it's not fully realized. The goal is to allow these communities to maintain their unique economic identities and governance structures while engaging in larger economic ecosystems. This capacity to interact on a larger scale without losing control over local resources or values fosters a form of digital sovereignty, empowering communities to navigate global systems on their own terms.

By embedding interoperability into their foundational infrastructure, communities can avoid isolation, enhance their resilience, and secure their economic independence, making it an essential consideration for any community-focused digital platform aiming for long-term sustainability and autonomy.

Savings Pools: A Mutual Lending Practice

Charity May

Summary

Savings pools are a mutual aid tool formed when a group of typically 10 to 20 people self-organize to aggregate their savings and offer interest-free multi-year loans among its members. Modeled after a cooperative loan and savings bank in Sweden, JAK Members Bank, savings pools are distinct from other mutual aid tools in their use of savings points, or reciprocity formula, instead of interest. The reciprocity formula encourages borrowers to pay back the amount they owe plus save an equivalent amount to lend the same amount to other members. While the pool of funds made available in any given savings pool varies by group, some groups have been able to support members in purchasing homes and business working capital.

Savings pools are successful when there is full participation by its members in administration and governance. Savings pools are informally organized, yet loan agreements are used to establish protocols such as use restrictions, default measures, and transfer rights in the event of loss. The group reviews and approves each loan request, amount, use, and repayment terms. Because of the high touch engagement and deeper level of transparency that comes with extending credit among a close-knit community, savings pools can be harder to implement. A high level of trust and transparency is required and can be difficult to cultivate if not pre-existing.

For example, borrowing $1,000 over 10 months requires $100 monthly payments. Thus, after the loan balance is returned, reciprocity payments kick in. The borrower repays the $1,000 and also contributes another $1,000 in savings to the pool to lend to others (the "reciprocity component"). They can then withdraw this $1,000 or keep it in the pool.

In this case study, we outline the inspiration that led to various communities of savings pools on the islands of Aotearoa, New Zealand, and follow this influence into North Carolina in the United States.

Fast Findings

- Inspired by international models like JAK Members Bank in Sweden, savings pools in New Zealand and the U.S., emphasize interest-free lending and mutual aid, highlighting a significant shift from conventional banking practices.

- While there is room for technology to play a core role in supporting the operations of savings pools, the essence of these groups—personal connection, mutual trust, and direct engagement—remains paramount.

- Efforts to expand savings pools across diverse communities encounter challenges related to trust-building and socioeconomic disparities.

- The dissolution of the National Savings Pool Association and the exploration of government-supported infrastructure for a cross-pool lending network highlight ongoing efforts to enhance the reach and impact of savings pools.

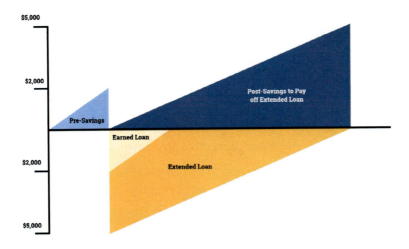

An Illustrated Model of Interest-Free Lending: The loan repayment includes a savings component with no interest incurred. Once the loan is fully repaid, the member has accumulated additional savings, which can be reserved in the pool or withdrawn.

Context

A Vision for Interest-Free Financing

Living Economies Trust, a non-profit enterprise, emerged in 2002 out of a group of community activists in New Zealand searching for ways to share and distribute financial resources. One of the board trustees, Bryan Innes, traveled to Sweden to study the member-managed savings and loan bank – JAK Members Bank (JAK). The bank's mission is to reduce indebtedness to encourage the production of a more sustainable economy. JAK Members' Bank was developed from a concept that grew out of Denmark which does not charge interest on loans or pay interest on deposits. The bank offers interest-free services to its members, making money just to cover its operating expenses through membership and administrative fees.

The bank manages its deposits and liquidity needs among its over 30,000 members through the use of a savings point system.[143] [144] [145]

Bryan brought this inspiration back to Living Economies Trust and formed a group with families pooling funds to build houses on community land and then expanded into offering workshops and roleplaying to educate others on savings pools. Living Economies Trust does not monitor, fund, regulate, or oversee the savings pools they seed. The primary focus of Living Economies Trust is to educate and provide group training to foster the seeding of new savings pools in Aoreatora, with reach into the U.S. and abroad. Phil Stevens, board member, and educator at Living Economies Trust, notes there are about 100 distinct savings pools across New Zealand that have been influenced by the education and inspiration of Living Economies Trust.[146] [147]

Motivation

"The whole purpose of savings pools is not just to provide interest-free lending, but it's also to build a community support system or mutual aid network that is founded on a lot of non-financial means of exchange."

– Phil Stevens[148]

---

143   Anielski, M. (2004). An assessment of Sweden's No-Interest Bank. The JAK Members Bank. http://www.monneta.org/wp-content/uploads/2022/09/JAK-An-Assessment-of-Swedens-No-Interest-Bank.pdf

144   JAK Bank (Sweden). (2024, February 8). Monneta. https://monneta.org/en/jak-bank-sweden/

145   Conaty, P., & Lewis, M. (2012). Sweden's JAK Bank liberating community finance from the ball & chain of compound interest. Makingwaves, 20(3), 51. https://base.socioeco.org/docs/mw200351.pdf

146   Phil Stevens of Living Economies Trust, personal communication, October 17, 2023.

147   Living Economies Trust. www.livingeconomies.nz.

148   Interview with Phil Stevens of Living Economies Trust, 17 October 2023.

This communal approach to saving and lending emerges from a collective desire to create access to capital for those who understand the value of credit but reject interest-bearing debt. Savings pools are deeply rooted in values of trust, mutuality, and a shared belief to the detriment of interest-driven growth, reflecting a conscious departure from conventional lending practices. Within these closely-knit groups, the act of sharing personal financial details becomes a core gesture of solidarity and reciprocity. This not only facilitates financial goals but also strengthens communal bonds and the sharing of risk, highlighting the profound impact of shared financial journeys on fostering community resilience.

Small Business Capital for North Carolina Ecovillage

About 30 miles east of Asheville, North Carolina is the town of Black Mountain, where an intentional permaculture community resides. Earthaven Ecovillage consists of about 100 adults (as of 2024) who have committed to living and sharing resources. After learning of the cost-prohibitive capital requirements needed to launch a mutual credit union, Zev Friedman and Courtney Allen turned to savings pools for their community to activate capital and resource distribution. They reached out to Phil at Living Economies Trust, who provided the necessary training and insight. About 18 community members participate in the savings pool. The initial focus of the savings pools was to provide the start-up capital to help members advance towards self-sufficiency through small business ownership. Since inception, through to 2024, the savings pool has aggregated over $70,000, issued several loans, and expanded the use of funds beyond small business support to include housing and debt relief.

Expanding this work further, Zev Friedman initiated Cooperate WNC, a local non-profit committed to supporting the development of other savings pools. Cooperate WNC has a keen interest in expanding small business loans through savings pools and is working with a local Community Development Financial Institution (CDFI) in Asheville to do that. What they are finding is that the savings pool loan can unlock access to additional small business capital at the CDFI.[149]

How it Works

Structure

Savings Pools are informal self-organized and self-governing bodies of people committed to saving and sharing these savings as loans among its members. Members contribute to a shared pool of funds that they can borrow from without interest. The funds are held in a shared bank account managed by multiple signatories. Instead of paying interest, they repay the principal plus an equal amount into the pool for others to borrow as their reciprocity contribution. This keeps the available funds balanced with demand and is a fair accounting method. The pools aim to build community support systems through non-financial exchange as well.

Governance & Decision-making

Lending parameters are designed and set using legal agreements between the borrowing member and the group. Each member has one vote. Every savings pool has discretion on how they handle absence when a decision needs to be made. For example, one group may decide that proxy voting or absent voting is permitted to get as close as possible to full participation, and consensus works best when membership is active and fully participating.

Meetings are scheduled regularly to gather and discuss members' lives and financial needs, as well as to assess the health of the loans issued. During these meetings, members who might be anticipating challenges in making payments, can bring these concerns to the group and respond with caring measures to support.

At Earthaven, meetings are held monthly and in person. There are rotating roles for each member to hold: notetaker, facilitator, and the "boss". The boss acts similarly to a committee chair, setting the agenda and

---

149   Zev Friedman and Debbie Lienhart of Earthaven EcoVillage, personal communication, November 3, 2023.

ensuring that the assigned notetaker and facilitator are present. Rotations are every three months, which allows each member to fulfill each of these roles. Another role that is assigned but held by the same person is the record-keeper. The record-keeper is tasked by the group to manage the financial and accounting records of contributions, loans issued, repayments, and reciprocity schedules.[150]

Loan Terms

Loan terms are outlined in the loan agreement that members sign when they take out a loan. The terms and conditions in the loan agreement are mutually agreed upon between the borrowing member and the rest of the group. Terms of repayment are established based on the borrowing member's capacity to pay. Loans can be secured with collateral or can be unsecured. The use of funds is also a component that members of the group have a say in. Some savings pools may mutually agree to restrict the use of funds for certain purposes. For example, Earthaven prioritized small business loans to its members when they started their community savings pool.[151]

Relationships

Phil stresses the importance of nurturing kinship bonds within a savings pool. Sharing personal resources in a mutual aid approach requires a deeper level of trust and vulnerability. The structure of the savings pools encourages trust building and exploration of people's relationships with money in a communal setting. Models of aggregating people together who do not already have established kinship bonds are not as successful. In their education and template guides, Living Economies Trust encourages the use

---

150   Zev Friedman and Debbie Lienhart of Earthaven Ecovillage, personal communication, November 3, 2023.

151   Review of Living Economies Trust Standard Template Loan Agreement as of October 2023.

of a membership agreement to acknowledge the individual commitment being made to the money collective.[152]

Friedman also highlights this in his observations of the Earthaven savings pool. He notes that starting within an intentional community enables them to have stronger relational dynamics. "We start each meeting with a pretty deep check-in for everyone to get a chance to speak about their whole life. Then we hone it down to what's going on in our finances. Because we know that whatever is going on in my relational life will affect my financial well-being. So people are willing to be pretty vulnerable. This leads up to the financial check-in where folks share "how much am I depositing" and "how much am I saving" for this month. These check-ins create a much more caring context than just the mechanics of depositing money. All this combined, we think, leads to the success of our pool."[153]

Regulation & Risk Management

Savings pools are not regulated or required to register as a financial service provider, as the structure and intention of the pools do not qualify due to the lack of service fees. In the Savings Pools playbook provided by Living Economies Trust, the following risk measures are adhered to for monitoring the pools' activities:[154]

- members pay their savings directly into the pool's account;
- monthly statements record all transactions – past, current, and pledged;
- members may access bank statements on request;
- every transaction requires the whole pool's acceptance;
- all transaction decisions are recorded;

---

152   Phil Stevens of Living Economies Trust, personal communication, October 17, 2023.

153   Zev Friedman and Debbie Lienhart of Earthaven Ecovillage, personal communication, November 3, 2023.

154   "The Common Sense Finance of Savings Pools." Living Economies Trust. Retrieved October 2023. (Contact authors for access.)

- a joint account is open in the name of a few volunteers;

- any withdraw requires at least two signatories;

- a record keeper ensures that all transactions correspond to pool decisions.

There is always a risk of delayed or no payments, even among savings pool members who are mutually aligned. Savings pools that utilize collateral register security interests in personal property. This gives the group the legal right to draw on the collateral in the event of a default. This is useful when issued loans are for equipment or other real assets. Rates of default are reportedly low, in large part due to the role that social cohesion plays in forming trust, mutuality, and responsibility. [155]

Members also hold the right to signal their risk appetite for each mutual loan issued. As an example, if one member feels the loan request is too risky or does not agree with the use of funds, that member's financial portion of the loan pool is excluded from the pooled amount issued in the loan.

Takeaways

Technology Integration in Savings Pool Operations

The integration of technology varies by savings pool. Phil acknowledges that the process of administering decision-making among a mutual self-organizing body is likely the most complicated component of operating a savings pool. Many savings pools in New Zealand utilize Loomio, a digital platform that enables distributed, transparent, and inclusive decision-making. However, financial recording is still largely governed by spreadsheets and manual tracking. An opportunity exists to create a savings pool app to assist in administering the loans, documentation, reciprocity points, and decision-making. Yet, any tool developed must serve the community and honor its agency. In-person engagement, while more difficult to manage

---

155   Phil Stevens of Living Economies Trust, personal communication, October 17, 2023.

for low participation, remains key to fostering the social connection, mutual trust, and reciprocity felt in the savings pool.

Barriers to Adoption Among Diversified Groups

While there have been attempts to bring disparate people together to start a savings pool, these efforts have been challenged given the relational and cultural dynamics that can be at play when trust is cultivated instead of enhanced. This can inadvertently lead to groups of savings pools that are more homogenous in terms of race and socioeconomic status.

Socioeconomic status can be a determining factor for initiation and ongoing participation in savings pools. Individuals and families with established savings, as well as individuals who are richer in time and capacity, are the demographics most likely to initiate an active savings pool group. There can be inherent power dynamics at play when wealth gaps exist among members. Cautious efforts are necessary to name these dynamics and address them with care. But efforts to ensure broader access are felt. Some groups may agree that the first rounds of loans offered are made to members with high-interest debt, allowing the community to come together and support others in eliminating their exposure to extractive financing.

Infrastructure Needed for Cross-Pool Lending

In some instances, members of a savings pool may need to borrow an amount that exceeds the capacity of their home pool (the pool they hold membership with). In this scenario, some pools partner together without organizing in a legal form to expand the borrowing capacity for this member. This has been done by allowing the borrowing member to become a guest member in a second pool. With one loan at their home pool, and a second loan to cover the balance in the second pool, repayment terms are staggered to facilitate full repayment of both loans. The loan from the member's home pool, for example, might extend the term longer given that the relationship and history are well established. The second pool, however, may request a shorter term for repayment as the relationship is not as rooted with the guest member.[156]

Living Economies Trust recognizes the need to develop infrastructure for cross-pool lending and has led efforts to explore this further with partners in New Zealand. In 2016, they formed the National Savings Pool Association to support the facilitation of cross-pool lending. The intentions were to increase the availability of mutual benefit among the scattered individual pools. However, legal interpretation led to the Association being dissolved, as savings pools are not legal entities and therefore cannot administer lending between the groups but only between individual members. Cross-pool lending continues, though the facilitation is not direct and is held through a process known as Groups Enjoying Mutual Support (GEMS).[157]

Efforts to streamline an approach to allow for cross-pool lending in New Zealand remain. Phil suggests there is a role for the government to play directly in the facilitation and establishment of infrastructure to support cross-pool borrowings and repayments between individuals and even small businesses. Careful considerations are needed to determine not only the appropriate governance structure for such a network but also the appropriate technology to facilitate the governance. Top of mind is preserving the autonomy and close bonds among the individual pools.[158]

---

156   Phil Stevens of Living Economies Trust, personal communication, October 17, 2023.

157   Lawler, M. (2023). Caring for each other through money: The story of two savings pools. Te Hiko: Centre for Community Innovation. https://assets-global.website-files. com/61677d4e818cfec6d372a655/64ee4e373c8b3953288477e7_ savings%20pool%20report%20August%202023.pdf .

158   Lawler, M. (2023). Caring for each other through money: The story of two savings pools. Te Hiko: Centre for Community Innovation. https://assets-global.website-files. com/61677d4e818cfec6d372a655/64ee4e373c8b3953288477e7_ savings%20pool%20report%20August%202023.pdf .

Sumitomo Group: A Keiretsu

Charity May

Summary

Keiretsu is a model of corporate organizing among Japanese industrial enterprises. The keiretsu in Japan is one of the most fascinating expressions of networked enterprising, where a loose affiliation is formed among diversified businesses through various ties that create multi-layered interlocking relationships. Descending from merchant family conglomerate holding companies (zaibatsu) in the 1500s, these networked organizations are characterized by the relationships formed among industrial enterprises, their supply chain partners, trading companies, banks, and insurance. These ties form without centralized corporate governance. The ties are often represented through group-affiliated bank borrowings, cross-shareholdings with core industrial enterprises, and social cohesion through the convening of member directors in a 'president's council'.

Academics and Western corporate leaders have been fascinated and humbled by keiretsu for decades, due to their complex form and ongoing stability against hostile market forces. Perhaps the most compelling testimony to explore is the social allegiances that have held strong across centuries, through war, pestilence, and the ever-evolving global capitalist markets.

Modern scholars identify two forms of keiretsu:

- Horizontal keiretsu – several companies across different industries owning shares in one another (cross-shareholding) with a main banking institution and trading company in the center. The six major historical family lines that formed today's horizontal keiretsu are Mitsui, Mitsubishi, Sumitomo, Fuyo, Sanwa, and Dai-Ichi Kangyō Bank (DKB).

- Vertical keiretsu – large companies that own shares in the companies forming their supply chain. Common in the auto industry, the Toyota Group is a classic example of a vertical keiretsu.

In this case study, we'll focus more succinctly on the evolution of the horizontal keiretsu and its prevalence in the Japanese economy. You'll find that we focus on relationships between firms in our description and analysis, and less on the inner workings of the individual firms and their relationship with their employees. Sumitomo, one of the largest and most prominent keiretsus thriving today, will be our model of reference.

Fast Findings

- The zaibatsu system, characterized by family-owned conglomerates with significant economic influence pre-WWII, evolved into the keiretsu system post-war, emphasizing a distributed network of mutual support and long-term stability over immediate profit maximization.

- The resilience of enduring social and business ties within Japan's economic structure is underscored by the transformation of zaibatsu family monopolies into keiretsu, despite efforts by the Allies to dismantle them during WWII.

- Keiretsu members, loosely organized through a web of relationships and interactions, benefit from a collective safety net, providing financial and strategic support to each other, ensuring the group's collective well-being and mitigating the impact of economic downturns.

- The keiretsu system's emphasis on collective benefits, operational stability, and employee loyalty challenges conventional conglomerate business models, focusing instead on long-term growth and sustainability.

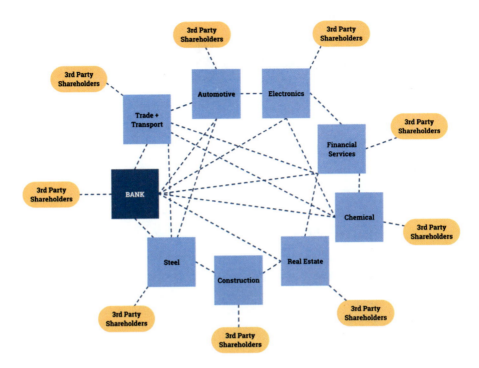

Cross-shareholding Network of Keiretsu Form: A keiretsu exists when there are diversified business enterprises that are loosely affiliated through several links, most notably through minor shareholdings in some or all of the core businesses.

Context

The Reign of Zaibatsu – Pre-War Era

In the tapestry of Japan's economic history, one will find the zaibatsu—translating to 'wealthy cliques' or 'wealthy clans'. This term encapsulates the essence of their role: dominant merchant family-owned conglomerates that, like cartels, wielded considerable influence over their respective industries before World War II. The prime expression of these economic powerhouses can be traced back to the Meiji Restoration Era, a period marked by great transformation and modernization. Initially rooted in singular trades, the zaibatsu families leveraged this era's opportunities to diversify and expand. Their ventures burgeoned into formidable networks, encompassing banks, insurance companies, trading entities, and a variety of other industrial sectors.

Sumitomo Group: A Keiretsu | 161

The operational philosophy of the zaibatsu was characterized by a meticulous balance between determined expansion and the preservation of operating control. Zaibatsu's growth strategies initially involved limited issuance of subsidiary and affiliate joint-stock, a practice that evolved over time. The symbolic issuance of stock served dual purposes. First, it diluted the perception of monopolistic family control by distributing shareholdings among affiliated firms. Second, these shareholdings were carefully orchestrated to ensure that these shares remained within a closed network of stakeholders committed to the well-being of the enterprise. The admonition by the Mitsubishi president in 1928, urging shareholders to regard their investment as a long-term commitment and to eschew immediate resale, underscores the moral and strategic framework within which these conglomerates operated. This model of economic dominion, rooted in both group identity and strategic expansion, laid the groundwork for the zaibatsu's significant influence on the pre-war Japanese economy.[159]

The Zaibatsu Dissolution from the Allied Occupation[160] [161]

The entry into World War II and the subsequent Allied occupation significantly altered the landscape of Japan's economy, and the zaibatsu conglomerates, which had been the bedrock of economic power and influence. These family-owned conglomerates were viewed by the Allied forces as emblematic of anti-democratic concentrations of power, reminiscent of the monopolistic practices they sought to dismantle in the post-war reconstruction of Japan. In response, the Japanese government (with strong support from the United States) formed the Holding Company Liquidation

---

159   Gerlach, M. L. (1997). Alliance Capitalism: The Social Organization of Japanese Business. Univ of California Press. https://www.ucpress.edu/book/9780520208896/alliance-capitalism

160   K. Frost, P. (2016). Debating the Allied Occupation of Japan (Part two). Education About Asia, 21(3), 47. https://www.asianstudies.org/publications/eaa/archives/debating-the-allied-occupation-of-japan-part-two/

161   Ericson, S. J. (2021). The Wealth of Zaibatsu owner families: The impact of Zaibatsu busting in occupied Japan. Shashi, 6(1). https://doi.org/10.5195/shashi.2021.48

Committee in 1946 with the single aim of dismantling the zaibatsu system. The implementation of this initiative forced zaibatsu families to divest their shares in exchange for 10-year non-negotiable bonds, while subsidiaries and affiliates were prohibited from bearing the family names. These actions severed the financial interconnections that underpinned the centuries of zaibatsu's dominance in the Japanese economy.

This deliberate dissolution of the web of intercorporate relationships marked the end of the zaibatsu era. However, this dissolution was primarily focused on the financial structures that united these affiliates. What was left intact were the social affiliations that evolved over decades prior and ran deep in the cultural centrality of loyalty and honor to ancestors. The relational connections among these firms proved resilient in the face of regulatory upheaval. The persistence of these networks facilitated the emergence of the keiretsu system, which, while distinct in structure from the zaibatsu, continued to embody the principle of closely knit business groups. This transition underscores the complexity of detangling entrenched economic powers and highlights the enduring nature of social bonds in shaping Japan's post-war economic landscape.

The Comeback and Keiretsu Formation[162] [163]

The influence of the zaibatsu family names stayed persistent, despite the government restricting families' involvement in the re-formation of corporate alliances post-war. Most of the alliances fell in step with the pre-war configurations, except that the notable ties were not through zaibatsu family holdings, but rather through keiretsu-styled cross-shareholdings and bank affiliations. While Japan was encouraged to embrace U.S.-style antitrust and anti-monopoly regulations during its post-war reconstruction,

---

162   Kobayashi, K. (2020). Effects of Japanese financial regulations and Keiretsu style groups on Japanese corporate governance. Hastings International and Comparative Law Review, 43(2), 339. https://repository.uclawsf.edu/hastings_international_comparative_law_review/vol43/iss2/7/

163   K. Frost, P. (2016). Debating the Allied Occupation of Japan (Part two). Education About Asia, 21(3), 47. https://www.asianstudies.org/publications/eaa/archives/debating-the-allied-occupation-of-japan-part-two/ .

such mandates often clashed with traditional Japanese business practices and thus many of these customary affiliation practices remained.

The remarkable economic resurgence of Japan, post-war, can be credited to the collaborative spirit inherent within these reconstituted groups, enabling them to compete on a global scale. Mutual reliance within the networks revitalized waning industries, promoted internal cooperation, minimized labor disputes, and mitigated the risk of business downturns without the need for extensive government intervention or subsidies.

In 1982, the then president of Sanwa Bank (one of the six main keiretsu groups) was quoted stating this truth held and exemplified in the post-war Japanese economy: "this type of mutually beneficial accommodation and exchange of territories, managerial know-how and clients is what we call good partnership, a true way of attaining maximum co-prosperity."[164]

A Brief Tale of Sumitomo Group[165] [166]

"It goes without saying that Sumitomo's businesses are in a family relationship, sharing a common "parent" from which they have separated. As such, the businesses are siblings joined by an inseparable bond. Therefore, although technically the businesses may be independently managed, I want you to form a spiritual alliance so that, come what may, you never lose your sense of brotherhood." – Shunnosuke Furuta, retired Director-General of Sumitomo Group to the group presidents when the Allied Occupation forced the dissolution of the zaibatsu.[167]

164　Gerlach, M. L. (1997). Alliance Capitalism: The Social Organization of Japanese Business. Univ of California Press. https://www.ucpress.edu/book/9780520208896/alliance-capitalism

165　Ibid.

166　Sumitomo Corporation History, Sumitomo Corporation. https://www.sumitomo.gr.jp/history/

167　"I want you to form a spiritual alliance so that, come what may, you never lose your sense of brotherhood." | Sumitomo Quotes with Enduring Value. Sumitomo Group Public Affairs Committee. (n.d.). https://www.sumitomo.gr.jp/english/history/analects/19/

This quote by a former Director-General of Sumitomo captures the essence that drove these deep inter-corporate bonds. These dynamics are best illustrated in tracing the lineage of the present-day Sumitomo Group, whose family ties begin in 1590 at a copper-crafting shop. The cash-flowing enterprise of the group was the Besshi mine in Shikoku in 1691. This enterprise carried the family and its business endeavors for over two centuries, making Sumitomo the world's largest copper producer and exporter.

During the Meiji Restoration in 1895, the merchant family started the Sumitomo Bank. This was immediately followed by the establishment of a formal holding company – Sumitomo Honten. It was at this time that the family also sought to bring more external professional management to oversee the expanding business units. The corporate structure was reorganized to resemble corporate holding companies with diversified operating companies, well known in the U.S. Sumitomo Honten became the family-held holding company to oversee the group's expansion into new lines of business including steel, electric wire, chemicals, and satellites, to name a few. The expanding network boomed across its industrial enterprises with the introduction of machinery, innovation, and processes from other parts of the world.

During the Allied Occupation, the Sumitomo zaibatsu forcefully dissolved and business names were changed due to the ban on using the associated family name. After the war, however, the relationships re-emerged and formed what is now known as one of the oldest and largest keiretsu, with the Sumitomo Bank and Sumitomo Corporation (the trading company) at the core of this reorganization.

As of 2024, the Sumitomo Corporation Group constitutes 900 group companies spanning 65 countries and producing an aggregate total of $4.2 billion annual net operating income. To this day, the Group honors the corporation's ancestral heritage, with a ritual ceremony occurring every year in April in the city of Kyoto.[168] [169]

Motivation

"The fact is that some Japanese firms derive substantial benefit from their keiretsu affiliations and others pay a price. Groups allocate resources among their members according to a long-term vision of collective welfare. They provide a safety net for their weak members, police profiteering by imposing penalties when a member firm does too well, and insulate their membership from the harsh scrutiny of tax authorities and investment analysts by managing the reporting of profits and losses to show steady, incremental growth."

– From Keiretsu Networks and Corporate Performance in Japan.[170]

Many studies have been conducted over the years to find the underlying motivation and impetus for why keiretsus prevail in Japan. These studies try to measure the benefits or challenges resulting from being a member of a keiretsu. In general, keiretsu firms, relative to conventional corporate firms, do exhibit lower growth rates, profitability measures, and stock market valuations. If value creation is measured solely by these metrics, as is the case in Western corporate finance, then the motivation to interact in a keiretsu would be quite low. However, as evidenced by the keiretsu's primary role in the global expansion and production of the post-war Japanese economy, value creation and the motivation to be a keiretsu member comes

---

168   About us. (n.d.). Sumitomo Corporation. Retrieved April 10, 2024, from https://www.sumitomocorp.com/en/jp/about

169   Gerlach, M. L. (1997). Alliance Capitalism: The Social Organization of Japanese Business. Univ of California Press. https://www.ucpress.edu/book/9780520208896/alliance-capitalism

170   Lincoln, J. R., Gerlach, M. L., & Ahmadjian, C. L. (1996). Keiretsu Networks and Corporate Performance in Japan. American Sociological Review, 61(1), 67–88. https://doi.org/10.2307/2096407

from elsewhere. The keiretsu model transcends the conventional corporate pursuit of profit maximization at all costs and favors an approach that prioritizes mutual benefits and the collective well-being of the network group. This ethos is not merely about becoming large entities to dominate markets and generate substantial profits; it's about fostering a symbiotic environment where access to benefits and opportunities contribute to the overall health of the intercorporate network.

These companies are known to cultivate greater employee loyalty and operational stability by adopting a long-term perspective on development, investment, and innovation. This strategic orientation reflects a commitment to a different measure of sustainable growth, where even profitability is distributed at will across the group, rather than being accumulated and benefiting one or two firms. By emphasizing stability, the keiretsu system demonstrates a profound understanding of value creation that extends beyond financial gains to include the welfare of employees, the resilience of operations, and the enduring strength of corporate relationships. This approach not only ensures a steady trajectory of growth but also reinforces the fabric of trust and cooperation that is fundamental to the keiretsu philosophy.

How it Works

Structure[171] [172]

The keiretsu structure is not like any known corporate structure in the U.S. Interlocking alliances through various ties among diversified enterprises formulate the network without formal legal ties (beyond cross-shareholdings). As exemplified in the Sumitomo keiretsu, the business types that make up a modern-day keiretsu include the following:

---

171   Ibid

172   Grabowiecki, J. (2006). Keiretsu Groups : their role in the Japanese economy and a reference point (or a paradigm) for other countries. Institute of Developing Economies, Japan External Trade Organization. No. 413. https://www.ide.go.jp/library/English/Publish/Reports/Vrf/pdf/413.pdf

- Multiple industrial enterprises (e.g., chemicals, metals, transportation, energy, machinery, etc.)
- A bank (e.g., Sumitomo Mitsui Banking Corporation)
- A trading and investments company (e.g., Sumitomo Corporation)
- An insurance company (e.g., Mitsui Sumitomo Insurance Company)

Each firm is incorporated separately as a joint-stock company or subsidiary and affiliates. The firms freely conduct their business outside of the keiretsu, while the ties to the keiretsu grant them special access to the services provided by the keiretsu firms. The cross-shareholdings demonstrate trust and affiliation and also ensure that these firms can share directors, maintain strong borrowing relationships, and obtain access to global markets through trading companies.

Roles and Responsibilities

Banks and trading companies are the firms that touch all other associated firms and are conceptually thought of as the keiretsu center because of this. However, these 'centric' firms do not act as a headquarters office to express greater authority or responsibility over any of the other firms, as would be the case with a conglomerate corporation with centralized functions. Here we'll describe in further detail the pertinent roles that trading companies and banks fulfill for the collective ecosystem of a keiretsu.

Trading companies (sogo shosha)

The sogo shosha is the trading company of the keiretsu, acting like a satellite, gathering and relaying information between the group and the outside world. These externally-facing firms serve the group as a market maker, distributor, and facilitator of global and joint venture projects. Sogo shoshas brings the goods and services of industrial production companies to the world. Due to their involvement in both imports and exports, they can collect real-time information from the global markets and support the collective's efforts in taking broader risks in business deals. These long-term implicit arrangements across industries and operations support the flow of information and can influence the pricing set for trades and transactions made within the network. Furthermore, with trading companies, "prices, wages, and rates of return are set, not so much by what the markets will bear, but according to what seems fair and proper given the identities of the transacting parties and the needs of the multi-firm community as a whole." [173] [174] Sumitomo Corporation is the trading company for the Sumitomo keiretsu and continues to operate as one of the third largest sogo shoshas today.

Banks

To understand the various roles that these banks play, we'll first describe the roles within the general banking system.

Economist Masahiko Aoki outlines three primary banking functions as follows: (a) credit underwriting for planned investments, (b) ongoing risk assessment and management, and (c) verification of the company's position to determine strategic activities. In the U.S. context, we may associate credit underwriting for debt or equity investments to be the role largely held by investment banks, venture capital firms, and other direct investment arms. For risk assessment and management, many banks rely on third-party rating agencies, as well as the fiduciary obligations of the company's board of directors to assess and manage risk. As for analyzing the company's financial position to take strategic action, this function is largely played by the capital markets in the monitoring of share prices

---

173   Lincoln, J. R., Gerlach, M. L., & Ahmadjian, C. L. (1996). Keiretsu Networks and Corporate Performance in Japan. American Sociological Review, 61(1), 67–88. https://doi.org/10.2307/2096407

174   Gerlach, M. L. (1997). Alliance Capitalism: The Social Organization of Japanese Business. Univ of California Press. https://www.ucpress.edu/book/9780520208896/alliance-capitalism

and company performance based on management decisions and market responses.[175][176]

In the Japanese context, keiretsu banks serve all three functions, as they are permitted under Japanese law to be both creditors and shareholders. The bank can monitor business operations more closely given its position and vested interest as an equity shareholder. In one way, this link supports the company's ability to optimize resources within and across the network. The Western analysis of a company's return on assets compared to its debt-to-equity ratio contrasts with the Japanese perspective: in a keiretsu context, heavy debt loads and strong banking affiliations can sometimes indicate a preference for investing in future growth rather than focusing solely on immediate earnings.[177] These banking relationships are more apt to invest further capital into the associated firms instead of calling on the loans or pursuing bankruptcy (as is the option for U.S. creditors when borrowers are not performing).[178]

Governance & Decision Making

Each firm within the keiretsu network houses an independent corporate governance structure, typically employing a dedicated board of directors which may consist of representatives from management, associated firms,

---

175   Aoki, M. (1995). Monitoring Characteristics of the main Bank System: An Analytical and Developmental view. In The Japanese Main Bank System: Its Relevance for Developing and Transforming Economies (pp. 109–141). Oxford Academic. https://doi.org/10.1093/0198288999.003.0004

176   Morck, R., Shivdasani, A., & Nakamura, M. (2000). Banks, ownership structure, and firm value in Japan. Sauder School of Business Working Paper. https://doi.org/10.2139/ssrn.219912

177   Lincoln, J. R., Gerlach, M. L., & Ahmadjian, C. L. (1996). Keiretsu Networks and Corporate Performance in Japan. American Sociological Review, 61(1), 67–88. https://doi.org/10.2307/2096407

178   Kobayashi, K. (2020). Effects of Japanese financial regulations and Keiretsu style groups on Japanese corporate governance. Hastings International and Comparative Law Review, 43(2), 339. https://repository.uclawsf.edu/hastings_international_comparative_law_review/vol43/iss2/7/

and even government officials. There is no central oversight board for the keiretsu group. However, unique to the Japanese way of doing business, keiretsu are known to have a president's council. The president's council, made up of presidents from core member firms, gives way for social engagements, trust-building and mutuality to be formed across the network. The council is solely a loose affiliation that acts more like a social club for the presidents than a board meeting. The presidents do not discuss or interfere with an individual firm's strategic and operational decisions. The gatherings are inherently social and build comradery among the presidents. Involvement in the close-knit circle builds 'credit' for when a firm is facing adversity. In times of trouble, member firms may look to other directors and call them to step in to assist in leadership. Sharing of strategic leadership is more streamlined because trust and mutual understanding are already in place.[179]

Equity positions do not warrant direct control in the same sense that activist investors might have in shareholder-centric capitalism. Instead, equity positions signal and permit influence and collective action to distribute resources, information, and talent, typically administered through the central connection held by the bank.

Relationships

Corporate group identity, social cohesion, and the underlying allegiance to the spirit of the group are deeply embedded into the Japanese cultural context, blurring the lines between business transactions and cultural expression. Loyalty to these social bonds of association among firm identity, the managers, presidents, and directors enter this mode of allegiance, even honoring the spirit of the founding family through ritual.[180]

---

179   Gerlach, M. L. (1997). Alliance Capitalism: The Social Organization of Japanese Business. Univ of California Press. https://www.ucpress.edu/book/9780520208896/alliance-capitalis

180   Gerlach, M. L. (1997). Alliance Capitalism: The Social Organization of Japanese Business. Univ of California Press. https://www.ucpress.edu/book/9780520208896/alliance-capitalis

For example, these sentiments are embedded in the original founding business principles adhered to by the Sumitomo Group to this day, reflected here:

1) Sumitomo shall achieve strength and prosperity by placing prime importance on integrity and sound management in the conduct of its business.

2) Sumitomo shall manage its activities with foresight and flexibility in order to cope effectively with the changing times. Under no circumstances, however, shall it pursue easy gains or act imprudently.[181]

Relationships between firms are revered and respected, with the firms, their directors, and employees committed to collective beneficial efforts of the networked ecosystem as a whole. The firms hold the responsibility to provide and care for their employees, as well as to conduct prudent business within the network.

Economic Interest[182] [183]

Member firms are a mixture of joint-stock companies listed on the public exchange or privately held as subsidiaries. Since the time of zaibatsu, equity share-holdings functioned more to preserve control rather than raise capital. Many keiretsu, including Sumitomo, gradually transitioned its subsidiaries and affiliates into joint-stock companies and eventually listed some on the Japanese and New York exchanges. Core companies sought to maintain close control over ownership and capitalization, shielding from

---

181   Corporate Mission Statement. (n.d.). Sumitomo Corporation Global Metals Co., Ltd. https://www.scgm.co.jp/eng/aboutus/ideology/

182   Liu, J. (2019). The Case Study of Cross-Shareholding between ZHENYE and CHANGCHENG. American Journal of Industrial and Business Management, 09(02), 342–353. https://doi.org/10.4236/ajibm.2019.92023

183   Kobayashi, K. (2020). Effects of Japanese financial regulations and Keiretsu style groups on Japanese corporate governance. Hastings International and Comparative Law Review, 43(2), 339. https://repository.uclawsf.edu/hastings_international_comparative_law_review/vol43/iss2/7/

mechanisms such as hostile takeovers and volatile market swings. As such, long-term holds were preferred and strongly encouraged by member firms. It was strongly frowned upon if any external shareholders sought out a short-term trade of stock among publicly listed companies that were also part of a keiretsu.

Even then, ownership shares remain tied to governance rights and give allowance for cross-shareholding companies to dispatch and trade directors for the benefit of the network. Redistribution of profits among any existing profit-sharing measures is initiated to support intra-network loans and deposits, offsetting capital needs met by the central bank.

Since reconstruction after World War II, the Japanese government and global market forces have encouraged the Japanese banks, especially keiretsu-related banks, to reduce their cross-shareholdings to improve balance sheet standing and circulation of capital. In 1977, Japan's anti-monopoly act curtailed banks' potential dominance over corporations by reducing the permissible equity stake from 10% to 5%, with a grace period until April 1987 for compliance. Banks are attempting to reduce shareholdings, reducing the focus on banks holding significant stakes in associated firms of the keiretsu. For example, the financial group of Sumitomo made a goal to reduce its cross-shareholdings by ¥ 300 million (or $2 billion) from 2020 through 2025. These efforts are underway but are presenting to take an extensive amount of time to get there.[184] [185] [186]

---

184   Yamaguchi, Y. (2020, August 16). Japan megabanks have slowed sale of stock in corporate borrowers amid pandemic. S&P Global Market Intelligence. https://www.spglobal.com/marketintelligence/en/news-insights/latest-news-headlines/japan-megabanks-have-slowed-sale-of-stock-in-corporate-borrowers-amid-pandemic-59929485

185   Oshino, S. (2017, July 15). Japan's cross-held shares fall below 10% of all holdings. Nikkei Asia. https://asia.nikkei.com/Business/Japan-s-cross-held-shares-fall-below-10-of-all-holdings2

186   Morck, R., Shivdasani, A., & Nakamura, M. (2000). Banks, ownership structure, and firm value in Japan. Sauder School of Business Working Paper. https://doi.org/10.2139/ssrn.219912

Member Benefits

The keiretsu structure provides three key benefits to its member companies. First, access to capital is streamlined within a keiretsu, thanks to the central positioning of banks. This arrangement alleviates the pressure on management to constantly seek external funding, allowing for more strategic, long-term, and less reactionary decision-making processes.

Second, companies within a keiretsu enjoy access to real-time market and trading information from their network, enhancing their competitive edge. This system facilitates advantageous intra-network trading arrangements, enabling price optimization and production adjustments to meet collective goals, without restricting external trade.

Lastly, the horizontal integration of keiretsu members across various sectors and industries ensures operational diversification. While no single company holds a majority stake in another, this freedom encourages broad market engagement. Simultaneously, it provides a safety net of economic and strategic support from the network, buffering member companies against the full impact of competitive pressures and economic downturns. This mutual support system underscores the keiretsu's emphasis on long-term stability and collective well-being over short-term gains.

Takeaways

Collective Well-Being over Profit Maximization[187] [188] [189]

Members of a keiretsu network contribute to and benefit from a collective safety net, a precautionary measure against the omnipresent threat of business downturns. This system of mutual aid and loyalty often transcends conventional financial wisdom, with companies within the keiretsu sometimes embracing short-term losses for the anticipated benefit of long-term stability and success. This approach, while fostering a deep sense of loyalty and social cohesion, has sparked debate among critics who question the financial prudence of decisions driven more by social and cultural allegiance than by strategic finance.

The impact of keiretsu affiliation on a firm's profitability is a subject of nuanced discourse, defying simple characterizations. The advantage—or disadvantage—of group membership is contingent upon a myriad of factors specific to each company, including its relationships within the network, the overall economic climate, industry-specific strategies, and governmental policies. This complex interplay of influences underscores the tailored nature of benefits or drawbacks that membership in a keiretsu can confer on a company.

Keiretsu structures can enhance the collective resilience of their businesses, and level the playing field between member companies, among many other multifaceted, practical outcomes. Keiretsu networks work to

---

187 Lincoln, J. R., Gerlach, M. L., & Ahmadjian, C. L. (1996). Keiretsu Networks and Corporate Performance in Japan. American Sociological Review, 61(1), 67–88. https://doi.org/10.2307/2096407

188 Kobayashi, K. (2020). Effects of Japanese financial regulations and Keiretsu style groups on Japanese corporate governance. Hastings International and Comparative Law Review, 43(2), 339. https://repository.uclawsf.edu/hastings_international_comparative_law_review/vol43/iss2/7/

189 Grabowiecki, J. (2006). Keiretsu Groups : their role in the Japanese economy and a reference point (or a paradigm) for other countries. Institute of Developing Economies, Japan External Trade Organization. No. 413. https://www.ide.go.jp/library/English/Publish/Reports/Vrf/pdf/413.pdf

redistribute prosperity and mitigate financial disparities. This is achieved through a series of mechanisms such as financial support during periods of difficulty, equity adjustments, and strategic personnel and resource reallocation. This process effectively acts as a form of internal voluntary taxation, where more prosperous entities support those in distress, ensuring the stability and recovery of the latter. Such solidarity was exemplified during crises like Mazda's financial troubles following the oil crisis, when Sumitomo, in a show of group loyalty, made exclusive purchases from Mazda to aid its recovery.

This keiretsu model of collective action and shared fate not only tempers financial inequalities among member firms but also strengthens the group's overall viability.

Urban Wealth Funds

Charity May

Summary

An urban wealth fund (UWF)[190] is a publicly-owned but privately managed corporation formed with a mandate to maximize the value creation of the public assets in its stewardship. The corporation is structured as a separate holding company owned by the local government to aggregate management of public assets from a network of agencies within a jurisdiction. These assets can be land, underutilized facilities, utilities, and transportation infrastructure. Through this structure, the government benefits from private sector methods through the engagement of an independent asset manager tasked to unlock the greatest value for each asset.

UWFs are tasked with recognizing the market value of assets on the government's balance sheet and creating another revenue stream separate from tax revenues to finance ongoing investments in public goods while maintaining public ownership of assets. Mechanisms deployed by the urban wealth fund to tap the value of underutilized assets take many forms and are determined by the local context, needs of the community, knowledge capacity of the local government, and any statutes or mandates put in place. These methods include land value capture, public-private partnerships, joint ventures, and asset sales.

UWFs offer a dynamic approach to managing civic assets, blending public ownership with private sector efficiency. By recognizing the market value of civic assets and implementing collaborative financing mechanisms across diverse stakeholders, UWFs have the potential to drive inclusive economic growth, enhance broader infrastructure development, and preserve shared ownership of public resources on a significant scale. This

---

190   There are different terms used in naming the function of an urban wealth fund. In his book, Public Wealth of Cities, Dag Detter coined the term 'urban wealth fund' to describe one type of public wealth fund.

makes them a compelling model for advancing sustainable and equitable urban development in diverse contexts worldwide.

Fast Findings

- The public sector can take a creative role to maintain public ownership in community and economic development projects.

- A combination of government mandates and independent management of assets shields the value creation of public goods from politicization.

- Blending public and private structures for commercial development calls for a mindset shift away from complete privatization of public goods.

- Holding companies are versatile and present the public sector a viable way to use private-sector financial mechanisms to generate long-standing public goods.

In this case study, we'll explore how urban wealth funds activate community wealth distribution with public sector actors, look at the international examples inspiring U.S. cities to take action and unpack the mechanisms that make public wealth funds a viable shared ownership tool in the public sector for local governments.

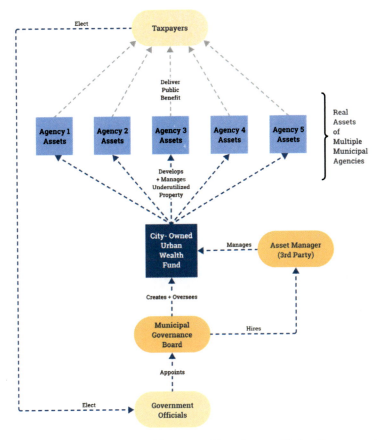

An Illustrative Urban Wealth Fund Structure: The urban wealth fund is arranged as a holding company which holds municipal assets that are managed by an independent asset manager to unlock value for public benefit. This structure ensures that short-term political influence does not interfere with ongoing management of the assets.

Context

Urban wealth funds are a type of public wealth fund. Perhaps more broadly understood are sovereign wealth funds, which is another type of public wealth fund. Sovereign wealth funds are investment pools created by countries or states to manage and invest their reserves, often derived from revenues generated by commodities like oil or natural gas. Classic examples would include the Texas Permanent Fund, the Norway Sovereign Wealth Fund, and the Alaska State Permanent Fund. These funds may invest in various asset classes, such as real estate, infrastructure, stocks, or bonds to preserve and grow the wealth. Urban (or national, if formed at that level) wealth funds are primarily focused on operational assets of a defined jurisdiction. Portfolio values are maximized through the commercial development and monetization of individual assets. Urban wealth fund examples that inspire cities worldwide include City & Port in Copenhagen, Temasek in Singapore, and MTR Corporation in Hong Kong.

Putting Assets to Work in the U.S.

Movements across U.S. cities are underway to bring urban wealth funds to life to tackle the dire infrastructure needs of the public. One civil servant in Utah took inspiration from Copenhagen and other international examples well documented by Dag Detter in The Public Wealth of Cities. Ben McAdams was Mayor of Salt Lake County from 2013 to 2019. McAdams was committed to several causes, such as early childhood education and recidivism, during his time and was eager to find ways to invest in prevention.

> "When I was working in that space, I saw that we had empirical evidence that we know that investing in early childhood, in addiction treatment, all these other things, will save us money. But instead, we are spending on remediation that is much more expensive on the back end. I was really frustrated by the fact that every penny we have was tied up to these inefficient, expensive 'cures'."[191]

This frustration led McAdams to dive further into the city budget. Given that the accounting standards of most governments hold assets at book value, or the historical value of the assets owned, McAdams learned that the balance sheet was grossly understating the value when compared to a fair market valuation. The estimated value was $45 billion, or 45 times the county's actual budget.

After he moved on from being mayor, this interest did not subside. He eventually teamed up with the Government Finance Officers Association

---

191   Ben McAdams, personal communication, December 19, 2023.

(GFOA) and started the Putting Assets to Work incubator in 2021 to help cities learn what he did in Salt Lake to unlock the value of underutilized public assets for funding investments in community priorities. McAdams and his team have worked with 12 cities, and two cities are taking the activation in stride.

In Cleveland, Ohio, Mayor Bibbs is using $50 million of American Rescue Plan Act (ARPA) funds to seed a $100 million evergreen urban wealth fund – the Site Assembly and Development Trust (SADT). The public good focus is to attract employers that will bring well-paying jobs into a region plagued with population decline and underutilized lands. SADT will be used to aggregate 20 acres held by the City to provide brownfield cleanup, remediating the land to make it "shovel-ready" for companies. The goal is to generate a source of revenue creation that will not waiver when tax revenues fluctuate. SADT will also source capital from local philanthropic funders and market rate investors to partner in the fund.[192]

The City of Atlanta used its time in the incubator to develop an affordable housing strategy. Through its assessment of city-owned vacant lots and underutilized government buildings, they've identified dozens of opportunities to develop thousands of affordable housing units towards the ambitious goal of 20,000 new units by 2030. The City will partner with developers through a public-private partnership by contributing land in exchange for hundreds of affordable housing units. Furthermore,

---

192   Daprile, L., & Astolfi, C. (2023, April 10). Bibb, in last big round of ARPA spending, unveils "60 million for job Creation, Violence Prevention, Infrast. Cleveland. https://www.cleveland.com/news/2023/04/bibb-in-last-big-round-of-arpa-spending-unveils-160-million-for-job-creation-violence-prevention-infrastructure-more.html&subscribed=google-oauth2%7C105451319944677478366

collaborative financing includes a $100 million commitment from the Woodruff Foundation and a city-issued housing bond of the same value.[193] [194]

Motivation

Urban wealth funds enable governments to fund public projects and optimize the use of public assets without increasing tax revenues through the implementation of private sector practices. Through the asset inventory and market valuation of book-valued assets, governments can develop an asset-rich balance sheet and expand their debt capacity. Additionally, instead of outsourcing the provision of public services and infrastructure to private parties, cities, and governments can retain ownership and utilize the urban wealth fund to borrow private sector mechanisms for proper stewardship of public goods into commercialization.[195]

Generating New Revenue Streams

Sources of revenues for local governments are primarily tax-driven. To increase revenues, governments are forced to look at increasing taxation based on property valuations, which can be a controversial issue among communities with varying degrees of tax bases. Many public goods, such as education, are financed through property taxation. If valuations decline, or the population decreases, those funds walk away. An urban wealth fund seeks to create economic value not sourced from tax revenues and available for recycling into funding new and ongoing development projects serving the community.

---

193   Smith, C. (2023, July 3). New uses of public assets are helping Atlanta fill its affordable housing gap. Governing. http://www.governing.com/housing/new-uses-of-public-assets-are-helping-atlanta-fill-its-affordable-housing-gap

194   Farmer, L. (2023, November 15). Helping cities flip money pits into gold mines. Route Fifty. http://www.route-fifty.com/finance/2023/11/helping-cities-flip-money-pits-gold-mines/392048/

195   Detter, D., & Kavanaugh, S. (2021). Putting Public Assets to Work. Government Finance Officers Association. https://gfoaorg.cdn.prismic.io/gfoaorg/fc756aef-e093-4034-a716-9e7062fb20a9_GFOA_UrbanWealthFunds_R7.pdf

Adoption of Private Sector Practices[196]

There are three practices common in the private sector that are imperative to getting the urban wealth fund right.

1) Take inventory of government-owned-assets: The fragmentation of ownership that exists among government agencies within a local community is antithetical to transparency and efficiency. As such, municipalities are often stocked with underutilized assets without a clear understanding of the extent of assets they hold. The first step is to conduct an assessment and create a centralized repository to track all assets owned. Once the government takes full stock of its inventory, then a fair market valuation can be conducted to inform the government of its potential to generate revenues.

2) Develop a Business Plan for Maximizing Value: With the fair market value illustrated on the balance sheet, the government can then develop a budget inclusive of maintenance and operating costs to inform what proposal types will be accretive to the immediate and long-term economic viability of its community.

3) Form the Structure with Arms-Length Governance: Financial responsibility, accountability and investment management of the assets is ideally delegated to an independent third party that will not be subject to 'short-term political influence'.

How it Works

Structure

An urban wealth fund is typically structured as a holding company owned by the local government. Once formed, the municipalities transfer real assets into the management of the holding company and hire an independent

---

196   Detter, D., & Kavanaugh, S. (2021). Putting Public Assets to Work. Government Finance Officers Association. https://gfoaorg.cdn.prismic.io/gfoaorg/fc756aef-e093-4034-a716-9e7062fb20a9_GFOA_UrbanWealthFunds_R7.pdf

asset manager to direct the commercial development of these assets strictly into a public beneficial use. This holding company can be structured as a non-profit and operate as a subsidiary of a government agency. When this structure is arranged, the municipality can transfer the assets over to the non-profit whose sole mission is to maximize value for the benefit of the public service mission defined or prioritized by the public. If not a nonprofit with an explicitly defined mission, a mandate or statute for the for-profit entity is an important factor to anchor the development and activities into public service.

A practical example of how this has been impactful in Denmark illustrates how an urban wealth fund can be transformative in the regeneration of cities. Copenhagen transformed a declining industrial port into a thriving commercial corridor equipped with over 30,000 housing units, over 100,000 workspaces, a university, parks, and cultural facilities. Spanning an area of nearly 1,300 acres, the regeneration of this corridor was entirely funded without tax revenues. In 2007, Copenhagen City & Port Development Corporation was established as an urban wealth fund and has since grown to over 100 employees with a $72 million annual budget, jointly owned by the city and national government. The national government instituted a mandate for the corporation to maximize revenues to generate capital for funding ongoing infrastructure projects in the region. The local metro system and other city developments continue to benefit from this purpose alignment through this urban wealth fund.[197]

Governance and Decision-Making

The urban wealth fund is governed by a board consisting of the appointment or election of public officials. This board decides which assets to hold and hires an independent asset manager to steer value creation. The establishment of independent management is crucial to ensure financial responsibility, accountability, and investment management. Shielding from

---

197   Noring, L. (2019). Public asset corporation: A new vehicle for urban regeneration and infrastructure finance. Cities, 88, 125–135. https://doi.org/10.1016/j.cities.2019.01.002

'short-term political influence' is a feature that this structure beholds. A publicly elected or appointed board not involved in the daily operations of asset management ensures continuity across projects regardless of the term length of public officials.

Economic Interest

> "The key to unlocking public wealth lies in the separation of governance of commercial assets from policy making."
>
> – Dag Detter

Corporate ownership of the holding company is held by the designated jurisdiction of the government, whether that be at the local or national level. Given the public ownership of the corporation, the idea is that any profits generated from the project become available to reinvest into existing or future commercial developments managed by the corporation, as the profits are not accumulating to one single private interest. One could view the economic interest and profit-generating capabilities of the corporation as essentially becoming a public good because the projects are usually directly related to serving a public use in that particular local jurisdiction. One example of this is when the ongoing revenue stream supports expansion or improvement in public transportation or the maintenance of lower use fees in fares.

Relationships

The relationships necessary for the activation of public assets are highly networked across government, the public, commercial developers and private investors. First, intra-agency relationships are necessary to address the fragmentation of government-owned assets. Secondly, capturing buy-in from the public in terms of what development needs are crucial for the region is necessary to continuously position the work and any revenue capture from development projects. And thirdly, these public asset commercialization projects still require a blend of capital sources. This blend may vary by region and strategic partners that reside in the region.

In the context of U.S. cities getting started with an urban wealth fund, McAdams sees the important role that the community foundation can play in these projects. "The community foundation seems to play an important role in these efforts because they want to be a part of helping solve a community problem. And the involvement of the community foundation supports the attraction of government capital and other philanthropic capital, impact capital and then private capital. We are starting to see deals get done under this scenario."

Takeaways

Empowering the Public Sector

The public sector is fraught with many challenges in delivering public benefits. The government sector is perceived to be bureaucratic, politically motivated, archaic in process, and slow to take action. The development of these sentiments over time leads to the management and delivery of public goods and services over to the private sector. The debate that privatization of public goods is caught in between is the perception and record of the private sector being more efficient and effective at taking action. However, these actions are sometimes conducted at the loss of broader community benefit, where the investment returns are concentrated in the hands of a few.

Many governments are eager to find ways to unlock these civic assets to generate more public benefit. The urban wealth fund structure is a proven tool that can be utilized to expand upon common practices such as public private partnerships (PPP) and tax increment financing (TIF), while maintaining public ownership and anchoring benefits to serve all citizens in the jurisdiction. The urban wealth fund brings the valuation of public assets to modern times, abandoning historical valuations no longer relevant through the adoption of Governmental Accounting Standards Board (GASB) measures.

Within the current context of divisive political discourse, urban wealth funds emerge as a pragmatic means to redefine individuals' roles as active citizens and integral members of the public sector. In a landscape where political representatives often prioritize special interests over broader public concerns, the structure of UWFs offers a potential solution. At the local government level, UWFs have the capacity to reorient public officials towards their duties of public service, transcending the short-term focus of individual political terms. As debates persist regarding nature-based financing and the urgent need to address environmental degradation, UWFs present a potential pathway for effectively stewarding common resources. Key attributes of UWFs include their ability to uphold public ownership of assets, empower local governments to direct revitalization efforts, and foster partnerships with the private sector that align with long-term public good outcomes and mandates.

A Shared Ownership Pathway to Combat Urban Blight

While Copenhagen has been touted as one of the richest cities in the world today, its public wealth creation did not occur overnight. In the 1980s, unemployment was over 15% and the city was facing the familiar woes of a declining industrial city, where migration away from the urban core wiped out the tax base. The city sold public land to private developers, who in turn formed single family homes. It was not until 1990 when the national and local governments formed an alliance to strategize on how to reimagine the city. In 1992, Orestad Development Corporation, the first iteration of City and Port, formed with the main goal to revitalize the former military base in the district. After this joint development effort was successful, the corporation began to address other areas of the city, eventually emerging into Copenhagen City & Port Development Corporation in 2007. The development and redistribution of public wealth creation continues, initiated by the mutual collaboration across the public sector, and the urban wealth fund mandate to transform the locale.[198]

---

198   Noring, L. (2019). Public asset corporation: A new vehicle for urban regeneration and infrastructure finance. Cities, 88, 125–135. https://doi.org/10.1016/j.cities.2019.01.002

Opportunities for Adoption in U.S. Cities

As of 2024, the Putting Assets to Work incubator has worked with two cohorts, serving 12 cities. Consistent feedback is that the incubator provides great onboarding, but most cities still need an extensive amount of capacity building to approach the next step in launching a jurisdiction-specific urban wealth fund. McAdams is looking into providing a fee-for-service to bring the capacity building the cities need. Still under development, the concept would support the pre-development work needed to launch a public wealth fund while also overseeing the implementation of the deals to prepare them for partnerships with developers.

Part III –

Patterns, Mechanisms, and Challenges: An Analysis

Purpose & Stewardship

Derek Razo

The Shared Ownership Renaissance

In recent years, there has been rapidly growing interest in business models that spread wealth, voice, and security more evenly to employees and communities. Concepts like employee ownership, cooperatives, nonprofit ownership, and community land trusts are gaining popularity across the political spectrum. This groundswell reflects a desire for a fairer and more sustainable economy. Regular Americans are increasingly open to reinventing systems they see as extractive, unfair, and disconnected from community well-being.

The reasons differ, from tackling rising inequality and disappearing quality jobs to calls for environmental sustainability. But common threads unite the yearning for change: More people realize short-term profits often undermine long-term prosperity. They want stable jobs, healthy communities, and a fair slice of the economic pie created by business and real estate. More people see economic growth concentrating wealth and control on a small and disconnected group of elites at the expense of themselves as workers, their children, and their communities.

Rather than one-off fixes, momentum is building for models that wire shared ownership and community stewardship into the core of economic life, in industry and communities. But, making this transformation will require surmounting some major obstacles.

The Difficulty of Imagining a Better Economy

So, while interest rises in alternative business models that share wealth and power more evenly, the surrounding legal and financial structures still concentrate on gains and control. Alternative models trying to empower people face immense inertia. The "immune system" of current structures resists newcomers that do not conform to profit-above-all norms. For example, even when supportive laws exist for employee-owned companies, the markets still impose demands undermining their stability. This imposes pressures towards premature growth and quick returns for outside investors rather than the interests of workers and communities.

Today's typical financial incentives exert intense pressure directly opposed to shared prosperity and dignity for all people. Dominant financial actors like monopolies and private equity acquire, dismantle, or subordinate alternatives once they gain influence. Attempts to spread equity face a steep challenge: The economy they hope to transform makes day-to-day life so precarious for ordinary people that it's difficult for most to imagine, much less fight for, something profoundly better aligned with their interests and values.

From the Ground Up

With systemic economic change so challenging to achieve top-down, transformation is bubbling up from creative grassroots solutions. Across businesses and communities, people are taking ownership of their economic futures enterprise-by-enterprise and place-by-place. The models gaining steam often convert existing institutions into stewardship structures centered on inclusive prosperity. For example, in 2022, Patagonia's founder, Yvon Chouinard, transferred ownership of Patagonia into a trust and a nonprofit organization called the Patagonia Purpose Trust and the Holdfast Collective. The Patagonia Purpose Trust owns 100% of Patagonia's voting stock and will guide the company's purpose and values. The Holdfast Collective owns the remaining non-voting shares, directing profits towards land stewardship and climate change mitigation. In essence, Chouinard restructured his company to become an entity required to uphold Patagonia's environmental values.

Many small and mid-sized businesses can now transition to trust ownership and employee ownership when founders retire, rather than selling to large outsiders focused on rapid growth for investors. A sizable portion of the American economy is already keen to change hands through a 'buy-in' to avoid losing their mission and values through an exploitative 'buyout'. Numerous models exist and provide options for how to implement this. Democratic worker cooperatives retain quality jobs in the community for the long haul. Community land trusts are also surging, where neighborhoods or nonprofits own land to preserve permanent affordability and prevent displacement. Residents own homes, but the land itself is forever a community asset. Ripples of smaller transformation are swelling to waves as the aim to structure business and growth for shared prosperity gains popularity.

Rewiring for Reinvestment

Reinvestment creates positive flow-on effects, while extractive incentives result in externalized costs. Redesigning ownership around long-term stewardship fosters reinvestment. Communities and workers have immense quality of life gains when companies anchor jobs and re-invest locally. Examples within this book, like Goodworks Evergreen, Clegg Auto, and The Industrial Commons, showcase present-day stewardship of American companies that prioritize people and place at scale. Purpose and stewardship ownership models also curb runaway wealth concentration and mitigate instability from constant mergers and offshoring. The whole economy becomes healthier when gains are recirculated rather than extracted remotely.

However, the reality is extractive financial models are still the norm. Pioneers of equitable models are constantly fighting to secure capital that aligns with their vision, rather than undermining it. Traditional investors overemphasize rapid growth and quick returns over deliberate stewardship for multi-stakeholder benefit. By extension, alternative models remain hampered by corporate governance laws largely written for passive, outside shareholders rather than engaged community and workforce stewardship. The immense gains from community-anchored enterprises are within reach, but it will take a coordinated, networked movement to rewire the incentives at large.

What We Must Build

Transitioning from extraction to equity requires progress on three interconnected fronts:

- Shared Ownership: More people need a direct financial and decision-making stake in enterprises critical to their livelihoods. For example, employees become co-owners of companies or residents co-owning real estate portfolios. This prevents capital concentration and keeps capital flowing locally.

- Stewardship: Institutions and assets require legal safeguarding from pressure to maximize outside shareholder profit over stakeholder wellbeing and sustainability. For example, company charters and ownership structures that insulate core purpose, from hostile takeovers, such as perpetual purpose trusts. This sustains their ability to provide long-term value without distortion and capture.

- Connective Infrastructure: Transformed enterprises must weave together into supportive consortiums, shared services vehicles, and investment funds. This helps companies coordinate needs like accessing capital without compromising autonomy to external forces. For example, community banking systems and jointly-owned supply chain logistics entities currently fill this need to some degree.

We need to transition from an archipelago model of one-offs to an interwoven fabric of aligned entities anchored in the interests of people and places. This bridges the gap between systems extracting human potential and systems nurturing it. We need entities that provide resilience and support to the development of durable ecosystems of equity and access. With these in place, citizens could lead lives of dignity and access real economic opportunity for their families.

By Design, Not By Default

The economic system we inhabit was designed by humans and can be changed. The rules currently governing business and finance ultimately concentrate both gains and control. The good news is if existing approaches lead to unfairness, modifications can be normalized, which leads to fairness and flourishing. Economies can proactively embed ethical orientation into their DNA at the single entity level, the coordination level, and the policy level.

Consider the founding principles codified in the corporate charter of the Japanese Sumitomo Group, drawn from an example in this book (See Keiretsu): "Sumitomo shall achieve strength and prosperity by placing prime importance on integrity and sound management in the conduct of its business. Sumitomo shall manage its activities with foresight and flexibility to cope effectively with the changing times. Under no circumstances, however, shall it pursue easy gains or act imprudently." This example, among many others, shows that we can architect economic logic to nurture ethics and prudent stewardship, rather than mandating endless growth above all else.

This kind of system has worked for thousands of years to create better outcomes. We must accept that inherited rules should never be mistaken for inevitabilities. Extractive economies aren't a natural law. Accountability, transparency, and integrity in our economic relationships are reliable approaches. The opportunity before us is to make changes to our economy that align its outcomes with today's needs, not just leaning on expired approaches because they're the default.

Coordinated Action

We know our economy is at a crossroads. Many business owners and citizens feel the current system concentrates wealth at the top while leaving too many communities behind. Promisingly, a wave of alternative ownership models is emerging to spread the benefits of economic success more broadly. Structures like employee ownership, cooperatives, land trusts, and benefit corporations, enable more people to have a stake and a voice in the enterprises that shape their lives. The core principles are clear:

- <u>Shared ownership:</u> Provide more individuals a share of the wealth they help create

- <u>Stewardship:</u> Orient firms toward long-term, balanced benefits for all stakeholders

- <u>Connective Infrastructure:</u> Create supportive ecosystems for these models to thrive and spread

Change will happen through leadership and cooperation: business owners deciding to sell to their workers as they retire, entrepreneurs opting for stewardship models, community leaders advocating for local ownership of vital assets, and policymakers enacting enabling frameworks. No one actor can transform the economy alone. The key is to link efforts so they become mutually reinforcing. As employee-owned companies, cooperatives, and land trusts proliferate in a region, opportunities emerge to forge connections between them. Suppliers, distributors, and service providers using similar models can preferentially do business with each other, forming an integrated ecosystem. This ecosystem, in turn, can exert market and political power to level the playing field further.

As business and community leaders, you have an important role to play. By adopting and advocating for these models in your context, you help bring them into the mainstream. You expand people's sense of what is possible. What is one viable step in this direction that makes sense for your business or community? However modest, it moves the needle.

The challenges we face are real, but so are the solutions available to us. Through our choices, we can grow an economy that produces good livelihoods while recycling wealth back into our communities. Not a utopia, but a practical vision for a system that better aligns incentives with our values.

Structures, Governance & Ownership

Charity May

In our exploration of these case studies, there were a few questions that we sought to understand. What were the motivating factors that led to the use of a particular company structure? How do these factors influence the relevant pathways for builders interested in advancing shared ownership?

We've identified three core motivations that shape corporate form in the pursuit of shared ownership.

1) <u>Firm Preservation:</u> Firstly, there is often a desire to preserve the firm, either to maintain its positive impact or to address an emerging threat. Commonly, business owners seek to prevent closure or private equity extraction, which becomes more relevant as they approach retirement. Retirement often prompts a strategic reassessment aimed at ensuring the continuity of the enterprise, growing its legacy, and protecting the livelihoods it supports.

2) <u>Employee Well-Being:</u> Secondly, there's a desire to prioritize and improve the well-being of workers in an enterprise. This motivation reflects a deeper commitment to fostering environments where employee welfare is paramount, leading to employees feeling empowered to contribute more than just their labor.

3) <u>Collaborative Value Creation:</u> Lastly, there's often a desire to innovate on how value is created and distributed among stakeholders. Our economy is obsessed with relentless growth at all costs. Could more collaborative business architectures build more sovereignty and resilience in communities, and between enterprises? This motivation leads

to prototyping new methods for how collective efforts and resources are leveraged among enterprises and the communities they operate in.

These underlying motivations are connected to a wider ecosystem of values and desires to establish a different economic logic. For example, values of solidarity and mutualism are common drivers of creative governance and ownership arrangements. Political economist Jessica Gordon Nembhard defines a solidarity system as "a non-hierarchical, non-exploitative, equitable set of economic relationships and activities geared toward the grassroots—that's of the people (people before profit), indigenous, participatory, based on human needs, humane values, and ecological sustainability." This definition reminds us that though much corporate ownership and governance design is conducted pragmatically, there is always a broader impact on society. Pursuing mutuality over extraction leads us to design our companies differently from the beginning, and results in different outcomes for direct and indirect constituents.[199]

This chapter covers how these values shape a diversity of governance (decision-making) and ownership (access rights and economic interest) structures. We will also provide a primer on some key concepts and types of structural arrangements that commonly appear. We will utilize examples from case studies within this book, and additional stories which illustrate these important concepts.

Organizational Structures for the Commons

To begin, we will introduce a few different legal structures and outline how each one achieves the three motivations presented. We also note that these models need not stand on their own, but rather can be blended to activate shared ownership at varying degrees of scale.

---

199   Gordon Nembhard, J. (n.d.). Building a cooperative solidarity commonwealth. The Next System Project. https://base.socioeco.org/docs/jessicagordonnembhard.pdf

Facilitating Firm Preservation: Holding Companies & Purpose Trusts

Holding companies (HoldCos) enable a sponsoring enterprise or entrepreneur to bring back-office and foundational resources together (e.g., legal, financial, and operational expertise). Small businesses strapped for cash and talent can benefit from the backing of a HoldCo equipped with the resources to bring other shared services and strategic insight to them. We include in this book several present-day examples showcasing the value of this approach. The Goodworks case study demonstrates this well with the HoldCo, Goodworks Evergreen, focusing extensively on improving and streamlining operations across a group of local businesses, including sourcing talent to fulfill managerial roles.

The utilization of purpose trusts to provide a mission-driven container for holding companies can serve as a promising solution, materializing multiple goals. The use of the purpose trust specifically for employee-ownership, known as employee-ownership trusts (EOT), is a fascinating blend of the first two primary motivations introduced: firm preservation and employee wellbeing. With the desire to preserve the company centered around employee agency, the EOT enables this in a way that is quite distinct from ESOPs and cooperatives. This approach is well illustrated in the case study of Clegg Auto, a group of auto body shops in Utah that transitioned from independent LLC enterprises to an EOT holding company. This approach provides a noticeable amount of flexibility in structuring incentive measures while preserving employee ownership and ensuring that the firm is never subject to a strategic or financial exit. This is made possible by implementing an EOT structure.

Pursuing Human Agency and Wellbeing: Worker Ownership & Cooperatives

The cooperative model is known for its emphasis on collective agency and the well-being of worker-members. At their foundation, cooperatives reconfigure the traditional hierarchical dynamics of industrial operations by prioritizing the welfare and participation of workers in all aspects of the enterprise. This is evident in the language used to describe workers of the cooperative – often they are not identified as employees, but rather worker-members. Additionally, the internationally recognized cooperative principles include inter-cooperative cooperation while upholding individual member autonomy. The cooperative structure champions democratic governance and places human dignity above the drive towards profit maximization, marking a significant departure from the exploitative labor practices that have characterized much of industrial history.[200]

We continue our emphasis here on EOTs and their ability to hold both firm preservation and employee well-being together. EOTs offer a creative way to ensure worker influence and well-being within a business by embedding employee ownership as a perpetual purpose, protected by the trust. EOTs allow employees to participate in company ownership without burdening them with an upfront capital contribution. They also allow for creativity in the formation of the governance structure, whether that be using a board or representative democracy model to organize employee participation as directors of the company. While U.S. tax laws have yet to fully recognize the benefits of EOTs compared to cooperatives and ESOPs, the alignment of values and flexibility of EOTs continue to attract business owners and employees towards its implementation.

Streamlining towards Collaborative Innovation: LLCs and Joint-Stock Companies:

Limited Liability Companies

Widely used legal structures can also offer positive benefits when structured thoughtfully. For example, under U.S. corporate law, limited liability companies (LLCs) can be managed by workers (worker-directed). LLCs can also be used to create platform services between companies like moving money, trading, making decisions, and prototyping interconnected systems to manage the growing complexities of these relationships.

---

200   According to the International Cooperative Alliance, there are seven main principles that cooperatives around the world subscribe to in their formation. We note only a few here, as the existing body of work describing cooperatives is extensive and rich. Learn more at International Cooperative Alliance's website, https://ica.coop.

Financial institutions have long since employed LLCs to facilitate joint venture investments and other business activities. When pursuing investment in the common good, LLCs present the possibility of multiplying the effect of collaboration among financial institutions. We explore these concepts through the case studies of the Calvert Investment Note and Credit Union Service Organizations (CUSOs).

Joint-Stock Companies

Joint-stock companies allow for the issuance of stock and typically take the legal form of a C Corp or S Corp in the U.S. context. These forms are distinct from LLC membership interest and its taxation parameters. Sardex, featured in this book, is a joint-stock company that operates a complementary currency and mutual credit system to facilitate the trade of goods and services among small businesses without fiat money. Initially a technology startup with cooperative ideals, Sardex chose the joint-stock model for flexibility and ease of attracting external investment and partners, ensuring founders' control over the product's direction and development. Over time, as the company evolved, efforts were made to broaden the 'public' aspect of its offerings.

The Networked Advantage of Blending Structures

Blending different enterprise structures within a regional economy showcases the potential for creative business arrangements that are grounded in meaningful purpose. It also promotes cooperation among businesses that may otherwise compete against each other. This helps them navigate complex legal frameworks that often favor larger entities that prioritize shareholder interest.

Regional economic development of this nature is demonstrated by The Industrial Commons (TIC) in Morganton, North Carolina. TIC used a non-profit as the convener and activator for the larger business ecosystem. They unlocked nearly $30 million of capital and enabled the capitalization of worker-member LLC cooperatives without being burdened with debt. Goodworks Evergreen, a for-profit holding company in Montana, owns independent but functionally related enterprises in the hardware and lumber industry. Additionally, it has a housing development entity that collaborates with a community land trust. The sole purpose of this collaboration is to develop community-owned housing. Again, we see the positive externalities of their legal structure bringing benefit to their region.

Multi-stakeholder cooperatives (MSC) also illustrate a powerful combination between charitable entities and for-profit enterprises. Margaret Lund, a consultant and contributor to alternative economic development and shared ownership strategies, offers a compelling example in the housing sector: "Affordable housing cooperatives, for example, often have difficulty attracting public subsidies in the U.S. because they are not structured as charitable nonprofits. A nonprofit housing organization could use a multi-stakeholder approach to this problem by using their non-profit status to be the recipient of subsidy funds from a grantor, and then use the limited cooperative association model to join a housing cooperative as an investor member. The housing non-profit would invest the subsidy funds as an investor member, and then use its governance powers within the cooperative to assure the grantor that the subsidy funds would be used for their intended purpose."[201]

Blending structures enables you to match purpose with pragmatism to come up with an actionable solution. Networked enterprises tend to benefit from this hybrid approach, building a bridge between conventional and alternative economies.

Governance & Decision-making

Governance refers to the systems, processes, and structures used to direct, control, and hold accountable an organization or group of people. Governance decisions set the overall direction and strategy of an organization, while management decisions focus on the day-to-day implementation and execution of those strategies. From corporate boards to advisory

---

201 Lund, M. (2011). Solidarity as a Business Model. Cooperative Development Center at Kent State University. https://resources.uwcc.wisc.edu/Multistakeholder/tool-oeoc-multistakeholder-coop.pdf

councils, decision-making, and its processes tend to take on the flavor of the leadership philosophies, which sets the tone for the approach.

We begin this discussion on governance by examining how one enterprise, Namaste Solar, allowed its governance practices to eventually evolve its legal structure. Namaste Solar is an employee-owned solar electric company based in Colorado that acted as the progenitor of a multi-stakeholder cooperative solar ecosystem. Jason Sharpe, the founder, began the enterprise as a conventional joint-stock company. However, even within this legal structure, the company opened ownership to employees, practiced democratic one-person, one-vote control, implemented open-book management, and had a graduated pay scale. With this collaborative governance culture in place, they eventually made the legal transition to align its ownership structure with the culture and internal processes.

In 2011, after starting as a joint-stock company in 2005, Namaste Solar transitioned to a cooperative structure. It continued the evolution through its expansion into a multi-stakeholder cooperative ecosystem. They were instrumental in forming a purchasing cooperative, operations, and maintenance shared services enterprise, credit union, and investment fund. This evolution from a traditional joint-stock company to a multi-stakeholder cooperative ecosystem underscores the profound impact that governance choices can have on the legal and operational framework of a business.[202]

---

202 Namaste Solar is not one of the case studies we cover in this book, however it demonstrates a relevant example of expanding shared ownership. A comprehensive case study was included in the Journal of Entrepreneurial and Organizational Diversity, which we link to here. Martins Rodrigues, Julia and Schneider, Nathan, Scaling Co-Operatives Through a Multi-Stakeholder Network: A Case Study in the Colorado Solar Energy Industry (January 31, 2022). Journal of Entrepreneurial and Organizational Diversity, Vol. 10, No. 2, 2021, pp. 29-53, Available at SSRN: https://ssrn.com/abstract=4038292

Democratic Governance Models

Conventionally, democratic governance is often tied to economic interest in the enterprise. This means the number of equity shares owned by the member would correspond to the weighted impact of this member's influence on strategic decision-making when decisions are put to a vote. However, in our case studies, we see more creative options. There is greater flexibility in the composition of the members participating in the decision-making of the enterprise. We observe that firms seek to collaborate while distinguishing who holds decision-making power relative to who has an economic interest in the company. From cooperatives to joint stock companies, different share classes can be established to provide diverse participation in governance. In some cases, economic interest and voting rights can be entirely separated. This allows for more nuanced governance arrangements that do not directly tie voting power to equity ownership. Here are a few examples of how these arrangements play out.

Governance in Multi-stakeholder Cooperatives

One such example is the multi-stakeholder cooperative mentioned earlier. An MSC involves various membership classes, such as producers, consumers, workers, partners, or investors, in the cooperative's governance and ownership. Each membership class in an MSC may have different weights assigned to their votes. The weighting is typically based on the primacy or proximity of the class to the purpose of the venture. This is also the case for joint-stock companies which may issue multiple classes of shares with varying degrees of governance rights.

Governance in Perpetual Purpose Trusts

Perpetual purpose trusts (PPTs) demonstrate a different approach. PPTs separate economic interests from voting interests. They achieve this by legally enshrining the purpose of the enterprise in a trust, placing primacy on its fiduciary duty to fulfill its purpose. Trustees govern this trust and oversee the strategic direction of the company held in the trust, ensuring decisions are taken in alignment with the purpose. As accountability, each PPT must elect an independent 'trust enforcer' whose governing authority overrides the trustees should they compromise the purpose. This enforcer is given veto rights that are not coupled with an economic interest, which eliminates issues of self-dealing and self-interest. Steward-owned entities using PPTs have an operating company (OpCo) entity owned by the PPT. This allows for investment shares and other share classes to be created at the OpCo level as needed. The OpCo is the venue for managing economic interests. With decision-making distributed across the trustees, the trust enforcer, and operating company leadership, agendas can remain unpolluted.

Participatory Governance

Participatory governance requires significant emotional investment from the members involved. This is particularly true in cooperative models and informal self-governing collectives. Additionally, the work of participating in decision-making is not always 'rewarded' with economic interest, but rather produces benefits of mutual understanding and commitment. This dynamic is also notable in the grassroots resource-sharing models of rotating savings and credit associations (ROSCAs) and savings pools. Members of these informal money circles make all decisions collectively on the parameters that are unique to each circle. They determine, upfront, what loan funds can be used for, and what the repayment terms or contribution amounts might be. While these resource-sharing models are more apt to take place between individuals, they are also the source of seeding new business endeavors. Small circles support each other financially and promote economic development and resiliency because of a foundation of trust. High trust networks, whether it be individuals or companies working together, enable braver and more purposeful endeavors to emerge.

For cooperatives, Margaret Lund notes that their success hinges on the ability of all members to look beyond immediate self-interests and towards a shared vision of mutual benefit. While this approach may not be time-efficient, it creates other meaningful benefits such as adaptiveness.[203] Daniel Fireside, the founder of Uncommon Capital Solutions, described democratic governance as "like a muscle". He said, "I've come to appreciate a certain planned inefficiency". Adding, "When I was at Equal Exchange, we would shut the whole company down and have Worker/Owner meetings where we would debate bylaws and governance stuff. A lot of people were like, 'I'm trying to package coffee over here! I've got to get an order out!' But you needed to do that sort of thing to keep worker democracy going. If people didn't have exposure to it, then it just became about letting the board or management decide everything. Democracy is like a muscle – you have to use it to keep it healthy."[204]

Distributed Decision-Making Practices
Many business owners are attentive to the cultural power of inclusive decision-making at the management level. Designing a management methodology that encourages employees to take part in business decisions can complement legal governance design.

Introducing participatory management practices can lead to a competitive advantage. One example is the disruptive management model called 人单合一 (rén dān hé yī). This concept emerged from the 20+ year evolution of Haier Group Corporation, a Chinese state-owned home appliance global manufacturer with over 70,000 employees. In 1984, Zhang Ruimin, the CEO and Board Chairman of Haier Group Corporation, was tasked with turning around the company, which was on the verge of bankruptcy at that time. His initiatives led to the formation of rén dān hé yī philosophy which has been instrumental to Haier's modern success. Rén dān hé yī promotes the establishment of micro-enterprises within a larger corporation, interconnected through contracts and collaborations. Each

---

203   Lund, M. (2011). Solidarity as a Business Model. Cooperative Development Center at Kent State University. https://resources.uwcc.wisc.edu/ Multistakeholder/tool-oeoc-multistakeholder-coop.pdf

204   Daniel Fireside, Founder of Uncommon Capital Solutions, personal communication, December 14, 2023.

micro-enterprise acts as an independent profit center with ten to twenty employees. The model values entrepreneurial capacity being developed at the employee level. By decentralizing decision-making and granting operational autonomy to individual business units, rén dān hé yī promotes an environment where employees are more than just executors of top-down directives. Employees are empowered stakeholders with a vested interest in their unit's success. This empowerment is enhanced by performance-based compensation and the use of open online platforms, encouraging a culture of innovation, accountability, and direct engagement with broader market dynamics.[205] Ruimin says: "With the rén dān hé yī model, we truly enter the network age. But the network aspect is not even the most important. What is more important is that we no longer try to delegate to, or 'empower', employees. It's now time for every employee to be his or her own boss. So, with the rén dān hé yī model we move away from being like an empire (with a traditional, closed pyramid) to being more like a rainforest (with an open networked platform). Every empire will eventually collapse. A rainforest, on the other hand, can be sustained."[206]

We also see a distributed decision-making process play out in Enspiral, one of the case studies in this book. The Enspiral network consists of entrepreneurs and independent businesses contributing to a shared financial pool. They share core values and remain connected through the use of online technology to share information, power, and collective decision-making. The Enspiral model illustrates blending the best of both worlds—time-tested collaborative strategies and cutting-edge technological tools—to create more inclusive, efficient, and adaptable ways of working together. This approach aims to enhance organizational agility, human development, and collective problem-solving.

---

205 Frynas, J. G., Mol, M. J., & Mellahi, K. (2018). Management Innovation made in China: Haier's Rendanheyi. California Management Review, 61(1), 71–93. https://doi.org/10.1177/0008125618790244

206 De Moree, P. (2018, September 26). RenDanHeYl: The organizational model defining the future of work? Corporate Rebels. https://www.corporate-rebels.com/blog/rendanheyi-forum

The adoption of distributed decision-making in the operations of a network of enterprises reflects a broader trend toward collaboration within and among corporations. Honoring autonomy at the employee and firm level facilitates new business opportunities and the reduction of transaction costs. These are a few of the practical benefits of fostering cooperative relationships within a competitive ecosystem. Other salient examples can be found in shared services business models, which are expanded later in this book.

Economic Interest in Networked Structures

Economic interest represents a stake or claim in the financial outcomes of an entity, whether it's a company, investment, or any financial venture. It encapsulates the level of investment, both tangible and intangible, that an individual or entity has in the economic success or failure of a business endeavor. This interest can manifest in various forms, including ownership of shares, rights to profit distributions, or any other financial benefits derived from the value created by the business. Economic interest is also the mechanism used to demonstrate the holder's vested interest in the health and longevity of the enterprise, as these can significantly impact financial outcomes.

In networked enterprises, the role of economic interest extends beyond traditional notions of ownership and profit. It can induce an interdependence between people, where they experience co-creating a shared economic destiny. The Japanese keiretsu model, for example, showcases how firms can be deeply invested in each other's mutual well-being, with economic interests representing a collective commitment to shared success over the long term.[207] This sense of responsibility and mutuality permeates within the enterprise and across partnering enterprises. This influences how the firms and employees perceive their role in contributing to the welfare of their colleagues and the broader ecosystem as a whole.

---

207   A keiretsu is the Japanese word to describe a loose affiliation between diversified businesses through cross-shareholdings. Learn more in the dedicated case study in Part 2.

Such models demonstrate how economic interests can transcend financial metrics to embody a broader vision of collective resilience, sustainability, and communal prosperity, marking a stark contrast from the conventional focus on maximizing profits for shareholders alone.

Ownership models can prioritize the longevity and sustainability of a firm by redesigning how economic interest is shared among stakeholders. This increases the desire to reinvest in the stability of an organization, and its stakeholders and community. When leaders consider the firm's role within the economy and society, it is logical to reevaluate the purpose of economic interests and their end goals. Networked enterprises invite us to explore the idea that wider distribution and recirculation of surplus is a signal of a company's health and success. Some models, like PPTs, enshrine reinvestment in their core documents. Another strategy we see in our case studies is the formation of pre-tax funding pools for internal support. Others may establish shared services companies or share profits between separate entities. Strategic and contractual interconnections between enterprises can activate a wider range of economic behaviors and more holistic benefit sharing.

Ownership in the Public Sphere

The public sector can play a more active leadership role in shaping values-driven economic development. Across our case studies, we note powerful examples of local and regional government or municipality collaboration for shared ownership infrastructure. The public sector can play a supporting role in connecting business and community initiatives, or it can step into directly initiating and creating them. Both are exciting forms of partnership in co-creating positive economic futures alongside local leaders. In this section, we explain a few different approaches the public sector is taking to support shared ownership and stewardship to grow.

Supporting Early Initiatives

When the public sector supports the formation of projects and businesses in shared ownership, it lends credibility and stability to these early initiatives. One example of this would be to act as the first mover of capital investment in a grassroots economic development initiative. For The Industrial Commons, both federal and state agencies rallied behind the vision of regional prosperity through employee ownership and market trading collaborations among textile industry partners. In addition to attracting $10 million from the Appalachian Trade Commission (a federal agency), TIC was also able to galvanize bipartisan support for a state-level appropriations bill. This allowed them to invest $5 million in the burgeoning multi-stakeholder cooperative ecosystem for the regenerative textile manufacturing innovation campus. This shows the immense leverage provided to local projects with scale when some of their first backers are municipal or public agencies.

Leading New Initiatives

The public sector can actively develop infrastructure for shared ownership and stewardship. The primary example of this in our case studies is Urban Wealth Funds (UWFs). UWFs are government-owned holding companies that manage underutilized public assets, primarily real estate, for the benefit of the community. Overseen by elected officials, UWFs aim to optimize these assets' use to generate revenue for reinvestment and promote public welfare. Asset management held by an independent party unties short-term political influence and activation of the newly valued assets for public benefit. This model offers an exciting possibility for representing the commons and tackling challenging civic development issues, such as creating permanently affordable housing.

An Acknowledgement of Public Banking

Delving deep into public banking goes beyond the scope of this book, but we want to point to the powerful role public banking plays in this movement. A public bank is a financial institution owned and managed by a government entity on behalf of the people within its jurisdiction, with the mandate to serve community needs. The parameters under which a public bank operates are determined by the public, for the public. Given that the assets backing the public bank are de facto civic assets, the goals of the bank do not seek to maximize profit for shareholders, but rather community benefit as a true mission-driven institution. This is achieved through new market formation, distribution of lending investment opportunities, and well-being monitoring.

Publicly owned financial infrastructure is key to aligning financial incentives with public good outcomes. Public banks can create financial products, such as favorable loan terms or local bonds, to facilitate the development of shared ownership infrastructure. Public banking can go hand in hand with urban wealth funds, as both position governments as active builders in the local economy.

Public banks are not a new concept. Many communities across North America are pushing for these systems to be established. One mature example is ATB Financial, Alberta's public bank in Canada. ATB focuses on financing Alberta's green and well-being economy. Fully backed by provincial assets and exempt from income tax as a government asset, ATB can leverage its balance sheet for community investment. It offers low-cost loans given its mandate to deliver for the public good, and non-profit maximization.[208] Local cities within the United States are inspired by the prospects of how a public bank could help close the financial gap not quite met by conventional banks, community development financial institutions, and private impact-investing funds. One such example is the concept and organizing group of the Municipal Bank of Los Angeles (MBLA), which in 2023 conducted a series of feasibility and assessment reports to understand how a public bank could change the trajectory of investment in and across Los Angeles' missing infrastructure, from affordable housing to the transition to employee ownership. This initiative is an attempt to realize this vision given the passing of the California Public Banking Act of 2019,

---

208   Anielski, M. (2016, November 6). ATB Financial: Opportunities for building a new flourishing economy of well-being for Alberta. Anielski Management Inc. https://anielski.com/atb-financial-albertas-golden-goose-that-could-finance-albertas-new-green-well-being-economy/

which enables local jurisdictions to establish public banks for community reinvestment.[209]

Activating civic assets through urban wealth funds and public banking illustrates an opportunity for the public sector to become direct and active stewards of the commons in partnership with private actors.

In Closing

Building toward shared ownership and stewardship relies on creative and values-driven governance, ownership, and economic interest arrangements. We must place priority on the purpose and the longevity of firms, and encourage a move away from founder-dependency, towards more inclusive decision-making frameworks. Shared ownership is not only about innovative structural models but also about empowering builders to forge stronger connections within and across enterprises. This evolution in enterprise structures invites us to rethink legal frameworks and business longevity, offering opportunities for diverse voices in governance, and increased stakeholder participation, including the public sector.

---

209   Ahmad, H., Feygin, Y., & Katz, P. (2023). What a Municipal Public Bank Can Do for Los Angeles and its People. https://jainfamilyinstitute.org/wp-content/uploads/2023/05/JFI-Berggruen_MBLA_Overview-Report_May-2023.pdf

Shared Services

Jay Standish

In this chapter, we explore how organizations are increasing their efficiency and connectedness by sharing services like HR, accounting, and purchasing. When firms share overhead, they increase their competitiveness in the broader marketplace.

We explore various models such as shared service cooperatives, internal shared services within holding companies, and strategic alliances, all forms of structural collaboration. Real-world case studies demonstrate how integrating specific business functions across organizations can lead to cost savings, operational efficiencies, and economies of scale. Additionally, we discuss how these collaborative models maintain institutional knowledge and working relationships.

What are Shared Services?

Shared services are business functions that service the needs of multiple organizations, or multiple divisions within a large conglomerate. For example, instead of each company having its own accountant, they may share a single accountant among the group. By sharing a function like accounting, organizations save money. Smaller organizations can also access higher-quality services, since the shared accountant can focus on their core competency, rather than also wearing the hats of bookkeeper, payroll admin, and CFO. Shared services also develop within larger companies when divisions, product lines, regional groups, or subsidiaries band together to share staff and resources. In a large corporate context, Bain estimates 20-40% cost savings from implementing shared services.[210]

---

210   Heric, M., Krafft, M., & Bhardwaj, P. (2023, January 31). How shared services organizations can scale up by earning internal customers' love. Bain & Company. https://www.bain.com/insights/how-shared-services-organizations-can-scale-up-by-earning-internal-customers-love/

Shared services companies work with a closed group of members who have a stake in the service company or unit. Shared services reduce overhead for their users by not having an external profit maximization incentive. Using shared services is not the same as outsourcing to a professional services firm in the open market. If a privately owned accounting firm is being run by a group of experts offering specialized value to a specific sector and charging an additional margin, this is just a vendor and is not considered a shared service. However, if a group of companies from within a sector agreed to co-invest, co-own, and co-manage an accounting firm with specialized knowledge, the incentive of that firm would be to provide high-quality services without pressure to increase margins. Instead, the "margins" are cost efficiencies that free up resources those companies can focus on their core business. Additionally, if the governance and ownership models of the shared services themselves are linked to the success of the companies they serve, the priorities become aligned across multiple entities to achieve overall net positive outcomes across the group.

Common functions for shared services:

- Accounting and bookkeeping
- Finance, forecasting, capital management
- M+A deal team & integration support
- Legal + compliance
- HR + payroll
- Recruiting + training
- Insurance
- Marketing, advertising & creative
- IT, website, operations software, automations
- Leadership development
- Specialty expertise & consulting
- Purchasing, distribution, supply chain management

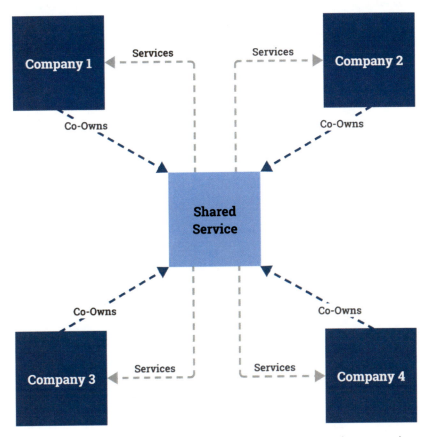

Basic Structure of a Shared Services Cooperative: Multiple companies or organizations co-own a Shared Services provider. Typically a capital contribution consummates ownership in the group, and services are only provided to member-owners. Excess cash produced by the Shared Services provider can be returned as profit distributions, usually pro rata based on the volume of use.

Models & Types

The Internal Model: HoldCos, Roll-ups and Conglomerates

One approach to implementing shared services is to provide those services inside a parent company. In this case, services are shared across either subsidiaries or divisions that share common ownership. In HoldCos, multiple companies with distinct operations may have started independently before being acquired. Once within the parent company, sharing functional teams drives cost savings that benefit the parent company and enables value sharing across subsidiaries, including institutional knowledge, trade secrets, and staff expertise. The strategy of a roll-up is similarly driven by the efficiencies of shared services on a single balance sheet. Common in private equity, a roll-up is when multiple "identical" companies are purchased and held together as a portfolio, usually integrating operations into a unitary force. A major aspect of this integration process is merging some functions into shared teams.

Within our case studies, Obran Cooperative is a holding company that has an internal services function that serves multiple companies within its portfolio. Functions like HR and investment are run by the same team members for multiple portfolio companies. Goodworks Evergreen did a hardware store roll-up and integrated a large portion of operations across them. Purchasing, hiring, inventory, and general management functions were all woven together into one operating entity and cohesive team.

The External Model: Shared Services Cooperatives

Shared Services Cooperatives are co-owned by independent organizations that form and manage the co-op to suit shared needs. As opposed to the internal model, where shared services can just be run by a team within an existing organization, shared service co-ops are third-party entities that provide the service to their members.

Criteria for a "true" shared service co-op:[211]

- Is member-owned
- Has a defined class of members (i.e. not just open to anyone)
- Has a democratic governance structure
- Participation is voluntary

The top factors that drive the need:

---

211   Clamp, C., R. Amendah, E., & Coren, . (2019). Shared-Services Cooperatives: Strengthening local economies through collaboration. In Cirec Working Papers (No. 2019/23). CIREC International. https://ideas.repec.org/p/crc/wpaper/1923.html

- Internal cost savings

- Administrative challenges + training

- Securing better-qualified professional staff

Many Credit Union Service Organizations (CUSOs) could be called shared services cooperatives. Credit unions have very similar and specific needs, which they can solve by working together to form a special-purpose entity. For example, credit unions have a shared national network of ATMs that allows even a tiny one-branch credit union to provide cash to its members 3,000 miles away.

The Federated Model: Shared Brands

Shared services aren't limited to back-office functions. Sometimes, one of the "services" that members can share is a brand. When multiple independently-owned companies co-own a shared customer-facing brand, we might think of this as a "federated brand cooperative." A well-known example of this is Organic Valley, which is a consumer-facing food brand co-owned by around 1,600 farmers and made over $1.2 billion in annual sales in 2023.[212]

We might think of this model as an "inverted franchise" where independent, local, small businesses co-own a brand and operations infrastructure that saves them money, rather than losing money to corporate franchise fees.[213]

Challenges in Shared Services

Adopting a shared services model presents opportunities for efficiency and cost savings but comes with its set of challenges.

Conflicts of Interest

In a shared services setup, differing priorities can lead to conflicts of interest. For example, when a shared HR service prioritizes recruitment for one

---

212   Organic Valley Cooperative website: https://www.organicvalley.coop/

213   Clamp, C., Romaric Amendah, E., & Coren, C. (2019). Shared Services Cooperatives: A Qualitative study. Oak Tree Books. https://www.successstore.com/shared-services-cooperatives.html

organization over another, tensions can arise. To mitigate such conflicts, establishing a clear agreement that outlines roles, responsibilities, and conflict resolution mechanisms would ideally develop clever long-term structural fixes that provide an elegant, permanent solution.

Governance Issues

Effective governance is key but can be complicated by combining different cultures and expectations of multiple-member organizations. For instance, governance issues might occur in a shared IT service, where one organization's demand for cutting-edge cybersecurity exceeds another's budget constraints. In healthy organizations, conflict resolution through governance processes are formalities that are rarely used, so addressing mismatched priorities early is important to avoid escalation to a time-consuming governance process.

Integration Challenges

Integrating systems and processes across organizations is fraught with hurdles, from incompatible IT systems to divergent operational procedures. A tangible example is the integration of financial reporting systems among different entities, where differences in accounting practices can lead to significant reconciliation issues. A dedicated integration team can work on harmonizing systems and practices, supported by training sessions to align staff to new processes. Complete standardization is not possible, so balance must be found between supporting unique practices and creating buy-in and alignment toward standardizing where it matters.

What Are Networked Enterprises?

While "shared services" is a well-defined term, we are taking some poetic license with the term "networked enterprises." We use this term to mean a group of organizations that have deep, strategic affiliations. Networked enterprises might own stock in each other, collaborate on supply chain financing, or partner on strategic investments. They might have for-profit and nonprofit bodies that serve different aspects of a broader mission. However, a certain degree of autonomy must exist at each organizational "node". By comparison, wholly-owned subsidiaries within a HoldCo

218 | Assets in Common

wouldn't qualify as a networked organization, But a shared services co-op would. Networked organizations seek to create value through alliances and symbiotic partnerships. They create a collaborative advantage, not just a competitive advantage.[214]

While many companies call their vendors "partners" and draft contracts that address mutual interests, we are pointing to something deeper. What does it look like when two organizations enmesh parts of themselves together? By "networked enterprises," we aren't talking about merging them into one but integrating specific functions of enterprises into structural collaboration.[215] In these interdependent relationships, organizations have a degree of operational independence but rely on one another in important ways, and the very corpus and form of the organizations are shaped around one another.

Throughout our research, most of the stories have a cluster of multiple entities at play. The degree of interdependence and the shape of the structure varies widely across our case studies. These multi-stakeholder networks have a better chance at solving seemingly intractable, complex problems than solitary organizations.[216]

Patterns + Qualities of Networked Organizations

Networked organizations aren't all formed for the same reason. They meet a broad and diverse set of needs. Below, we've outlined some of the driving forces behind networked organizations and the value they create.

---

214   Kanter, R. M. (1994). Collaborative advantage: the art of alliances. Harvard Business Review, 72(4), 96–108. https://training.pcsaonline.co.uk/wp-content/uploads/2.-Collaborative-Advantage-Ross-Kanter.pdf

215   Castañer, X., & Oliveira, N. (2020). Collaboration, coordination, and cooperation among organizations: Establishing the distinctive meanings of these terms through a systematic literature review. Journal of Management, 46(6), 965–1001. https://doi.org/10.1177/0149206320901565

216   Dentoni, D., Bitzer, V., & Schouten, G. (2018). Harnessing wicked problems in multi-stakeholder partnerships. Journal of Business Ethics, 150(2), 333–356. https://doi.org/10.1007/s10551-018-3858-6

Interdependent Resilience

When a company is dependent on a single, unique supplier, this vulnerability presents a risk to its resilience. When backup suppliers are not an option, a networked enterprise approach will seek to strengthen that bond, since both parties are now invested in each other's existence. In the example of keiretsu, the companies might own shares in one another and provide generous financing and payment terms to ensure the other's welfare.

Standardization and Formalization

Networked organizations can act similarly to a trade association or a voluntary regulatory body in defining consistent processes and standard operating methods. By "speaking the same language," member organizations can work in compatible ways, accelerating volume and improving quality, rather than trying to collaborate with third parties who do business differently, causing friction and cost.

Operational Cost Efficiency + Quality Control

A massive benefit of networked organizations is the cost savings unlocked when one company can lean on the specialization of another, rather than a small team wearing many hats. This specialization improves quality and efficiency. By plugging multiple specialized teams and organizations together, groups like the Enspiral freelancer network build off one another's strengths.

Economies of Scale

Almost every network takes advantage of economies of scale somehow. In Carpet One, for example, a network of flooring stores aggregate purchasing to get lower pricing. COOP Services, a Credit Union Service Organization, has enabled tiny credit unions to use each other's ATMs, creating a massive national network. Networking small groups together is a way to access the benefits of scale while maintaining the agility and authenticity of smaller teams.

Liquidity Pooling + Shared Balance Sheets

Cash flow can make or break a small business or organization. The Savings Pool concept of interest-free lending addresses liquidity needs through mutual support. Industrial Commons uses the balance sheet of a well-funded non-profit to take out equipment loans on behalf of tiny sewing cooperatives that wouldn't qualify for financing. Keiretsu companies have heavy cross-shareholding and supply-chain financing deals within the "inner circle" of their alliances.

Public, Private and Philanthropic Partnerships

Many networked organizations have a for-profit and a foundation that operate semi-independently. Goodworks Development is a real estate program (and sibling to Goodwords Evergreen, one of our cases) using private capital to develop workforce housing and convert municipal land into a land trust. This type of partnership requires deft collaboration among parties who see themselves as part of a broader civil society, not just narrow-minded careerists pushing for the interests of their organization or personal success. There is a great opportunity for philanthropies to amplify their grants through a blended capital strategy for providing patient capital for viable projects that perform somewhere on the wide spectrum between market-rate investments and donations.

Incubation + Innovation

Networked organizations are fertile soil for starting new projects and companies because they already have experience in an industry or geography, and can easily identify opportunities to create new value. With a variety of organizations, infrastructure, capital, and people at their disposal, networked organizations can marshal the resources required to launch new initiatives and incubate new companies and organizations. Industrial Commons incubates new sewing cooperatives and feeds them customers with their shared sales pipeline. Credit Union Service Organizations (CUSOs) are special entities launched as partnerships of multiple credit unions who have the same problem that pool resources to build a solution together. CUSOs have incubated new products and services together, like building online banking software that can be used by multiple small credit unions.

A Regional Identity

Many of the cases we studied serve relationships in a local community and are driven by a commitment to one's hometown, region, or state. Sardex is a complementary currency in Sardinia that enables businesses on the island to trade their goods inside a network without using up regular cash. Goodworks Evergreen has bought 7 small hardware stores in Montana to preserve local character and jobs. Industrial Commons started the Carolina Textile District, which feeds client work and provides job training to sewing + textile companies in the region. These projects expand their radius of concern beyond employees and see themselves as members of a place and its people. As relationships strengthen between people in the region, the collective becomes more capable of successfully managing resources, innovating new projects, and achieving positive shared outcomes.[217]

Internal Cooperation to Enhance External Competition

One of the qualities of networked organizations is that they can work among themselves internally to gain a competitive advantage externally. Keiretsu groups absolutely prioritize members over outsiders. Shared services associations lower costs for members to give them an edge in the market. CUSOs bolster the credit union industry as a whole so it has a chance to compete with for-profit banks for customers. All of these relationships involve inward-facing camaraderie that enhances and supports the collaborators. This loyalty mirrors the dynamic in a single company or organization, where members work together on the same team, and then the organization as a whole competes in the outside world. There can also be instances where members compete with one another in some areas, but collaborate on others.[218]

---

217 Lorentzen, A. (2008). Knowledge networks in local and global space. Entrepreneurship and Regional Development, 20(6), 533–545. https://doi.org/10.1080/0898562080246212

218 Osarenkhoe, A. (2010). A study of inter-firm dynamics between competition and cooperation – A coopetition strategy. The Journal of Database Marketing & Customer Strategy Management, 17(3–4), 201–221. https://doi.org/10.1057/dbm.2010.23

Making Institutional Knowledge + Working Relationships More Portable

Useful knowledge is shared knowledge. Consider the example of two people who have established a deep, shared understanding of the process of making knitted wool hats at high volumes. They have worked together for two years as the key people producing hats in a factory. Although they could write down a detailed manual describing that process, institutional knowledge only truly lives in its full fidelity through experienced people. If both hat makers quit on the same day, institutional knowledge would be lost even if the production process was well-documented. Institutional knowledge gathers strength as more people understand it. Additionally, positive working relationships enhance culture, stability, and performance. If these hat makers have a healthy working relationship, it benefits both them and the company. There is less conflict, smoother collaboration, more joy, and the satisfaction of productive teamwork. If they were to leave the factory to start their own venture, the working relationship would be maintained, and they would take the informal institutional knowledge with them.

Institutional knowledge and working relationships are preserved effectively through organizations with intimately intertwined operations and staffing.[219] If the knitting factory is part of a networked organization, and the factory goes out of business, the two hat makers might get quickly hired by a sock factory that is part of the network. Much of the value of their know-how is transplanted, and the sock factory benefits from the social capital and shared knowledge that would have otherwise been lost. Just like how a forest ecosystem composts dead material into nutrients for new growth, organizational ecosystems can make more efficient use of lessons learned from failed projects.

There is social and economic value in healthy, functioning, interpersonal relationships that exist throughout networked organizations. This

---

219   Ortíz, B., Donate, M. J., & Guadamillas, F. (2021). Intra-Organizational Social Capital and Product Innovation: The mediating role of realized absorptive capacity. Frontiers in Psychology, 11. https://doi.org/10.3389/fpsyg.2020.624189

may be called the "extitutional value"[220] that is extra-institutional – it exists beyond the confines of the formal systems of an institution. This extitutional value is portable, not limited by the boundaries of an organization's formal structure. When organizations do not leverage tacit knowledge, friendship, and cultural ties, they lose value when key people leave. Whereas in networked organizations, if staff shift to roles in other teams and even organizations of the network, the network as a whole retains that value.

Final Thoughts

The tactics outlined in this article show how various forms of **structural collaboration** drive value in networked organizations. But in a winner-takes-all business culture, would intimate collaboration with other organizations seem risky to most companies and even non-profits? Will these models become more commonplace in the coming decades? What industries are most ripe for the emergence of shared services groups? If your organization were to form a shared services group, who would you partner with? How do these alliances get started, and what does it take for structural collaboration to be successful? We'll explore these questions around the implementation of shared services in a later section of this book.

---

220   Schingler, J. K., & De Fiippi, P. (2021, January 18). An Introduction to Extitutional Theory – Berkman Klein Center Collection. Medium. https://medium.com/berkman-klein-center/an-introduction-to-extitutional-theory-e74b5a49ea53

Holding Companies

Jay Standish

Concept + Context

A Holding Company – or HoldCo – is a parent company that owns subsidiary companies and assets. HoldCos don't directly operate a business themselves, as opposed to Operating Companies – or OpCos. Berkshire Hathaway is an example of a very large HoldCo. At the other end of the size spectrum, an entrepreneur who owns a small business might hire a general manager to free up their time, and then go buy a second company and have both companies structured as wholly-owned subsidiaries of a tiny HoldCo.

At its simplest, a HoldCo is an entity that exists primarily as a capital structure to own assets, under which a subsidiary OpCo may conduct business. HoldCos also represent a combined strategy – thinking like an investment fund and building like an operator. Throughout this book, the case studies have shown HoldCos to be a useful way to establish infrastructure for shared ownership. In this chapter, we'll examine the idea, look at examples, and understand trends with the use of holding companies. We look at how these models have been used for private profit, and then we explore how they have been modified and used for values-driven purposes and mission-driven organizations.

Examples

To showcase the diversity of holding company structures, we have provided a few short examples here. They span across legal structures and demonstrate both hyper-local versions of HoldCos and very large-scale HoldCos.

Private SMB HoldCo: Chenmark

To get a sense of the "pure" small business HoldCo, Chenmark Capital is a helpful example. The group was founded by siblings who quit private equity because they wanted to own 100% of their companies, and to hold them in perpetuity rather than flip them to the highest bidder. They bought their first company, a landscaping company in Maine, with an SBA loan and a seller note. After about 9 years in business, the group has acquired over 30 small businesses in 7 industries and is now making new acquisitions with excess cash from their portfolio.[221]

The Worker Cooperative HoldCo: Obran Cooperative

Obran is structured as a worker cooperative at the HoldCo level, and employees share profits across all the companies in the group. They have three divisions, reflecting their strategy. They focus their acquisitions within three industries with partial integration in each vertical, as well as shared services across the entire umbrella. The group has also started companies from scratch. Obran uses internal and external capital to fund their acquisitions.

The Family Office Impact HoldCo: Goodworks Evergreen

Goodworks Evergreen has private ownership but serves a community purpose. It buys very small businesses that would otherwise shutter to preserve local jobs and small-town character. Its governance is centralized but benevolent. Their strategy is mainly a roll-up. A steward ownership transition is a likely exit outcome. Goodworks used internal capital for its early acquisitions but started bringing in outside capital for its later deals.

The ESOP HoldCo: Sammons Enterprises

Sammons is a diversified HoldCo founded in 1938 as a life insurance company that started acquiring other companies in the 1950s. The ESOP was launched in 1978 and now owns 100% of the company. It is the 44th largest privately-held company in the U.S. with 6,000+ employees and $123 Billion in assets. It has four sub-HoldCos and operations in four countries totaling $7B in annual revenue, with shared services among them. The employees make $5M in impact investments each year alongside philanthropic giving.[222]

---

221 Weekly Thoughts. Chenmark. https://chenmark.com/weekly-thoughts/

222 Sammons Enterprises, Inc. https://www.sammonsenterprises.com/

Benefits + Advantages

Holding companies are used across many industries. There are clear benefits to using these structures, which have enabled efficiency gains and increased competitive advantage. We've compiled a few key benefits to the holding company model here.

Balance Sheet Aggregation

By combining multiple assets under one ownership umbrella, a larger pool of resources sits on a single balance sheet. With a larger balance sheet, it is easier to access debt and equity investments. Banks like to see assets on the books and healthy volumes of cash flow. Due to the increased scale and diversification, investors perceive lower risk and there are more assets available as security.

Let's say a subsidiary company needs a $2M loan to buy a building, but it only has annual earnings of $500,000 and has only been in business for 3 years. Even though the subsidiary can afford the monthly payments, the bank is not willing to write a mortgage because it's a young company with meager earnings. In this situation, the HoldCo steps in and goes to the bank showing a diversified balance sheet totaling $10M in annual earnings, a corporate track record of 20 years, and an average monthly cash balance of $1M. The bank is happy to loan the HoldCo the $2M to buy the building, which the HoldCo can then provide to its subsidiary at cost.

Shared Services, Economies of Scale + Integration

We've covered shared services previously, and HoldCos are probably in the most straightforward place to take advantage of shared services. A roll-up almost always implements shared services by integrating small new companies into a larger existing company. When a HoldCo has businesses in different industries, shared services will still be possible for more generic functions like HR, accounting, and legal.

In some cases, the larger purchasing power can lower supply costs when there is an overlap in needs. For example, if a HoldCo has two solar companies that both buy a lot of panels, they can buy larger orders together and get volume discounts.

Integration is the process of merging the operations of companies, and it can be a tricky skill. By merging the operations of multiple companies into one, best practices can rise to the top, economies of scale can be enjoyed, and staffing can be more specialized and efficient.

Growth through Acquisition

A single operating company must grow by investing in sales, developing new products, and driving other tactics to increase revenue and grow organically. But HoldCos can take advantage of "inorganic growth" when they buy additional companies and assets to add to their portfolio. Raw revenue numbers are not the only benefit, HoldCos can also buy companies that help with problems in their existing companies. These strategic acquisitions complement their existing portfolio companies, perhaps by buying a supplier or customer that helps them streamline their value chain or improve the quality of their service. HoldCos can also be in a position to reinvest profits from existing businesses as down payments to acquire new businesses, which can be a wise way to re-invest excess cash.

Multiple Arbitrage

When profitable companies are acquired, they are typically priced at a multiple of their annual earnings, usually an "EBITDA[223] multiple" on the private markets. You divide the acquisition price by the annual EBITDA earnings to calculate the multiple that was paid. So if you pay $4M for a company that makes $1M a year, you paid a 4x EBITDA multiple for that company.

Smaller companies are bought and sold for lower multiples, and larger companies trade at higher multiples. This is because small companies are higher risk, require more hands-on management, and are less resilient to problems, shocks, supply issues, etc. Larger companies have more resources to solve problems, more marketing budgets to help grow, and can be owned more passively, without the need for hands-on management.

---

223   EBITDA is Earnings Before Interest, Taxes, Depreciation and Amortization

Arbitrage refers to buying something for less and selling it for more, usually in different markets. In this case, the asset is being aggregated with other small companies and sold at a higher tier in the market.

For example, imagine you have four landscaping companies that each make $1M/year, and the market values them individually at a 3.5x multiple, or $3.5M each for a total of $14M. If they merge under a HoldCo and then go to sell the new conglomerate that makes $4M/year, the market values that $4M at even just a 5x multiple, they could sell the company for $20M, achieving $8M in additional value by restructuring.

In the lower tier of the market, companies with profits under $1M of EBITDA typically sell at 2.5x-4.5x. Larger companies that do $2-5M in EBITDA trade at higher multiples, like 5x-7x, so just by placing multiple small companies into a HoldCo, the group is immediately worth more. In the case of a permanent-hold strategy, multiple arbitrage is still relevant even if you don't sell the company. As a larger platform, you can buy a smaller company and plug it into your existing systems, customers, marketing channels, etc., and improve its performance. The financial reward comes as regular profit, not the terminal value of the company.

Governance & Ownership Modularity

Holding companies can have a variety of governance designs, levels of centralization, and levels of stakeholding in their subsidiaries. HoldCos don't have to be monolithic and centralized. Many HoldCos we researched have a very small "head office" that uses a light touch, with most of the activity and decisions sitting with the underlying companies. Although many HoldCos prefer to have a controlling stake in their portfolio companies, it's common to see stock carve-outs in individual companies for key staff, outside investors, or even the founders. So it's possible to be creative and flexible with ownership. In the case of Obran (a cooperative HoldCo) employees in the portfolio companies get exposure to the entire HoldCo, not their individual workplace. At Clegg Automotive, there was a sophisticated plan crafted for sharing some, but not all, profit across individual locations so if one shop did better than another, its staff would get a kicker, while also spreading some benefit out to employees at the other shops. However, their employees opted to just pool and split profits equally.

Similar to the flexibility in designing ownership structures, governance, decision-making, and management can be crafted to suit the unique needs of each business and its culture. Some HoldCos may have extreme autonomy, where each OpCo has an independent board and the HoldCo only imposes through its seats on the board. In some cases, when the operating companies share a common identity and use many shared services, it may be more effective to manage the holding company as a unified entity.

Professionalized Leadership + Asset Management

Small, one-off companies can only afford to pay for one or two leaders or managers. Usually, their time is spent running operations and putting out fires, meaning important bigger-picture opportunities sit on the back burner indefinitely. With a HoldCo, this may still be true in the portfolio companies, but the size of the overall group can support an additional layer of professional support. This can come in the form of a handful of "head office" staff who sit at the HoldCo level and are focused on big-picture strategy, growth, performance improvements, and new acquisitions. This means that general managers have someone to turn to for special projects, and there is capacity to get off the hamster wheel of the daily grind and invest in opportunities to grow and improve the company.

These head office staff can also ensure that the best finance and legal structures are in place, and bring a level of rigor and sophistication that is easily neglected when managers are bogged down in day-to-day operations. The HoldCo core team can raise capital, apply for lines of credit, get in front of compliance issues, and court strategic partnerships. They ensure that the company is investible, bankable, compliant, and solvent so that operating staff can focus on running their businesses.

In the case of Goodworks Evergreen, we saw the critical role played by just 3 head office staff in acquiring 7 very small businesses and working hands-on to improve operations and support general managers in their success. The general managers were capable operators but didn't have the level of legal, financial, and operational skills that the head office team brought to the table. These tiny companies greatly benefitted from the additional investment and support from the Goodworks head office, support that would not otherwise exist for a hardware store producing only $200k a year in profit.

Liability Shielding

A subsidiary structure helps limit some liability throughout the group. If one company were to go bankrupt, losses could be contained to that entity. This is possible if a clean legal and financial firewall exists between the two balance sheets and there aren't any credit guarantees going back to the HoldCo. Legal risk is also improved by layered entities which serve as additional liability shields.

Succession & Tax Strategy

Owner succession plans are a major vulnerability in small businesses. Even for companies large enough to sell to private equity, the founders may cringe at the prospect of their life's work being handed over to a faceless corporation. Team and relationships are very important in small businesses, and many owners want to make sure their employees are treated well and are respected for the expertise they bring to the table. HoldCos are desirable buyers for small businesses, acting as stable institutions with professional managers.

Portfolio Strategies

There are different approaches to bringing multiple companies under one roof. Some HoldCos are focused on key sectors or industries, while others are highly diversified.

Roll-up

When multiple companies are acquired and merged, it's called a "roll-up." This strategy is most commonly applied to businesses in the same industry where they can merge all their operations, and is frequently employed by private equity(PE). PE usually seeks to sell the whole group after only 3–7 years, extracting terminal financial value through arbitrage. However, roll-ups have benefits beyond merging businesses and selling them for a profit. Roll-ups also improve stability through professionalized management, increase margins through economies of scale, and can take advantage of shared services.

Accumulator

When portfolio companies are in the same general category, but don't offer the exact same product or service, it can be called an Accumulator play. In these cases, the entire company's operations can't be merged, but some functions can be shared because they are similar. An accumulator might buy home services companies, and have a mix of plumbers, electricians, roofers, and landscapers. These companies have different services, but similar operations, business models, staffing problems, and billing cycles.

Strategic + Bolt-Ons

When a company adds complementary value to an existing portfolio company, this is a "bolt-on" acquisition. A shipping pallet manufacturer might buy a lumber mill that helps them normalize their supply of raw materials. Many bolt-ons might be moved toward vertical integration, where the company controls more and more of its value chain. "Strategic acquisition" is a similar idea, and generally means there is a complementary value that unlocks new opportunities, lowers costs, expands markets, etc.

Multi-Industry Portfolio

Many HoldCos branch out to multiple specialties as they grow. Obran has three industry portfolios, each with its own investment thesis and division manager. This is a way of adding diversification while still benefiting from the specialty industry knowledge gained over years of running companies in a specific space.

Heavily Diversified

Larger HoldCos may be heavily diversified and take a passive role, only sitting on boards of their portfolio companies. These companies might have one-off acquisitions in an industry and move on to buy something entirely different. It's rare that a small business HoldCo would not have any industry clusters within their portfolio, because there's so much value in specialization and the synergies listed above.

Final Thoughts

The Rise of Search Fund HoldCos and "HoldCoBros"

The world of "search funds" and "entrepreneurship through acquisition" or ETA has gained momentum over the past 10 years. Independent entrepreneurs called "searchers" raise capital or use their own money to buy a small business, usually with annual profits between $500k-$2M. They tend to be white-collar types buying blue-collar businesses. Conferences[224], investment funds[225] and podcasts[226] have cropped up to articulate the space. Some more established searchers, like Chenmark, have bought multiple companies and formed them into a HoldCo[227], which is the aspiration of many searchers.

Overall, it's a good thing to preserve the small businesses that these searchers buy, and for more market share in our economy to be on small balance sheets rather than huge private equity groups and public corporations. Many of these entrepreneurs build meaningful relationships with their employees, and are carving out equity plans for key employees. With the rising interest in the SMB acquisition route, there's an opportunity to expand the conversation into considering employee ownership and social impact in the ETA space. As more attention, expertise, and capital go into acquiring small businesses, hopefully, the conversation can expand beyond the usual well-educated, in-the-know professionals that currently dominate the space.

---

224   Self-funded search conference: https://www.smbash.com/

225   One of the strongest search equity funds: https://sigpartners.com/

226   One of the best podcasts on ETA: https://acquiringminds.co/

227   A conference was held on the topic of SMB HoldCos: https://www.youtube.com/@holdcoconf

The Spectrum of "Pure Capitalist" to "Visionary Benefactor"

In our cases, we see a range of motivations and attitudes behind the leaders of HoldCos. On one end of the spectrum, we have the "HoldCoBro's" playing the traditional profit game and are predictable, reliable, and intellectually honest about what they are doing. On the other end, we have the visionary benefactor types who are excited to transition their companies to steward ownership, so much so that they give sweetheart deals to sell to their employees. But it seems that most people fall somewhere in the middle, operating with a sense of "enlightened self-interest." In this large gray area, the devil is in the details of governance models, compensation incentives, and company culture. Working with the right people becomes paramount when navigating through these fertile gray areas.

The Frontier of Steward-Ownership for Small Business

While holding companies have traditionally been employed to serve private equity investors through lucrative exits, steward ownership presents an intriguing opportunity to repurpose HoldCos to drive social benefit. By embracing steward ownership, HoldCos can redefine themselves around a meaningful purpose, aligning operations with broader societal objectives and fostering economic democracy.

Steward ownership positions ownership as a responsibility to safeguard the long-term well-being of the enterprise, its employees, and the communities it serves. This approach resonates particularly well with small and medium-sized businesses (SMBs), which often form the backbone of local economies.

Imagine a holding company that acquires locally-rooted SMBs, not for eventual resale or personal profit, but to preserve these businesses as permanent community fixtures. By transitioning ownership to structures such as employee trusts, perpetual purpose trusts, or cooperatives, the holding company ensures that the wealth generated remains embedded within local economies. This approach safeguards jobs, fosters shared ownership, and cultivates a culture of self-determination.

We detail actionable steps toward implementing steward-owned HoldCos later in this book.

Liquidity, Resource Sharing & Risk

Charity May

Building a resilient shared ownership economy requires resource pooling. Throughout this book, we observe companies and communities pool resources to unlock liquidity. Liquidity from traditional sources is often fraught with misaligned interests and compromise. The case studies demonstrate that it is possible to source aligned liquidity. However, this is not without complexities or risks.

In this chapter, we explore the role of liquidity from multiple viewpoints, how resources are shared between parties, and how risk sharing can be facilitated in these situations. We will illustrate each point through reference to case studies and other learnings.

The Value of Liquidity to Different Stakeholders

From the Enterprise Viewpoint

Every enterprise needs cash to continuously flow in and out of the business. However, there are times when a specific event creates greater demands on the normal day-to-day cash flows. One example might be a business seeking to buy out a misaligned investor. Another example of this might be an employee who has worked at the firm for seven years and has contributed to their capital account with contributions from their salary. Now, they want to leave the firm and take this accumulated capital with them. Over those years, the company might be paying interest on the account to allow the operating business to access those funds in the interim. However, the company cannot predict when or how many employees will want to cash in on their capital accounts. Funding the capital needs of enterprises in these moments can be challenging. In general, funding the capital needs of companies that choose not to take the quick exit route continues to be a challenge. There's ongoing education necessary to help capital providers relate to the deeper motivation behind alternative structures which facilitate shared ownership among enterprises, and steward ownership more broadly. We delve into these possibilities more elaborately in Part 4: Opportunities for Action.

Noah Thorp, Founder of Upside[228] and former VP of Engineering at NASDAQ Private Markets' secondary platform, helps collaborative ventures using tokenization to facilitate the democratization of market trading participation. He notes that the goal of liquidity alone isn't always good for private enterprises. He attributes this to the impact volatile share price swings can have on setting valuations for raising capital in the future as well as for the pricing implications of employee stock incentives. The impersonal volatility of a passive investor market influencing the strategic decision-making of an enterprise is exactly what the Japanese keiretsu sought to reject by using cross-shareholdings as a defense mechanism between the related firms.[229]

Companies seeking to benefit from liquidity while raising capital can create their own rules to avoid being subject to unpredictable market forces. Noah identifies that tools like periodic trading windows, price range restrictions, and tradable share percentage restrictions are helpful so long as they comply with regulations. These mechanisms can be used by a variety of company structures, as we note, from joint-stock companies to cooperative firms. One example of a periodic trading window is the redemption prohibitions or specific redemption periods. This tool comes into play when the enterprise restricts investors from selling or trading their shares for a specific period. An example of price range restrictions might be when a governing board is tasked with setting the annual dividend rate or share price valuation, instead of external market forces making these determinations. These mechanisms are creative options worth considering for the management of liquidity.

---

228   Upside. https://www.upside.gg/

229   Noah Thorpe, Founder of Upside, personal communication, November 28, 2023.

From the Investor Lens

Investors often want to understand how liquid their investments are, as access to liquidity can be an indication that a company is operating well. Companies managing their operations need to monitor a healthy amount of liquidity in terms of cash and assets. At times there is a need for asset accumulation, but when there is a need for capital to flow, how quickly can this occur? Traditional investment's singular focus on means to prioritize exits and returns is misaligned with the dynamics of interconnected businesses. Investors stepping into the arena of more networked enterprises' shareholdings will need to trade their conventional approach for a more holistic set of success measures. In ecosystems of connected assets held in shared ownership, liquidity is not just about securing an expedient exit and immediate return. It is also about aligning with the broader and ongoing health and ambitions of the enterprise itself. In the keiretsus of Japan, liquidity eventually became an issue for some of the banks as they held onto shares in affiliated companies long-term, with little trading action. Long holds were encouraged and promoted from the vantage point that any shareholder had a 'moral obligation' to the well-being of the enterprise. Conducting a quick trade to gain shareholder benefit was antithetical to the underlying principles holding the keiretsu firms together.[230]

This shift in perspective requires investors to embrace a sense of stewardship, recognizing that their investments are one part of sustaining the infrastructure that provides resilience to the company systems. Like the keiretsu model, where long-term holds and a moral obligation to the collective well-being of the enterprise prevail, investors are called to prioritize the enterprise's interests alongside, if not above, their own financial gains.

Liquidity for Employees in Shared Ownership

For employees, liquidity creates flexibility and reward. In shared ownership models, employee well-being and long-term commitment are central

---

230   Gerlach, M. L. (1997). Alliance Capitalism: The Social Organization of Japanese Business. Univ of California Press. https://www.ucpress.edu/book/9780520208896/alliance-capitalism

to the company's mission. Employees embody the values of enterprises, especially in companies championing democratic principles. Employees tie their personal financial futures to the company's longevity. Their incentives are not only cultural but structurally enshrined in dedicated equity share classes and governance rights. This alignment can serve as a powerful motivator for employees to invest their efforts and commitment over the long-term.

However, the reality of life's unpredictability means that circumstances may necessitate an earlier departure than initially anticipated. This presents the need for companies to manage the liquidity of employee capital accounts and profit-sharing formulas efficiently. For employees who participate in ownership structures that use trusts, retirement plans, and capital accounts to hold their portion, the potential inability to access their capital accounts until retirement can emerge as a significant concern. It's a scenario that underscores the importance of exploring interim solidarity mechanisms, such as enabling loans, or other measures that allow employees to unlock this stored wealth when needed. These mechanisms can offer a lifeline, ensuring that employees can benefit from their contributions to the company's success without having to wait until the end of their careers. The absence of a secondary market for employees to liquidate their capital accounts outside of the company may limit employee flexibility. There needs to be a balance between encouraging long-term commitment and providing employees or worker-members with timely access to capital.

Lastly, on the topic of employee interests in liquidity, we have also seen numerous examples of companies that are interested in becoming employee-owned, but require a capital injection to buy out existing investors. Many employees do not have access to capital at the scale they would need to internally crowd-fund the amount needed. The brokerage of capital within these kinds of transactions requires professional support from services firms like Common Trust. There is a growing interest in finding aligned sources of liquidity for this situation to empower employees to steward their companies into the future.

Balancing investor and employee interests

Differences between employee and investor interests can result in strategic tradeoffs. The tension is most significant for enterprises wanting to take a less extractive route to growth or business development, but need significant capital requirements that go beyond what their constituents can provide.

One relevant example from the case studies is Sardex, the digital mutual credit system and complementary currency based in Sardinia, Italy. The company juggled investor growth targets while operating a highly mutualistic and publicly beneficial business-to-business exchange system. Initially, the vision of Sardex was to establish a digital platform company that operated as a public service across the region. However, this required substantial external capital to build the digital infrastructure and team capabilities. To fund the project, Sardex entered a relationship with venture capital investors (VCs). VCs often have expectations and strategies that diverge from the ideals of conscious growth and democratic governance. Sardex's term sheets reflected a push towards a more traditional business growth trajectory, one that prioritized rapid scaling with an eye toward an eventual public offering. The shareholder's agreement outlines the intended pathway to an initial public offering (IPO) as a strategic goal for the enterprise.[231]

Jason Wiener, in his work with cooperative enterprises, acknowledges access to liquidity as a large concern for companies structured as cooperatives. "There's no secondary market for [their investor class shares], it's more like a waiting list. If the co-op doesn't have to worry about retaining earnings to buy back shares, it solves a major challenge related to redemption or repurchase liability. Many co-ops have to think about freshening up their capital stack. If they didn't have to focus on this all the time, that would be huge. It would mean that all retained earnings can go

---

231   Sardex. (2021). Sardex S.P.A. Shareholders' Agreement. In Sardexpay. https://www.sardexpay.net/app/uploads/2021/11/03-SARDEX-Crowdfunding-Round-Shareholders-Agreement-EXE-v-3_Omissis.pdf

to sustainability and growth."[232] This showcases a possible opportunity for adjacent marketplaces to be developed to aid in the generation of liquidity.

Equal Exchange, one of the largest worker-cooperatives in the U.S., pioneered the issuance of different class shares in the States. They implemented restrictions on trading within their investor share class. It was a structural attempt to align investors with the values and needs of the company. The price of shares was fixed, and dividend payments were not guaranteed in any year, though the target was typically 5% (within the range of 0% to 8%).[233] [234] Namaste Solar, a worker-cooperative solar electric company, adapted this design of multiple classes of shares for their direct public offering in 2016.[235] These examples not only demonstrate that there are investors willing to take on more illiquid investments in this manner but also illustrate how to use bespoke arrangements to bring diverse stakeholders to the table and come to an agreement with the long-term goal of the enterprise.

Resource Sharing

Numerous case studies show that sharing resources among multiple stakeholders is a key pattern driving the success of shared ownership infrastructure. Whether it's banks, loan funds, digital platforms, or currencies, the structures for resource sharing are central to ecosystems of entities thriving together. To create new incentives for this economic paradigm shift, we must investigate how resources are structured, aggregated, and

---

232   J. Wiener, personal communication, December 2023.

233   Brodsky, G., & Azhar, S. (2020). Equal exchange: creating Non-Voting investor shares for co-ops. Start.coop. https://www.start.coop/case-studies/equal-exchange

234   Daniel Fireside, Founder of Uncommon Capital Solutions, personal communication, December 14, 2023

235   Namaste Solar. (2017, June 6). Namaste Solar raises over $3.1 million in unconventional stock offering. Namaste Solar. https://blog.namastesolar.com/3.1-million-unconventional-stock-offering

distributed with the spirit of mutuality between enterprises, people, and the broader economy.

Networks of connected enterprises create resilient, sustainable models of operation that benefit a diverse array of participants and members. In a sense, when we connect our entities, we create a microcosm of the broader shift to a sustainable and regenerative economy. An economy that values people and the planet requires us to reimagine our economic systems as interconnected networks of cooperation and mutual benefit, where one entity's success contributes to the overall vitality. In this section, we will explore trends in resource-sharing methods and how pooling resources is integral to this broader vision.

Sharing Assets through Balance Sheets

One of the most interesting resource-sharing trends is how private and public enterprises leverage shared balance sheets to achieve mission-aligned goals.

Unlocking Value for Smaller Enterprises[236]

Smaller companies benefit from accessing shared resources to enable them to compete with larger companies. This is especially true in industries that involve a lot of specialized equipment and hardware. The Industrial Commons (TIC) utilizes its non-profit structure to attract investments and uses these capital injections to acquire industrial machinery and equipment on behalf of the for-profit worker-member cooperatives within their network. These assets are made available to the cooperatives under a user agreement, allowing them to access essential industrial equipment for their growth and development without incurring debt. With a lack of a capital-intensive setup process for each company, they can also distribute more cash flow back to their members. Interestingly, TIC uses this support selectively, primarily benefiting the cooperatives they have directly founded. While TIC offers cooperative development services to any business owner in the region interested in transitioning to employee-ownership

---

236   Aaron Dawson, Director of Workforce Development at The Industrial Commons, personal communication, January 17, 2024.

cooperative structures, they reserve balance sheet leverage for internally formed cooperatives.

Public Goods Asset Inventory[237]

Methods like the case study on Urban Wealth Funds (UWFs) help reveal resources held by governments. When you can account for your resources, you can measure and monitor their value for use. Many U.S. municipalities struggle to leverage their assets for the public good. This is primarily due to a lack of comprehensive asset accounting within their jurisdictions. Municipalities can undertake a systematic asset inventory to visualize all asset ownership across uncoordinated agencies. This enables a more cohesive strategy for asset management and development. Following an inventory, municipalities can conduct a fair market valuation to reveal the realistic financial value of these assets. This often uncovers a valuation multiple times higher than what is recorded on the original balance sheet, which may be severely out of date.

After conducting an inventory, resources can be structured to put those assets to work for community benefit. The creation of an urban wealth fund facilitates the transfer of these assets into a holding company, governed by elected officials and managed by independent third-party asset managers. This structure empowers municipalities to collaborate with communities and the private sector on infrastructure projects like afford-able housing, economic development centers, and educational facilities. Urban wealth funds can also significantly enhance the municipality's ability to generate new revenue streams beyond traditional taxation.

Sharing Legal Infrastructure

Beyond holding multiple assets on a single balance sheet, we have identi-fied other resource-sharing mechanisms. These include using legal enti-ties to contain shared resources among autonomous groups, developing

---

237 Detter, D., & Kavanaugh, S. (2021). Putting Public Assets to Work. Government Finance Officers Association. https://gfoaorg.cdn.prismic.io/gfoaorg/ fc756aef-e093-4034-a716-9e7062fb20a9_GFOA_UrbanWealthFunds_R7.pdf

specific financial products to increase access, and programming social processes for shared utilization of this infrastructure.

The Calvert Community Investment Note illustrates the legal infrastructure required to craft a financial investment tethered to social good. Calvert Impact Capital developed regulatory-compliant methods for pooling investor capital into large-scale impact investments. The case study explores the formation of the community investment note, but the key point here is that Calvert ultimately supports other investment vehicles and initiatives by 'lending' its legal infrastructure and guidance, otherwise, the regulations would make it extremely difficult for any other parties to participate. Calvert holds the backing, track record, and time in the field to take on the legal investment required to be able to offer these investments and securities in all fifty states.[238]

Another example briefly referenced in the Enspiral case study is the model of Open Collective. Open Collective is a digital platform that enables grassroots organizations to use its legal infrastructure and financial management tools to run their projects. At the time of this writing, they support over 15,000 collectives worldwide. Their online platform facilitates fundraising, provides access to nonprofit status, and offers a suite of money management services without the traditional hurdles of legal incorporation or bank account setup. This democratizes the infrastructure needed to efficiently manage funds, ensuring every dollar's path is fully traceable and aligned with collective goals. Their fiscal sponsorship model allows unincorporated groups to operate under the umbrella of established legal entities, removing administrative burdens and enabling these groups to focus on their missions. Their growth indicates the need for technological,

---

238   Emmeline Liu, General Counsel of Calvert Impact, personal communication, November 6, 2023.

legal, and financial support tailored to the needs of groups active in the solidarity economy.[239] [240]

Sharing Social Capital Flows and Capacity Building

Throughout history, resource sharing has extensive roots in many cultures worldwide. However, many of these examples are resource sharing between individuals and families, rather than legal entities. In our efforts to seek out ways in which businesses pool resources together, we came across the models of savings pools and rotating savings and credit associations (ROSCAs). We found that both of these approaches are effective in their approach to aggregate and distribute resources. These stories invite us to discover how these methods may spark more business-to-business resource sharing in similar manners. Both models promote lending among a trusted group of community or a kinship circle. Both reject the notion of interest or accumulation of value in money and prioritize circulation. These models are grounded in the principles of mutual trust and community support. They work because they're taking place in a circle of known and trusted individuals. Despite their informal nature, they serve as an inspiration for modern collaborative ventures.

ROSCAs and savings pools are particularly noteworthy for fostering organic practices of reciprocity and care, which predate formalized cooperative enterprise structures. These models not only facilitate the pooling of resources for mutual benefit but are also critical for seeding capital investments in small businesses. There is evidence that this kind of crowd capital has fueled permaculture ecovillages in North Carolina and immigrant groups supporting each other's arrival and flourishing in Western countries. By prioritizing social connections and regular, meaningful engagement, these practices create a supportive environment conducive to personal and collective financial growth.

---

239   Open Collective. https://opencollective.com/

240   Open Collective Docs. (n.d.). Open Collective. Retrieved February, 2023, from https://docs.opencollective.com/help

Risk Management

Financial cooperation is often perceived as risky, especially when it involves cooperating with potential competitors. However, many of our case studies show that networked businesses thrive long-term as mutual support buffers them through crises. The reality is that risk is inherent in both going it alone and cooperating. In the following sections, we emphasize practical success factors for risk management in networked business environments, including culture, transparency, and long-termism.

Culture & Participation

Pooling resources and helping one another access liquidity involves risk exposure. To mitigate this, participating parties and financial products undergo robust vetting against a measure of principles and procedures. In a number of the resource-sharing examples we investigated, we found actors setting criteria for entry to ensure overall resilience in the performance of the asset pool. This is especially true in small-scale, resource-sharing environments. Successful financial cooperation requires early participants to set a culture that promotes cohesion. Building a culture that focuses on relational connection, reciprocity, and collective benefit is a success factor for resource aggregation and sharing.

Trust and Transparency

An efficient flow of information between entities can mitigate risk. Transparency ensures that knowledge and insights can circulate and educate all involved. Transparency also allows for a collective to adapt to challenges that arise.

Intercompany entities can facilitate the flow of information. These entities can include trading companies, mutual credit platforms, and specialized shared services. For information sharing to be successful, information cannot be monopolized by any single entity within the network. When successful, these mechanisms decentralize power and build collective capacity to determine a network's needs and issues. These connective entities act as conduits through which information can be disseminated in multiple directions, reinforcing the network's adaptive capacity. Transparency not only empowers firms within the network to manage risks but also enhances their collective ability to pursue opportunities for collaboration and value creation.

On Legacy and the Long Game

Managing risk in a network of enterprises is not just about safeguarding against potential losses, but also about creating a supportive ecosystem that gives way to new ideas. Innovation is directly supported through safety nets, solidarity measures, and a collective vigilance that benefits all involved.

Shared ownership companies and networks benefit from prioritizing future value and impact over immediate gains. Leaders can define a company's success not only as steady profitability but also as the stewardship of its values over time. As seen in the enduring businesses of Japan, taking a long-term view and revering the business' holistic contributions to the broader society preserves its priorities well beyond a founder's lifetime. This shows the power of honoring a legacy.

Resilience through challenges preserves a company for the long run. Ensuring a company or network can progress beyond any issues that arise is a test of durability. A combination of mutuality and autonomy enables greater durability. Each unit of a network needs to be able to maneuver to its circumstances, while also offering to buffer any downside for others in the network. Autonomy enables dynamic risk distribution, ensuring that a setback for one does not spell disaster for all. This is demonstrated by the cooperative model of Mondragon, where the collective has navigated challenges inside and between individual cooperative firms without jeopardizing the entire ecosystem. This underscores the importance of balancing shared responsibility with individual agency.

Transitioning the economy toward shared ownership and stewardship is a legacy of its own. Building this future is a long game and we are already seeing challenges inhibit the process. One challenge is navigating antitrust regulatory landscapes, as the distinction between collaborative efforts and monopolistic behaviors becomes increasingly nuanced.

The risk of a shared ownership model being perceived as an exclusive and anti-competitive approach should be explored within the movement. Understanding the intentions and motivations behind the adoption of shared ownership frameworks is crucial. We must ensure that collaborative tools generate positive externalities for all stakeholders. The long-term legacy of the shared ownership movement should be in creating shared upside for our communities and places.

In Closing

In summary, managing liquidity, sharing resources, and mitigating risk is crucial for building successful infrastructure for shared ownership. Innovative approaches to resource sharing, such as shared balance sheets and pooling capital, demonstrate the power of collaboration in unlocking value and supporting smaller enterprises. Effective risk management through social cohesion, transparency, and a commitment to long-term success emphasizes the resilience of interconnected systems. Adopting a mindset of stewardship, adaptability, and collective well-being is essential for equitable and sustainable resource sharing.

Marketplaces & Value Chain Integration

Charity May

Money and markets are not neutral – they run on rules that can be reformed. This chapter outlines the inner workings of interior and exterior markets and proposes the benefits of purposeful markets. We will showcase the role of trading companies and currencies as bridges between interior and exterior opportunities. We'll also look at the activities of closely held marketplaces such as matchmaking, dynamic aggregation, and consistent transparency. We will also explore how value chain integration can turbocharge both business efficiency and communal prosperity.

The Role of a Marketplace

An economy does not exist without a medium for exchanging value. The notion of value in the context of shared ownership extends beyond transacting with and for money. This gives way to the infrastructure for shared ownership to host and grow exchanges of value between aligned actors. Our case studies and wider research show that the gathering points where financial exchange occurs can also be the home of rich cultural exchange. The marketplace is the activity hub, where transformation of the inputs and matchmaking can occur. The models and stories we explore in this book give us an expansive definition of what a marketplace is, the epicenter of exchange. To build a shared ownership and stewardship economy, we will need marketplaces to include not only products between creators and users but also ideas, finances, and skill sets, among many other services. Whether a marketplace is hosted internal to an enterprise, between two or more enterprises, or within a value chain, this function enables the distribution of information and activates the power of relationships.

Marketplaces require pre-determined rules and boundaries to guide participation. In the conventional capital markets economy, marketplaces tend to favor the highest bidder and the maximum rate of growth and return, while disregarding negative externalities. What builders of shared ownership infrastructure can take away from this is that generating values-aligned rules is possible and can have an outsized positive impact. Keep this in mind as we move on to discuss the design of interior and exterior markets and the ways to make them work for the commons.

Interior Markets

Interior markets are pre-tax exchange ecosystems operating within and among interrelated firms. Interior markets emerge where exchange redistributes value communally rather than being exclusively transactional. This is often orchestrated through a carefully constructed conduit, facilitating redistribution first to its participating members. The exchanges occur within a company or its immediate circle of influence in a semi-closed network. These systems also operate like an internal town square for collaboration, challenging normative beliefs about market competition and corporate governance. Interior markets are established by networks of allies coming together with shared values and ideas. These networks tend to operate based on a set of values such as trust, transparency and shared economic destiny. These markets challenge the traditional economic models by demonstrating that collaboration and mutual benefit can coexist with competitiveness and innovation.

Interior markets are unique and reflective of the ecosystems within which they operate. The Industrial Commons in Morganton, North Carolina, exemplifies an interior market thriving within the textile industry. The Carolina Textile District, formed by The Industrial Commons, acts as an aggregator and distributor of textile manufacturing opportunities among its regional constituents. Similarly, regionally-based enterprises like Sardex in Italy, Mondragon in Spain, and Goodworks Evergreen in Montana demonstrate how a vision for a region can foster interior markets that benefit from localized networks of trust and cooperation.

The creation of interior markets can also offer protection from external market volatility. This is typically derived through more structured arrangements, such as cross-shareholdings. The Japanese keiretsu use cross-shareholdings among firms to fortify against hostile takeovers. Additionally, the mutual holdings of each other's shares embed a system of mutual reliance and shared destiny that transcends mere financial transactions. Keiretsu members establish interior markets through their banks, among other methods. This allows for support and knowledge transfer from across the network to mobilize in favor of a member firm's needs. Additionally, there are interior markets for strategic management when needed, facilitated through the president's council. At times, member firms might deploy other firms' directors to support challenged firms. This example shows how interior markets can protect against the volatility and adversarial nature of impersonal external markets, promoting stability and long-term alignment among participants.

Exterior Markets

In contrast, exterior markets operate as platforms for exchange between enterprises and the broader global economy. These markets are where enterprises engage with entities outside their immediate network or eco-system, including global customers, partners, and suppliers. In this section, we focus on key mechanisms that increase the capacity for shared owner-ship models to thrive in exterior markets. We highlight two examples from our case studies, trading companies and complementary currencies. These illustrate the need for external trade systems alongside interior markets to enable infrastructure for shared ownership to thrive.

Global Representatives: Trading Companies

Trading companies act as market makers and facilitators on behalf of groups of companies. Much like a purchasing co-op or a shared brand, the united front of a shared trading company enables market influence (e.g., price setting). These entities run interference between interior and exterior markets to broker suitable opportunities. To illustrate this, we review the Sogo Shoshas. Sogo shoshas, the trading arms of keiretsu, play a key role in creating external markets for their groups. Functioning as satellites, they are the outward face of the keiretsu in global ventures and joint projects of scale. Their key contribution lies in bringing the products and services of keiretsu's industrial entities to the international stage, leveraging their unique position in both imports and exports to gather vital, real-time global market insights. This intelligence is crucial for the collective's strategic risk-taking in business dealings. Sogo shoshas underpin the flow of information across industries. This influences pricing strategies within the network, not just based on market dynamics but also on considerations of fairness and the collective needs of the multi-firm community. This approach to setting prices, wages, and forecasting returns is a reminder of the communal ethos and strategic objectives of keiretsu. The trading companies play a key role in extending the keiretsu's reach and competitive influence in external markets.[241]

Financial Technologies: Complementary Currencies

Complementary currencies facilitate the formation of purposeful exterior markets. When creating a new exterior market, there is an opportunity to enshrine specific values and norms into how money derives its value and how it is ultimately used. This provides a profound opportunity for reprogramming economic priorities. Here we will go over the basics of complementary currencies, and look into the details of a successful implementation.

Complementary currencies are exchange mediums that can operate alongside a dominant currency. They prove themselves most valuable during times when the money supply is constricted due to macroeconomic forces. Few of us think about our dominant monetary policies. Consider that when using a U.S. dollar bill, you agree that the trading value is equivalent to one tangible unit of the dollar. Without mutual understanding and agreement on this trading value, it would become weaker and prove to be a poor means of exchange.

---

241   Lincoln, J. R., Gerlach, M. L., & Ahmadjian, C. L. (1996). Keiretsu Networks and Corporate performance in Japan. American Sociological Review, 61(1), 67. https://doi.org/10.2307/2096407

When creating a currency, there needs to be an initial agreement among its users about its value and use parameters. Complementary currencies rely on how much trust users place on the exchange unit itself. In the early years of developing the Sardex Unit, the founders worked hard to gain buy-in from the local small business community. Sardex units are not fiat money, however, the value of a Sardex Unit is set to be equivalent to the Euro. Sardex units allow businesses to move goods and services through the platform and set the value of their offerings. A large amount of time, effort, and energy was invested in building trust for the marketplace to work. Once they had critical mass, the participants spread the word and invited other business owners within their regional community to join. Sardex formed a complementary currency to create an exterior market. This exchange network created new value. These goods and services may not have been traded without the introduction of the Sardex unit, as many opted in because liquidity in Euros was not required. We can also argue that the Sardex circuit simultaneously functions as an interior market because the Sardex unit is only made available to participating members. While this is true, the point to emphasize here is that the financial technology of a complementary currency is powerful enough to create exterior markets where fiat money carries limitations and may fall short in distressed regions and economic conditions.

New currencies enable transactions that might otherwise be hindered by the mainstream economic system, especially during economic downturns, or when the money supply is constrained. In an analysis of the social impact of this system, observers note that "Sardex enables users to question their practices and reconsider what money is doing for or against them, what values it should embody, how it should make them feel, and how it lubricates social relations. Instead of having money as a taken-for-granted feature in society, users discover how it influences their personal behaviour and social organisation. Sardex makes people curious about their financial life and education, and how these relate to their way of life and their values."[242]

We have discussed the role of both interior and exterior marketplaces. Mechanisms like trading companies and complementary currencies give builders of shared ownership infrastructure creative tools to navigate the balance between internal cohesion and external outreach that is required in the modern economy.

Characteristics of a Thriving Marketplace

Throughout this book, we reveal success factors and tools for building infrastructure. When we look at the success factors for marketplace development, we find two notable highlights, matchmaking and transparency. Matchmakers optimize and curate opportunities in a market. We see examples where this function is so important it's a dedicated and staffed capacity. This appears to be even more important in designer markets which have been established around specific purposes and values.

Unlike 'free market' approaches, coordination is important in markets designed around more communal values. Relational brokers become central to the process of managing match-making within the market. This approach is a move away from the impersonal, growth-centric global market. These brokers link interior and exterior markets and facilitate the creation of a cohesive network. Their goal is not volume-based transactions but ensuring the best possible connections. They emphasize the importance of relationships, connections, and human interactions over algorithmic determinations.

Priorities like reciprocity and continuity of capital flows change the definition of success for market behaviors. Brokers are a critical component in building markets like this, in part, due to the need to form a complete circuit. We define a circuit as one complete trade or full exchange of value

---

242 Motta, W., Dini, P., & Sartori, L. (2017). Self-Funded Social Impact Investment: An interdisciplinary analysis of the Sardex Mutual Credit System. Journal of Social Entrepreneurship, 8(2), 149–164. https://doi.org/10.1080/19420676.201 7.1321576

between parties. Brokers who are not incentivized by transactional volume can focus their energy on making the most optimal match. This kind of brokerage is more relational and its success is reliant on connection and human interaction. This is achieved through information gathering and ongoing facilitation. Market brokers curate connections between distributed nodes and between interior and exterior market opportunities.

To make this practical, here are a few cases that have staffed this relational broker role. At Equal Exchange, they have a dedicated capital coordinator who ensures continuous investor compatibility. Sardex has brokers who are engaged to ensure the circuit of exchange is completed. Enspiral has dedicated personnel called "Catalysts" who are responsible for knowing the needs of the network and mobilizing people, funds, and efforts toward meeting those needs. Relationships and coordination offer a valid alternative to conventional free market mechanisms.[243][244][245]

Transparency of Information

To create a marketplace, participants must agree to share the same level of information. The development of purposeful digital exchange service platforms like Sardex and Enspiral are excellent examples of how digital platforms can facilitate the dissemination of information. This in turn facilitates the movement and flow of connectivity for a marketplace to thrive. In other cases, like the multiple multi-stakeholder cooperative and holding company examples, this transparency is primarily facilitated through agreements, bonding the social arrangements into ongoing commitments of transparency from participants. Participating members may agree to

---

243   Dan Fireside, personal communication, December 18, 2023.

244   Littera, G., Sartori, L., Dini, P., & Antoniadis, P. (2017). From an idea to a scalable working model: merging economic benefits with social values in Sardex. International Journal of Community Currency Research 21, 21, 6–21. https://doi.org/10.15133/j.ijccr.2017.002

245   Motta, W., Dini, P., & Sartori, L. (2017). Self-Funded Social Impact Investment: An interdisciplinary analysis of the Sardex Mutual Credit System. Journal of Social Entrepreneurship, 8(2), 149–164. https://doi.org/10.1080/19420676.2017.1321576 .

open book budgeting and accounting (as in the cases of TIC and Obran Cooperative), contributions to collective funds (Mondragon Corporation), and sharing of director leadership (Sumitomo keiretsu).

What these case studies illustrate is that the rules that run our economic exchanges can, in fact, be rewritten. We can have purposeful markets designed to fit the values and needs of our communities. Values-aligned marketplaces are critical infrastructure for shared ownership.

Value Chain Integration

Value chain integration represents another strategy for building infrastructure for shared ownership. Value chain integration involves connecting the primary producers of goods and services to their processing and distribution partners, and ultimately to the end consumer. This connectivity can enhance the efficiency and competitiveness of an enterprise or group by optimizing the flow of goods, services, and information. This enhances value creation and distribution across the entire chain.

Monopolistic global conglomerates and extractive private equity roll-ups are not the only way to achieve certain benefits of integration. Enterprises can employ various approaches and given trends in our case studies, we'll elaborate on three: conscious consolidation, cooperative development, and capital access.

Conscious Consolidation

Goodworks and Obran demonstrate the use of acquisitions as a means to integrate through conscious consolidation. Goodworks utilized the structure of a holding company to transition Montana business owners into retirement while preserving the companies. Early on, the most viable businesses ready to undergo this transition were in the hardware supply sector. One lumbar hardware company became the seed company through which the conscious consolidation could take form. The strategy organically evolved in response to the readiness factor of both the sector and the holding company's operating capacity. At the time of this writing, Goodworks is slowing down its acquisitions' strategy to focus on integration within the subsidiary operations.

256 | Assets in Common

In the case of Obran, a growing diversified worker-cooperative, the goal is to maximize surplus distribution to individual members. Obran does not have a regional focus, instead its acquisition approach is to assess what is the appropriate next venture to add to the enterprise network that can lean into its broader cooperative function. Obran began consolidation in the healthcare sector and has slowly expanded to adjacent sectors.

These are both highly intentional consolidations of previously independent businesses that share a value chain. They are not consolidating for purely extractive motivations, but to achieve holistic improvements to the spaces they work in.

Cooperative Development

Cooperative development is another strategy for value chain integration, exemplified by many of the cooperative case studies. Cooperative development refers to the deliberate creation of a new cooperative company to meet a need. This is often more intensive than typical entrepreneurship due to the involvement of the coordination and shared vision development of a founding group of worker-owners. Cooperative development is often conducted by an agency that specializes in facilitating this process alongside a founding group. Some of our case study companies perform this process within their holding company or network to address opportunities for value chain integration. The Industrial Commons facilitated the formation of the Carolina Textile District. This aggregator was created in-house as a cooperative business that dynamically collects textile orders and efficiently distributes them among regional manufacturers. The Industrial Commons develops new cooperatives to meet supply chain needs, such as Good Books (a worker-owned, minority-focused, women-led accounting services firm) and Material Returns (worker-owned textile manufacturer transforming waste into new products). Similarly, Namaste Solar formed a purchasing cooperative to address common challenges faced by solar electric companies.[246] This further evolved into an operations and maintenance cooperative (a shared services company), and participation in financing cooperatives, like credit unions. Obran also exemplifies how cooperative development can propel extension and diversification within and across sectors. These examples all underscore the efficacy of cooperative development in integrating the value chain.

Capital Access

As the final point on value chain integration, we discuss how access to capital up and down a value chain can enable integration even without creating new legal entities.

Unlocking Cash Flows: Supply Chain Financing

In a complex and globally interconnected supply chain, suppliers may find themselves in a competitive bidding war, vying to supply a large corporation that has a substantial balance sheet. With such power dynamics at play, major buyers can use their purchasing power to extend the payment terms, in some cases longer than what is prudent for suppliers. The extension of payment terms may create a bottleneck for smaller suppliers, locking up their working capital needed to fulfill the next round of orders. Supply chain financing (hereafter referred to as SCF) is a tool that uses a buyer's typically strong balance sheet to unlock capital for the potentially cash-strapped supplier. We'll briefly describe how it works here.

SCF is a cash flow management solution initiated by a purchaser with a strong credit profile, who facilitates incoming and outgoing payments among purchasers and suppliers. A tool of treasury management, SCF

---

246   Namaste Solar is not one of the case studies we cover in this book, however it demonstrates a relevant example of expanding shared ownership. A comprehensive case study was included in the Journal of Entrepreneurial and Organizational Diversity, which we link to here. Julia, M. R., & Schneider, N. (2021). Scaling Co-Operatives through a Multi-Stakeholder Network: a case study in the Colorado solar energy industry. Journal of Entrepreneurial and Organizational Diversity, 10(2), 29–53. https://papers.ssrn.com/sol3/papers.cfm?abstract_id=4038292

supports the efficient use of working capital while also reducing supply chain risk.[247]

There are broadly three types of SCF arrangements:

a) Reverse factoring – an arrangement between three parties: the purchaser of goods and services, the financial institution, and the supplier of those goods and services. The supplier is paid by the financial institution earlier than the purchaser pays the financial institution.

b) Dynamic discounting – an arrangement directly between purchaser and supplier whereby the supplier gives a range of discounts that varies based on when the purchaser decides to settle the payment. For example, maximum discount if paid immediately to no discount if paid on standard payment terms.

c) Supplier inventory financing – an arrangement where the financial institution buys inventory from the supplier and sells it to the purchaser.

Japanese auto manufacturers often use these methods. Commonly structured as a vertical keiretsu, auto manufacturers offer inter-company support similar to the model described in supply chain financing. Toyota, for example, may identify an innovation in-house that they want their trusted suppliers to provide for, however, these suppliers may not have the investment capital or know-how to retool their processes to integrate these upgrades. Toyota leans into these existing relationships by bringing suppliers together to educate them on the innovation or process

---

247 Hoffman, E., Y. Korde, R., Leuschner, R., Rogers, D., & Templar, S. (2021). Supply chain financing and Pandemic: Managing cash flows to keep firms and their value networks healthy. Rutgers Business Review, 6(1). https://rbr.business.rutgers.edu/article/supply-chain-financing-and-pandemic-managing-cash-flows-keep-firms-and-their-value-networks

improvement and will seed the investment these suppliers need to meet the new demands.[248]

Optimizing Investments: Internal Financing

Internal financing refers to capital movement among subsidiaries of a parent company. Internal loans allow enterprises within a holding structure to leverage the parent company's balance sheet for growth and innovation, bypassing the often extractive external financing routes. Similarly, cooperatives engage in an analogous practice by redirecting member contributions into solidarity funds, which are then strategically deployed across the network for various purposes. This model of internal financing is exemplified by Mondragon's inter-cooperative funds, which circulate capital among cooperative members to foster mutual support and financial stability. Additionally, multi-stakeholder cooperatives are often involved with a cooperative credit union, further increasing access to friendly capital through cooperative membership, and enhancing the community's financial resilience. In Japan, keiretsu incorporates centralized group banks that not only hold equity shares in network companies but also serve as a primary financial artery, offering loans and fostering interconnectivity within the ecosystem. The essence of all these capital practices is leveraging internal networks for strategic growth and resilience.

In Closing

This discourse offers four powerful concepts: 1) Market rules are not set in stone—they can be rewritten. 2) Purposeful markets can be designed with values. 3) Money's definition is ours to reshape. 4) Capital can be mobilized to bring vitality to many. Together these ideas can be made practical with mechanisms like markets, internal finance, currencies, and integration. We can use these tools for shared ownership infrastructure.

---

248   Aoki, K., & Lennefors, T. (2013, September). The new, improved Keiretsu. Harvard Business Review. https://hbr.org/2013/09/the-new-improved-keiretsu

Relationships, Capacity & Culture

Charity May & Chelsea Robinson

In this chapter, we explore the textures of relationships and culture in shared ownership infrastructure. We acknowledge the principles driving shared ownership to be from the broader lineage of the solidarity economy. This movement was birthed from struggle, misunderstanding, and fights against the collusion of power in centralized or oppressive authority. We look at culture, reciprocity, trust, and the various roles that people and firms can play in shared economic futures. We propose that the human elements of a group's culture and established norms are equivalent influences as a legal structure or financial system in a company's ultimate success or failure.

Shared Ownership as an Expression of the Solidarity Economy

The Solidarity Economy is rich with examples of resistance against the centralization of power and economic exploitation. Political economist Jessica Gordon Nembhard chronicles the history of black-initiated cooperatives in the United States in her seminal work "Collective Courage." She explains the extensive, systemic opposition to alternative economic paradigms throughout U.S. history, and the impact on those who dared to defy the status quo. The creation of cooperatives was a direct challenge to the oppressive structures of capitalism. This was met with violence and sabotage by those who feared the empowerment of Black communities. These coops were beacons of independence, offering a glimpse into the transformative potential of shared ownership in fostering economic resilience and community solidarity.[249]

---

249   Sherman Rogers, W. (2020). Building social and human capital in the Black community by increasing strategic relationships, cooperative economics, the Black marriage rate, and the level of educational attainment and targeted occupational training. UC Law Journal of Race and Economic Justice, 17, 211. https://repository.uclawsf.edu/hastings_race_poverty_law_journal/vol17/iss2/3

Additionally, the history of complementary currencies, as highlighted by Charles Einsenstein in "Sacred Economics," showcases the innovative spirit of the Solidarity Economy. The Wara currency in Germany emerged as a lifeline for a mining town during the Great Depression. Its use revitalized the local economy through a system of shared value, transcending traditional monetary frameworks. This initiative was met with hostility from the central government, which perceived it as a threat to the established economic order. Yet, the very resistance it encountered underscores the disruptive power of collective economic action. It also demonstrates the potential of alternative currencies to reconfigure the foundations of economic exchange.[250]

The struggle for agency, redistribution of power, and collective wealth creation in these examples underlines the revolutionary essence of the Solidarity Economy, which shared ownership extends from. Through shared ownership and stewardship forms, communities worldwide are reclaiming their right to economic self-determination, challenging entrenched power dynamics, and ultimately rewriting the rules of economic engagement.

Symbiosis of Place and Cultural Economy

The culture of the Solidarity Economy is dynamic and continues to evolve. This culture is enriched by the diversity of its constituents and the narratives of the people and places it represents. This culture is a foundation for envisioning alternative organizational structures and challenging traditional economic paradigms. Culture, in this sense, is more than a backdrop, it is a central actor in shaping the economy, reflecting the interplay between people, their environment, and their economic practices. The influence of place on culture, and vice versa, is significant. The evidence from numerous case studies points to a symbiotic relationship between place and culture, where the natural, physical, and social environment plays a decisive role

---

250   Eisenstein, C. (2011). Negative-Interest Economics. In Sacred Economics: Money, Gift, and Society in the Age of Transition. North Atlantic Books. https://sacred-economics.com/ sacred-economics-chapter-12-negative-interest-economics/

in molding the economic infrastructure. For instance, rural or small towns facing industrial decline due to globalization and exploitative labor practices have leveraged their cultural cohesion to develop economic development strategies. In strife, solidarity principles inspire many leaders to build structures that enhance worker agency. We note a few examples from our case studies. The Goodworks Evergreen holding company safeguards small-town Montana, aiming to sustain transitioning family businesses. Immigrant communities in Western cities develop peer-to-peer financial structures to support mutual aid practices rooted in their cultural heritage. In New Zealand, the ethos of mutualism and interconnectedness permeates the business landscape, as seen in the Enspiral network and the savings pools movement, illustrating a profound cultural emphasis on collective well-being and shared resources. Moreover, the remarkable longevity of businesses in Japan, where a significant percentage of enterprises over 200 years old thrive, reflects a cultural reverence for heritage and ancestral honor. This culture manifests itself in the enduring structures of keiretsu and the historical zaibatsu, which successfully mitigated many extractive impacts of economic colonization.[251] All of these examples give a taste of how the structures and formation of networking emerged from the context unique to the place in which these firms and persons find themselves.

Roles for Infrastructure Building

There are a range of roles for people and companies to play in building infrastructure for shared ownership. Throughout this book's stories, we have seen brokerage, coordination, communication, financial management, and many other kinds of connective roles. The roles played by companies are also analogous to roles that people can take on: A bank; A social services organization; An educational institution; A shared services digital platform; A trading company. This list is not comprehensive, rather it is illustrative of the diverse entry points into forming a thriving ecosystem

---

251   Lufkin, B. (2020, February 11). Why so many of the world's oldest companies are in Japan. BBC Worklife. https://www.bbc.com/worklife/article/20200211-why-are-so-many-old-companies-in-japan

among enterprises. Each of these can be seen as parallel to the capabilities brought by an individual contributor's strengths and gifts.

A bank is a connector that allows capital, knowledge, and market insights to flow. Banker Ladies also serve in this capacity in the case of rotating savings and credit associations. Social services organizations are nurturers, forming the conditions for a culture of collaboration to take root and evolve with the enterprises themselves. Digital platforms can be multifaceted in the roles they take on. In the case of Sardex, the mutual credit system allowing small and medium enterprises to buy and sell production goods and services without fiat money, this digital platform was simultaneously an activator, facilitator, and agitator within an impersonal monetary system.

As mentioned previously, these roles are not comprehensive, but a teaser for us to discover what other roles might emerge. It is impossible to paint a complete picture of everything that is required to shift our economy and the way it works. For now, we can say that as we invest in the connective entities needed to erect infrastructure for shared ownership, so too should we invest in the new kinds of leadership roles needed to lead our communities.

Pragmatic Leadership as Dreamer and Architect

In every transformative movement, there is a core of individuals who spearhead the journey from conceptual visions to tangible realities. These leaders are distinguished by their resilience, their willingness to give freely, and their flair for innovation, often carrying the burden of being misconstrued by others. They bring an entrepreneurial zeal necessary for driving forward initiatives.

Our case study exploration reveals a common thread – the absence of a self-indulged archetype, and instead, the presence of a benevolent leader or leaders who role model values and actively build systems. These leaders are ahead of their time and may be misunderstood, yet they are deeply collaborative and open to experimentation. They are motivated by a desire to shift from extraction to equitability, and they identify as builders driven by questions like: "How can we use today's tools to serve values and purpose?", "How can we unlock a win-win between stakeholders and create value for all of us?", and "How can I help redistribute wealth and opportunities within my community?" These pragmatic visionaries are not the usual suspects highlighted in Forbes lists. Rather, they are individuals deeply committed to servicing their employees, a local economy, or even the broader welfare of a nation or demographic.

The early leaders of shared infrastructure projects have proven to be not only values-driven but also very practical and willing to make tradeoffs. Across many case studies, we see these leaders convert their inspiration into action through technical efforts to design structures aligned with their vision. An example of this is Sardex, which may be the most successful modern complementary currency in the world. Arguably, their success is due to the unlikely combination of monetary policy, software, and VC funding, all operating within a highly mutualistic cultural context. Sardex took a highly technical approach and professionally staffed it with investment dollars, despite it being largely motivated by the mutualist desire to provide for local community needs. Their progress was more important than adhering to an ideologically pure process. Similarly, the early leaders of Enspiral took a high-trust, mutualistic approach to pooling pre-tax funds, but did so using typical legal structures like LLCs and individual owners, rather than collective ownership. There is an uncomfortable and paradoxical nature to the kinds of risk-taking and structural design needed for these ventures when they start. Pioneering leaders of these projects are often more capable of handling contradictions and finding fit-for-purpose solutions that others might decry as not purely 100% values-aligned. As a result, pragmatic visionaries build working versions that can be iterated and improved upon, starting with what is available and pushing the boundaries along the way.

Transitioning towards shared ownership necessitates moving away from glorifying singular figures, challenging the "central figure syndrome" prevalent in current economic narratives. While bold leaders are often needed to outline a vision and gather collaborators at the start, their role evolves as these initiatives grow. In shared ownership, cultural emphasis on participation and collective direction-setting often reduces the reliance on founders more quickly than in a typical business culture. In a mature networked enterprise ecosystem that truly embodies shared ownership and stewardship structurally, the spotlight fades away from any one individual, contrasting sharply with celebrity founder culture. Yet, it is precisely this hard work of fostering mutual support, reciprocity, and conducting business through relational lenses that is often undervalued in a market driven by competition and dominance. Those catalytically collaborative leaders are personalities we need to recognize and uplift.

Among those leaders who embrace shared ownership, there's a palpable sense of determination. Community leaders like Molly Hemstreet and Sara Chester exemplify this resolve. They witnessed their community's economic downfall and chose to stand firm and innovate. Similarly, Giuseppe Littera of Sardex, the Banker Ladies of Toronto, Joshua Vial and Alanna Irving of Enspiral, and Joseph Curaton of Obran Cooperative highlight holistic leadership styles in this body of work. Included in this leadership arena are small business owners seeking to transition in a manner that extends the wealth creation opportunity to employees more broadly, as in the case of Clegg Auto. The work ahead of us is not just to spread awareness of ideas, but to support the voices of those already dedicated to fostering a more deeply connected and equitable economic model. These leaders, who dream and build with reciprocity and trust, are the cornerstone of shared ownership infrastructure, meriting support and advocacy in broader investment and policy discussions.

On Reciprocity and Trust

Reciprocity is fundamental in many collective and indigenous cultures, reflecting their strong sense of interconnectedness with nature. This principle is an acknowledgment of the interdependence that defines living relationships and our bond with the natural world. In these cultures, reciprocity is seen as a way of living that mirrors the cyclical give-and-take inherent in the natural world. It is an acknowledgment that what one contributes to the community or the environment will, in turn, support the individual and the collective well-being. This practice is embedded in the social fabric, where the sharing of resources, knowledge, and support is not only encouraged but expected, thus fostering a strong sense of unity and mutual respect.

Trust plays an indispensable role in the dynamics of reciprocity. The foundational belief is that giving, whether material or intangible, is anchored into a greater cycle of support that benefits all. This trust implies a certain level of vulnerability, an openness where individuals give without a guaranteed or direct return, trusting that their contributions will be reciprocated in times of need. This level of trust is essential for the maintenance of a culture of mutuality, where the focus is on the collective good rather than individual gain.

However, the cultural nuances of stark individualism present in many modern economies can make the practice of direct or indirect reciprocity more challenging to embrace. In societies where the economic system is heavily centered on individual achievement and competition, the intrinsic value of reciprocity and trust can be overshadowed by a focus on personal gain. This emphasis on individualism can lead to a weakening of communal bonds, as interactions become more transactional. The contrast between individualistic and collectivist ideologies highlights a significant cultural divide in the structure and value of economic and social relationships. While reciprocity and trust generate mutual support that is more inherent in collectivist societies, cultures oriented towards individualism may struggle to lean into these practices without a greater mindset shift. This perceived dichotomy underscores the challenges and opportunities in bridging these cultural differences to foster a more inclusive, reciprocal, and trusting economic and social landscape.

"So the notion is that we don't really have any one group, or one person running off with all the spoils, right? The spoils are truly recirculating in the community. And the community itself is the one who decides what happens to those resources."

Jessica Gordon Nembhard, Political Economist[252]

There are also promising examples of cultures achieving a balance between a mutualistic code of conduct, and activating individual advancement and self-actualization. Casting the general ideas of collectivism and individualism in immutable contrast is incorrect. Many indigenous and land-based cultures have been oversimplified by Western observers, and long-standing cultures often contain complex overlapping values of reciprocity and personal development. One example is the misunderstanding that occurred in the work of Maslow's hierarchy of needs. Maslow, a Western cultural scientist, studied the philosophies of the Blackfoot nation. His popularized conclusion was that once basic needs such as food and shelter are met, human potential can be reached. However, this indigenous community explained that they see self-actualization as the starting point. Their support of the unique essence within each individual in their communities was a precursor to successfully building shared systems that provide material needs for their community. Rather than the pinnacle of their culture being well-developed individuals fed by material inputs, they strive to pass on knowledge, cultural, and intergenerational insight. They achieve it through the collective power of individually talented and culturally nourished

---

252   Quote from Jessica Gordon Nembhard's interview with Keane Bhatt, refer to Bhatt, K. (2015, October 7). Dangerous History: What the story of Black economic cooperation means for us today. YES! Magazine. https://www.yesmagazine.org/economy/2015/10/07/dangerous-history-what-the-story-of-black-economic-development-means-for-us-today

people.[253] [254] This shows a feedback loop between collective and individual success, shattering the purported polarity between mutualism and individualism. The takeaway here is that personal development and collective health and wealth can co-exist. The journey is to recognize the part and talent each of us has to offer for the mutual benefit of the community, instead of the endless pursuit of self-gratification at the expense of others.

In the case of Enspiral, the acknowledgment of individual agency within the collective is well evidenced. Enspiral is made up of voluntarily cooperating individuals and companies pooling money together and helping each other's visions as well as investing in shared needs. Common pool resources in Enspiral are not only used to fund accountants or buffer rainy days, they are also deployed for personal development of individuals and individual projects. The thriving of each person, their family, and their work, is seen as indivisible from the success of the group.

Conclusion

Shared ownership draws from the cultural lineage of the solidarity economy, and would not be possible without the reimagining of relationships by and between enterprises and people. The principles rooting the struggles, comradery, and reciprocity of the solidarity economy are expressed in a variety of ways, challenging centralized power dynamics. Pragmatic leadership, which seeks out mutually beneficial outcomes, enlists collaboration, and decentralizes power over time, deserves more recognition and investment. Our relationship with places and with each other is the bedrock of shared ownership culture. Harmonizing philosophies of service and reciprocity with our beliefs about money and growth can produce a well-adjusted group culture and capacity from new infrastructure can be built.

---

253   Michel, K. L. (2014, April 19). Maslow's hierarchy connected to Blackfoot beliefs. A Digital Native American. https://lincolnmichel.wordpress. com/2014/04/19/maslows-hierarchy-connected-to-blackfoot-beliefs/

254   Ravilochan, T. (2021, April 26). Maslow got it wrong [gatherfor. org]. PACEsConnection. https://www.pacesconnection.com/blog/ ravilochan-maslow-got-it-wrong

Part IV –

Opportunities for Action

Launching Shared Services Cooperatives

Jay Standish

Anatomy of a Shared Services Co-op

Earlier in this book, we outlined the overall concept of shared services, which could be internal to a single organization or serve multiple enterprises.

A Shared Services Cooperative is a specific form of the shared service concept. It is an alliance of multiple organizations that co-own and co-manage a shared services group. What makes something a shared services cooperative is a shared ownership and governance structure and a focus on passing through the upside and efficiencies gained to members. Members and users are not just customers, they are co-owners. An accounting shared services cooperative is owned by all its members and governed to suit the needs of the members. A shared services cooperative has either a zero-profit model or redistributes profits back to its owner-members, driving savings either way. [255] These user-owned services firms have formed in government, business, and civil society, so any organization, sector, and industry could be ripe for the model.[256]

This is distinct from hiring an external vendor. Many small businesses use outside companies to fulfill certain functions like tax accounting, creative design, advertising, and even HR functions and payroll. Think of an accounting firm that prepares taxes for multiple companies, has an independent owner, and is a standalone company focused on generating profit

---

255   Crooks, A. C., Jr., Spatz, K. J., Warman, M., & RBCDS Agricultural Economists. (1995). Basics of organizing a Shared-Services cooperative. In Service Report (Vol. 46). https://resources.uwcc.wisc.edu/Shared%20Services/ BasicsShared-ServicesCoop.pdf

256   Butzen, J. (2010). Shared Services Alliances: Part 1. Stanford Social Innovation Review. https://doi.org/10.48558/C2H6-GR24

for its owners. It is run by its owners, not its customers. This is a vendor, not a shared services organization.

Origin Stories

Before diving into a recipe for how to start a shared services platform, let's learn from the stories of some of the strongest shared services cooperatives that have emerged between for-profit businesses in the U.S. There are also examples of these cooperatives that serve government and non-profit groups, but the context of business provides a clear example of multi-firm cooperation as a strategy in what is otherwise a competitive arena.

Carpet One

Carpet One demonstrates how a shared services group enables small, independently owned flooring businesses to compete against big-box competitors like Home Depot and Lowes. It is a powerful example of how small businesses can use internal collaboration to enhance their external competitiveness.

Carpet One Floor & Home is a cooperative, shared services platform that is co-owned by its 1,000 independent members and aggregates their purchasing, marketing, merchandising, and management systems. It lowers supply costs through bulk purchasing, produces ad campaigns, and builds operations systems to help its members run their small businesses.

The cooperative was started in 1985 by two retail carpet store owners who were both former presidents of flooring industry association groups. The founders Howard Brodsky and Alan Greenberg were looking for solutions in a competitive industry where smaller independent retailers found it increasingly difficult to match the prices of larger-volume corporate competitors like Home Depot. The pair spent a year researching the existing franchises and co-ops in the industry and interviewed dozens of store owners. Based on both their own deep experience and the input of dozens of their peers, they fused concepts from franchises and purchasing cooperatives to form Carpet One.

Brodsky and Greenberg saw a cooperative model as a fair and effective way for independent businesses to form an alliance. This innovative approach aimed to consolidate the fragmented efforts of individual carpet and flooring entrepreneurs across the nation, offering a unified, collaborative platform for competitiveness and growth.[257]

The launch of Carpet One began with a bold move. The founders raised startup funds to launch a nationwide advertising campaign. The campaign's goal was to collectively sell $1 Billion of flooring in 10 days. They used this campaign to gain buy-in by showing the tangible value of co-branding and recruited 13 initial carpet businesses into the cooperative. After its first year, the group had around 25 members, and after the second year, it had 50 members. The campaign succeeded in its $1 Billion sales goal.

Members of the cooperative have equal decision-making power, but receive dividends based on the volume they run through the cooperative. The dividend is essentially a reimbursement of the surplus that the co-op generates. This is a key point, the co-op isn't set up to maximize its own profit as an intermediary. The independent members' interests are prioritized, and the co-op serves to their benefit.

The shared services model is not limited to lowering the cost of goods sold through aggregated purchasing. The group uses a strategy they termed 'the equilateral triangle': incorporating purchasing, marketing, and management. This triple value proposition means that Carpet One lowers supply costs, executes marketing tactics, and provides operational best practices to reduce operating costs for its members.[258]

---

257   Clamp, C., Romaric Amendah, E., & Coren, C. (2019). Shared Services Cooperatives: A Qualitative study. (pp. 207) Oak Tree Books. https://www.successstore.com/shared-services-cooperatives.html

258   Carpet One Floor & Home. (2019). Carpet One Case Study. Cooperative Curriculum. https://cooperativecurriculum.org/resources/Carpet_One_Case_Study-(final).pdf

In 2001, they expanded and rebranded as CCA Global Partners, marking a significant evolution in their mission and scope by acquiring another shared services co-op under the umbrella. This transformed it into a powerhouse that now runs 14 different similarly structured cooperatives across a variety of industries, extending its reach beyond flooring to include lighting, bicycles, home improvement, and more. Today, CCA Global Partners could be thought of as a conglomerate of industry-targeted shared services cooperatives. As almost a "HoldCo of shared services," it boasts around 4,000 stores across the United States, Canada, and other countries. The umbrella has around 400 employees, within which Carpet One Floor & Home remains a vital subsidiary. Because some of the groups have similar needs, some staff are shared across multiple shared services groups, meaning CCA has two layers of shared services, it is a shared services co-op for shared services co-ops!

The story of Carpet One gives us some powerful lessons about how shared services can strengthen small businesses. Shared services prove to be an attractive alternative to the franchise model by driving greater cost savings by aggregating purchasing. Additionally, the founders launched Carpet One with a bold vision, which reminds us that launching a shared service is just as much an entrepreneurial lift as starting a "normal" company. Carpet One is somewhat unique in its use of a public-facing brand as a shared asset, which creates the mirage of a recognizable national brand. The cooperative's success at parlaying the model into other industries demonstrates that the core strategy is versatile and adaptable to many different contexts, geographies, and business models.

Johnstone Supply Company

Johnstone Supply transformed a single-owner chain of heating and cooling (HVAC) supply stores into a cooperative of independently owned stores. This is an uncommon narrative within the business world. In Johnstone's example, we see the "before and after" structural changes of how a business looks under centralized ownership, and after it is adapted to a shared services model with distributed ownership.

Initially, Johnstone Supply was set up with a traditional business model as a supply store for contractors in the HVAC industry. It comprised about 30 stores primarily located on the West Coast of the United States. The founder and sole owner, John Shank, needed a succession plan as he approached retirement age. Instead of selling the company as a whole, Shank broke up the company into regions and transferred ownership of each regional group to different individuals within the organization. Many of the subsequent owners were family members or employees with extensive experience in the company's operations, management, and logistics. This model allowed for specific geographic territories to be operated by independent business owners, ensuring a basic but effective organizational structure. This was the first phase of the cooperative, an alliance of family businesses.

Over the years, the group shifted into more of a true "one-member-one-vote" egalitarian co-op and exhibited less of the former family business structure. Fully embracing the shared services model allowed member participants to collectively improve their business practices by leveraging shared services for distribution and ordering processes. Additionally, the shared service model facilitated extensive training programs for the members' employees, adding another layer of value that contributed to the cooperative's overall success.

Johnstone Supply's evolution illustrates the viability of a shared service model in playing roles previously accomplished through a traditionally structured business.[259] In 2020, the co-op had around 90 independent member-owners comprising 450 locations, with most members owning multiple locations. These 90 members collectively owned and managed the cooperative. During its 40-year cooperative phase, Johnstone expanded

---

259   Clamp, Christina; Amendah, Eklou Romaric; Coren, Carol. Shared Services Cooperatives: A Qualitative Study: Exploring Applications, Benefits & Potential (p. 187). Oak Tree Press. Kindle Edition.

the number of locations from 30 to 450 – over ten times the amount of the original family business.[260]

With over $4 billion in annual sales, the scale of Johnstone attracted the attention of private equity. In 2021, co-op members made the pivotal decision to partner with an outside investment group called Redwood Capital. This deal converted them from an Oregon cooperative entity to a Delaware LLC, providing a more capital-friendly structure. This shift marks the end of Johnstone as a pure member-owned co-op, although the 90 or so members did retain a significant equity stake in the new entity. There is no public information on whether the former co-op members also partially cashed out in the conversion.[261]

Johnstone Supply shows us how a company can transform its organizational structure through shared services. Their 40-year track record under shared services shows how the model is capable of tenfold growth. The Johnstone example also demonstrates how a mature shared services group can evolve into a private-equity-backed engine for growth.

Key Factors for Launching a Shared Services Co-op

The Catalyst: Founding Leaders

We see strong founders in nearly every successful shared services group we studied. In some cases, a keystone organization played a catalyzing role, but even then, there was usually a pivotal person or small team within that organization who brought vision and gumption.

In the case of Carpet One, the founders were already business owners in the flooring industry, and starting the co-op was a way to solve their

---

260   About Johnstone Supply. Johnstone Supply. https://www.johnstonesupply. com/our-history

261   Johnstone Supply, Inc. (2021, September 24). CORRECTING and REPLACING Johnstone Supply approves definitive conversion agreement with Redwood Capital Investments [Press release]. citybiz. https://www.citybiz. co/article/148008/johnstone-supply-approves-definitive-conversion-agreement-with-redwood-capital-investments/

needs. They put in a major entrepreneurial effort by raising capital and launching an advertising campaign to start the co-op. Carpet One became their primary professional focus for the rest of their careers. In the case of Johnstone Supply, the original owner of the company was the catalyst for the conversion to a co-op, and dictated the shift.

Starting a shared service is just as much a heavy lift as starting any other organization or company. It is also an exercise in facilitation, the founders must "herd cats" and facilitate convergence on solutions to common problems. It's no small feat to enroll busy managers to agree to shift major aspects of their work into the hands of what can feel like a third party. However, a shared services co-op is really a "second party" and there is a mindset shift for members to view it less as an arms-length vendor relationship and more as an extension of their team.

The character and grit of a capable entrepreneur are not a formulaic commodity that can be easily taught. It should be emphasized that, without a sufficiently entrepreneurial person or team, it is unlikely that a shared services co-op will emerge organically from a well-meaning but disorganized group. Vision, risk tolerance, and the sustained motivation to execute toward that vision are success factors.

The Design: Solving the Right Problems

Carpet One founders were diligent about understanding the biggest problems in their industry. They could have jumped to conclusions and pushed loosely formed ideas, such as creating a less expensive franchise or starting a marketing agency targeting flooring shops. Instead, the founders took an entire year having exploratory conversations with owners of flooring stores, some fully independent, some franchisees, and some participating in purchasing cooperatives. They put considerable thought into solving multiple pain points and created a very attractive proposition that solved the biggest pain points that were common to most stores.

It is wise to choose an industry that is genuinely ripe for shared services; forcing a cute idea in the wrong circumstances could fail. Below are critical factors for designing the core value propositions of a shared services cooperative.

Identify Vital, Unsolved Shared Needs

Organizations have a host of problems; some are mission-critical, while others would be nice to solve but don't demand attention. Many people and organizations neglect things that are "important but not urgent".[262] These are projects that don't have major time sensitivity but would be very impactful if solved. Many times these important issues aren't solved because they require significant effort and investment. These kinds of problems aren't "putting out fires" and don't always have a single source. They can be tricky, multi-faceted issues that require thoughtful consideration and design. These kinds of problems are ripe for shared services because you would be solving an important issue that is being neglected because the organization is too small, and they don't have time to deal with it.

It's important to ask whether it makes sense to shift a function into a shared team. A shared services team tends to work best when it is specialized within an industry or business type. For example, the marketing needs of a hipster coffee shop are wildly different from those of a smartphone app for in-home health. Shared services make sense when similar businesses, facing similar problems, join together so they each don't have to reinvent the wheel to get their needs met. We'll explore the viability and implementation of shared services further towards the end of the book.

Start the process by talking to stakeholders and staff in your chosen field who know the real problems, and won't sugarcoat. Try to get these "boots on the ground" team members in a conversation without their boss or the leader of the organization. Ask seemingly basic questions and begin to understand why certain important issues aren't being addressed. Understand the priorities and motivations, and learn the lingo if you don't already. Then look for the patterns across multiple organizations. What

---

262   Introducing the Eisenhower Matrix. Eisenhower. https://www.eisenhower.me/
       eisenhower-matrix /

pain points keep coming up? Of these, which problems seem the most important? Which issues drive the most financial impact?

Bridge Non-Competitive Parties

It's unlikely that organizations that view each other as competitors are going to join a shared service and expose their "dirty laundry" to one another. If you can, focus on industries and fields where there is already a culture of collaboration and openness. Non-profits may seem collaborative but are competing for limited grant funding if they work on the same issues. You could also look at industries with natural separation and clear boundaries. As discussed previously in this book, exploring the value chains and supply chains of a given product can be a source of allies. For physical goods and services, most companies only serve certain geographies, so outside a reasonable radius, they see peers, not competitors. You want to find the sweet spot between groups that identify with the same problems and speak the same language but aren't bracing for confrontation.

Solve a Standardizable Problem

Look for problems that lend themselves to repeatable solutions. The whole point of shared services is to solve redundant problems once so that multiple organizations aren't wasting resources reinventing the wheel. If you try to deliver value that needs to be highly customized for each member, you won't be able to "rinse and repeat" and you won't save much time and money. A good shared service will be relevant and applicable to a broad group, and not require too much customization or modification for each member. Usually, a shared service isn't meddling in the primary function of an organization, but is streamlining the back office. Many of the administrative functions and some professional services are good candidates for sharing.

Aggregate Economies of Scale

When a process is well-defined, or a supply chain is standardized, it becomes easier to do things at a larger scale. So, by providing a standardized solution, you're also able to unlock economies of scale. At both Carpet One and Johnstone, the supply chain was a major aspect of the shared service. The groups combined purchasing power to unlock bulk discounts. Scale can also take the form of the volume of a service. Imagine if 100 organizations all pool their data entry workflow, it becomes worthwhile to spend 5 hours improving the process, whereas if only 1 organization by themselves does 3 hours of data entry each month, they probably wouldn't bother spending 5 hours to improve the system.

Drive Financial Impact

Shared services are about more than money, however, if they don't move the needle financially, they have a weak value proposition. Even in non-profit shared services, there is always a meaningful improvement in finances as a result of shared services. Sometimes it's very clear cost savings, but other times shared services might make a financial impact indirectly such as improving reliability, increasing quality, or speeding up delivery. Operators who know their industry well will understand the financial impact of making performance improvements. But ideally, a shared services alliance should have a strong "no-brainer" financial logic that is more than speculation. You should seek to have multiple financial benefits, look for compounding opportunities, and use shared services to get leverage.

Summarized into a single sentence:

Clarify shared needs among non-competitive parties, and provide a standardized solution that makes a financial impact by taking advantage of economies of scale.

The Members: Coalition of the Willing

Don't build castles in the sky, shared services need to be built hand-in-hand with potential members. Ideally, multiple organizations are bought in early on, fanning the flames and encouraging the entrepreneurs working to stand up the service. Finding the right champions and evangelists might be the most important part of the process. They are the source of intelligence on what problems are worth solving. The right early adopters are incredibly powerful in signaling to the rest of the industry that the project is legitimate and valuable. Make sure to get a sense of who is respected in the industry and try to align yourself with the trusted leaders in the space.

The Startup Resources: Money + People

Once the groundwork is laid and the idea has traction, a new organization needs to be birthed, and that takes time, money, and people. In the credit union world, service organizations are founded by multiple credit unions who co-invest to launch a new shared service organization. In other cases, service co-ops may have a one-time buy-in fee that might be around $50k to help resource the ramp-up. The fundraising structure and amount will depend on the specific needs and context, but it's likely going to need some fuel since new value is being created. A fundraising campaign also helps validate whether stakeholders are willing to support the project in a tangible way. Floating this question early on, with potential members, could be a good way to solicit no-nonsense feedback.

Tensions at Different Stages

Like any organization, early-stage groups face different problems than mature ones. When starting a shared service, it's wise to consider the future issues that are likely to arise. These considerations might even inform the initial design, and help avoid major problems, down the line, that could have been anticipated and avoided.

Small Scale

At the smaller scale, shared services groups work to get traction and adoption with members. They are likely improving their core value proposition and recruiting members. They are trying to get larger to reach economies of scale that provide more savings and value to members and make the cooperative more viable itself. At the small scale, delivering value to a core group of constituents should be the focus. There isn't room to get distracted and thrown off course, so you have to know who your main audience is and not try to please everyone.

Medium Scale

As a shared service approaches escape velocity, the question of basic survival fades into the rearview mirror. Things are working, members aren't calling to complain, they are calling with new ideas and opportunities. Once there is viability and sustained traction, there can be competing forces and visions at play. Some members may want to keep things the same, while others may be enthusiastic to add new services and keep building momentum. There might be disagreements about what to prioritize, and the formal governance model may be tested. Can this group of independent organizations orchestrate the juggling act called the democratic process? Will the organization be driven by the loudest voices in the room, the biggest pockets, the popular kids, those who work the most, or hopefully, those with the best ideas and most practical approach?

Large Scale

At the larger scale, a shared services company becomes resilient. The focus is on optimization, systemization, efficiency, and cost control. Now with large volumes of transactions and a larger base of members, things get more formal, and innovation happens slower. There is a clear sense of what is within bounds and out of bounds, and any one member has less influence. More projects, products, and services are taken on, and the scope of the organization can bloat. The company makes most of its decisions internally and has significant staff and a full management team. At this scale, there can be a temptation to take on third-party clients outside the membership, blurring the lines of whether it is truly a shared services company, and whether it should consider becoming a stand-alone vendor on a path to scale. Thoughtful governance will determine future scenarios, no longer bogged down in operational trade-offs and putting out fires.

Reflections

The heroic entrepreneur who builds a disruptive brand is an alluring story, but perhaps we've heard that tune enough. In these trying times, entrepreneurs could focus more on rallying participation and collaboration among their peers. By pursuing shared services schemes, entrepreneurs can roll up their sleeves to repair and improve existing systems rather than starting yet another company. It may not look as sexy as a shiny new startup, but we need more glue holding together the vital functions of our society.

Organizational change can be hard when there are firmly established processes, people, and politics driving the ship. Shared services can act as "scaffolding" for institutional change. We can imprint new and better ways of working into the shared services we create, and see these positive changes feed back into the organizations they serve. There is also an unmet opportunity for support organizations to help shared services entrepreneurs navigate the startup process. Because they transcend organizational boundaries, shared services can act as vehicles for institutional knowledge to be passed on so that more people can benefit from lessons learned.

We need new solutions and new infrastructure in our society today. The traditional sectors of government, business, and civil society may need new intermediaries, and shared services almost represent a fourth sector. By building a network of shared bridges between organizations, we fortify our collective foundation and amplify existing strengths instead of fragmenting efforts by building isolated new entities.

Building a Steward-Owned Holding Company

Jay Standish

Concept + Context

This section unpacks the opportunity to use Holding Companies (HoldCos) to drive economic democracy and deliver social impact. We look into the feasibility of acquiring companies in the small and midsize business (SMB) space earning between $200k + $10M in profit each year and assembling portfolios of SMBs into HoldCos under steward ownership.

As discussed elsewhere in this book, steward ownership is when a firm is owned for the sake of a specific purpose and mission. In steward-owned companies, the profits serve that purpose and can benefit a broader group of stakeholders than just financial investors, which might be employees, foundations, community members, or customers. The group of stakeholders who are actively engaged in the business are those who govern it. In some cases, third parties also play a role in governance, enforcing adherence to the rules of an ownership trust. In its purest form, a steward-owned firm can never be sold.[263]

HoldCos offer an immediately actionable opportunity to build permanent capital vehicles with steward ownership. We see the potential for this concept as missing infrastructure that could help fund civic projects, secure local jobs, and recycle dollars in local economies. This solution is exciting and timely. As the older generation retires, thousands of businesses need new owners. There is a great opportunity to shift these small businesses into the hands of local people. Otherwise, they will either be devoured by private equity or will go out of business, and their market share will go

---

263 Purpose Foundation. (n.d.). Steward-ownership: Rethinking ownership in the 21st century. (pp. 3–132). https://purpose-economy.org/content/uploads/purposebooklet_en.pdf

to corporate big-boxes, exporting profits from communities and further dismantling Main Street.

Holding Companies are a brilliant way for small businesses to take advantage of the benefits of scale and diversification enjoyed by their larger competitors. In the context of shared ownership and collaborative networks, holding companies are a potent tool for building durable and financially resilient entities. Below, we outline how a private equity strategy can be repurposed to benefit employees and communities, not just investors and executives.

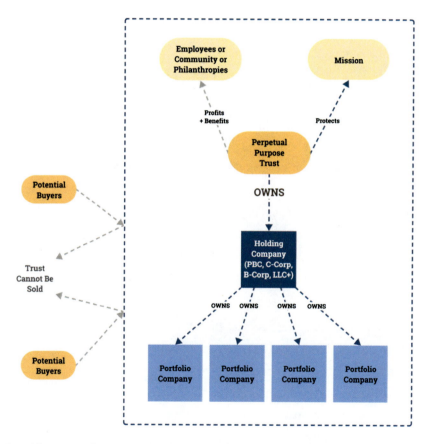

Legal Structure of a Hypothetical Steward-Owned Holding Company: A Perpetual Purpose Trust is the sole shareholder in a Holding Company, which has equity interests in a portfolio of subsidiary companies. The Trust agreement bars the sale of the HoldCo and its assets, and profits are distributed to various stakeholders on a case-specific basis.

288 | Assets in Common

Structures for HoldCos

There are a number of models for holding companies, each with different pros and cons. From private ownership to purpose trusts, we have listed the main approaches to HoldCo architecture in this section. Use it as a reference point for considering how your assets might cohere within one of these frameworks. We have ordered them from privately owned, through co-ops and ESOPs, to steward-owned. We are unabashed proponents of stewardship models and hope you see the relevance and added value they provide.

Private Ownership

A classic HoldCo is owned by a small group of private individuals. Cash flows are either distributed pro-rata to shareholders or can be re-invested to acquire new companies or assets. We might think of these private HoldCos as the "traditional" form to which the current economy is most accustomed. Privately-held HoldCos can be set up with a range of corporate entities, like C-corps, S-corps, LLCs, partnerships, or trusts. Private HoldCos can also make equity grants to employees and other community stakeholders, so the structure can be adapted to include stakeholders in upside.

Employee Stock Ownership Plan (ESOP)

The ESOP structure has had special government treatment in the U.S. since 1956. [264] In this model, a trust is also used as the custodian that holds the stock. ESOPs are regulated by Congress, which sets limits on how employees can participate and benefit. ESOPs are more expensive to set up correctly and require more work to stay compliant than Employee Ownership Trusts (EOTs). However, business owners who sell to ESOPs don't pay capital gains on the proceeds if they reinvest the cash. So ESOPs

---

264   Rutgers School of Management and Labor Relations. (2015). The origin and history of the ESOP and its future role as a business succession tool. CLEO. https://cleo.rutgers.edu/articles/the-origin-and-history-of-the-esop-and-its-future-role-as-a-business-succession-tool/#:~:text=The%20first%20 ESOP%20(employee%20stock,members%20in%20the%20private%20sector.

tend to be used for ownership transitions in cases where owners are more economically motivated. If a HoldCo were created under an ESOP structure, the HoldCo could offer tax-free buyouts to companies it wishes to acquire. Although this tax advantage is a beautiful tailwind for growth, it would require creative legal customization to also protect the mission and culture at the same level possible in an EOT or PPT. Sammons Enterprises is a diversified HoldCo 100% owned by an ESOP, outlined later.[265]

Worker-Owned Cooperative

Cooperatives have been driven by a social movement toward worker empowerment and a culture of direct democracy. The "one-member-on-vote" governance mantra typifies the egalitarian and consensus-driven ethos of many worker cooperatives. The cooperative is also a specific legal entity in the United States. Many cooperatives pay dividends based on the hours worked by each employee. Cooperatives have some tax deferment advantages when an owner is selling to a cooperative, somewhat similar to an ESOP. Obran Cooperative is incorporated as a worker cooperative at the HoldCo level.

Perpetual Purpose Trusts (PPT)

Holding companies can also have trusts as parent entities stewarding their long-term missions. Most commonly, this is achieved through the use of a perpetual purpose trust (PPT). In these models, all or part of the stock is moved into a trust that owns that stock, and the trust is designed to serve a purpose, rather than profit maximization for shareholders. You may be familiar with trusts that are created for individual beneficiaries, such as heirs to an inheritance. PPTs broaden what you can define as the beneficiary, making them perfect containers for mission-driven holding companies.

PPTs were historically used for unique circumstances like entrusting an art collection for perpetual preservation, such that the "purpose" of the

---

265 Bauer, J. M. (2014). Unique tax advantages of ESOPs. In ABA Section Of Taxation Newsquarterly. https://www.americanbar.org/content/dam/aba/publishing/aba_tax_times/14sum/5-bauer.pdf

trust is to steward the safekeeping and appropriate usage of the art in perpetuity. Recently, PPTs have been repurposed to steward and protect the mission of a private company. The clothing company Patagonia converted its ownership into a PPT whose purpose is to support nature conservation. Profits from Patagonia will go to organizations working on conserving nature because the purpose of the organization is not to produce income for owners, it is to produce impact for the environment. For these reasons, PPTs are often referred to simply as "purpose trusts". Purpose trusts are the primary way to achieve steward ownership in U.S. law.

Employee Ownership Trusts (EOT)

In holding companies focused on employee ownership, the purpose of their trust may be maintaining the company's financial health and distributing benefits to employee-owners. Employee Ownership Trusts is a model using a purpose trust structure to serve employees. EOTs position employees as the beneficiaries, where they often receive a share of company profits. The trust owns the stock such that new employees don't need to buy stock from former employees. Clegg Auto is an example of an EOT that distributes profits to its current employees. EOTs are increasing in popularity due to being cheaper to set up and more flexible than alternatives such as ESOPs.

Foundation / Hybrid

Nonprofits and foundations can also own HoldCos, either partially or in full. This is another way to achieve steward ownership. We've seen that structures between for-profit companies, non-profit foundations, and family offices are rich with possibility. When a non-profit foundation owns a for-profit, the cash dividends of the company fund the charitable work of the foundation. This provides the non-profit with a strong, stable source of philanthropic dollars. Since the for-profit can grow organically and acquire other businesses, the foundation can expand its impact without requiring additional or ongoing grants from individuals. There are too many options for structuring hybrid ownership models to outline here, but one notable example is Bosch, the German industrial and automotive company. Bosch is 93% owned by a charitable trust that was created by the founding family.[266]

A Recipe for Implementation + Feasibility

Implementing a steward-owned holding company for small businesses requires combining strategic vision, operational expertise, and a commitment to economic democracy. By adapting the framework to your unique context, you can create a holding company that generates financial returns, cultivates thriving local economies, empowers employees, and contributes to community well-being.

Formative Ingredients

The following recipe outlines the key ingredients and steps to embark on this transformative journey.

A Meaningful Vision

As with any new venture, there needs to be a compelling motivation behind starting a Holding Company with a steward ownership structure. This depends heavily on the founding team, but a fundamental question is profit allocation. Is there a charitable foundation behind the effort looking for a permanent endowment? Is a family office looking to make a seed investment that helps to redistribute wealth? Is a business owner looking to leave a legacy of impact by exiting to employees?

Industry + Geographic Focus

A blank canvas is overwhelming. It is important to narrow the focus when searching to buy a business. One might select industries that are ripe for consolidation but still deeply embedded in the fabric of local economies. The management team might bias toward industries in which they have expertise. However, it's also crucial to assess whether the industry has a strong business model and "strategic moat" or if it's vulnerable to too many external forces. When considering geography, prioritize areas with high potential for economic revitalization and populations large enough to

---

266   Wikipedia contributors. (2024a). Bosch (company). In Wikipedia. https://en.wikipedia.org/wiki/Bosch_(company)

provide a sizable customer base. That said, many of our case studies don't choose a market academically. Instead, they are rooted in place, and their efforts serve their allegiance to that location. In such cases, the projects take their place as a given, making the choice of the right industry even more critical.

Entrepreneurs with Finance + Operations Savvy

Entrepreneurs steering Holding Companies must possess a unique blend of financial acumen and operational expertise. The existence of an entrepreneurial core team is critical in the formation of a HoldCo. Their role demands more than just strategic oversight; it requires an intimate understanding of the nuances of each subsidiary's operations and the ability to identify synergies within the portfolio. This dual competency ensures that the holding company can effectively allocate capital, manage risks, and drive operational efficiencies across its subsidiaries. Entrepreneurs with a background in finance and operations are better equipped to navigate the complexities of scaling small and mid-size businesses, optimizing performance, and sustaining growth. Their expertise is crucial in building a cohesive, efficient, and resilient portfolio that delivers on both economic and social impact objectives.

Anchor Investors + Advisors

The foundation of a successful Holding Company, especially one aimed at fostering economic democracy, is solidified by the presence of committed anchor investors and advisors. Capital is almost always necessary to acquire businesses, and forward-thinking ownership structures require forward-thinking investors. These stakeholders bring more than just capital; they offer a wealth of experience, strategic guidance, and a network of potential partners and resources. Anchor investors who share the vision of steward ownership and social impact can provide the aligned capital necessary for long-term growth and stability. Meanwhile, advisors with expertise in various fields—ranging from industry-specific insights to governance and legal structures—can guide the holding company through growth phases, ensuring that its mission coheres with operational practices. These allies create a vital support network that helps the holding company achieve its goals while staying attuned to market conditions and its social purpose.

Time + Patience

It can take 6–12 months to find the right company to add to a HoldCo. HoldCo managers must give ample time for the careful selection and integration of SMBs into the HoldCo portfolio, ensuring alignment with the overarching mission and operational compatibility. Many steward-owned companies took multiple years to figure out their ownership and governance designs. It takes thoughtful engagement with stakeholders to establish governance structures that reflect a commitment to shared values and objectives.

Time plays a critical role in realizing the benefits of scale and diversification, as these advantages accrue through sustained efforts in operational optimization and strategic growth initiatives. Patience is essential for stakeholders to witness the compound effects of their investments in community resilience, employee well-being, and local economic empowerment. In this context, a long-term perspective is not just a virtue but a strategic necessity, allowing the HoldCo to navigate challenges, seize opportunities for meaningful impact, and ultimately, contribute to the broader goal of sustaining vibrant local economies and communities.

Deal Inception: The Seed Company

Acquiring the first company is crucial for launching a holding company. Rather than an arbitrary acquisition, a carefully-chosen "seed" company sets up the HoldCo for success. This initial cash-flowing asset, sometimes called a "platform investment," is selected for qualities that provide a strategic foundation for future growth and acquisitions. Usually, this means that the company is mature and stable and can either absorb new acquisitions in the same industry, and/or generate enough cash to fund future buyout deals.

The process begins with an entrepreneurial deal team sharing the holding company's mission and vision. Finding and acquiring that first company can take 6–18 months of dedicated effort. The deal team must be appropriately incentivized and funded during this search period.

The seed company could serve as the platform for a roll-up strategy within its industry, or represent a starting point for adjacent bolt-on acquisitions. It should align with the holding company's investment thesis, and possess a solid business model, profitability track record, and growth potential.

Aligning the interests of the seller, deal team, and stakeholders during the acquisition process sets the stage for a successful transition and future growth within the holding company.

Capital Stack + Deal Economics

When a profitable small business is purchased, the money for buying the business is paid back from the cash profits generated by the company once it's acquired. That's why acquisitions are priced as a multiple of earnings. The lower the multiple, the quicker it should take for the company to pay for itself (the "payback period"). All the details of how the investment is structured are essentially various ways of dealing with the risks and timing associated with making that payback process work in a way that's as fair and attractive to all parties involved.

When buying a company, success is when you've paid off all the debt and have met all investor obligations. So crafting a workable deal means assessing all the risks, making educated assumptions about how the company will perform, and striking the right balance of capital sources to fit that company. If you use debt for 90% of the deal, you'll have to use a lot of the free cash flow to service the debt, so you have to either pay a low price for the company or be confident that performance won't dip. If cash flows do drop below what you need to pay your loans, you're probably going to regret not bringing in more equity, or trying to get the seller to give a bigger seller note with a more forgiving repayment schedule.

Unless one person has 100% of the cash necessary to buy the company, some kind of outside capital will be necessary, and that investment can be set up in many different ways:

Equity Investments

Equity is the cash invested directly into the deal, like the down payment for a house. If you buy a house without a mortgage, you've acquired it with 100% equity. Another example is when you buy a share of stock in a publicly traded company, you've bought equity in that company. The term "equity" can refer to both the cash used and the resulting ownership stake that is purchased. When investments are made into deals to acquire companies, there are a variety of terms and agreements you can use creatively to design an equity investment. At its simplest, if a company is bought for $100 and you put in an equity investment of $20, you own 20% of that company. Equity investors are a lower priority, they get paid "after" loan payments, and take more risk on the performance of the company.

Debt: Banks, Private Loans, SBA Loans, Mezzanine Debt

Debt sometimes provides the majority of the cash needed to buy a company, but regular payments are required, so they introduce risk and a burden to perform well to be able to make payments.

Acquisition debt can take various forms, both in terms of who the lender is, and the terms of the loan. Bank loans are a common source of debt financing, offering relatively low interest rates but more stringent lending criteria and strict repayment terms. Private loans, on the other hand, may come from individuals or institutional investors, often providing more flexible terms but potentially at higher interest rates.

Small Business Administration (SBA) loans are attractive for very small business acquisitions as they offer favorable terms and government backing, making them accessible to a broader range of buyers, however, they require a personal guarantee from the borrower. Mezzanine debt, positioned between equity and senior debt, involves higher interest rates but can be valuable for bridging the gap between equity and traditional bank financing, especially when the buyer's equity contribution is limited.

Seller Notes + Earnouts

Seller notes involve the seller financing a portion of the purchase price, often at favorable terms such as low interest rates or deferred payments.

Although this is technically debt, the seller doesn't loan cash, they essentially loan the business itself to the buyer, who then uses the business to make payments to the seller. You could almost think of seller financing as a "rent-to-own" arrangement. This not only reduces the upfront capital required by the buyer but also demonstrates the seller's confidence in the business's future performance.

Earnouts, on the other hand, tie a portion of the purchase price to the future performance of the acquired business. This arrangement incentivizes the seller to help maximize the company's value post-acquisition, ensuring a smoother transition and alignment of goals between the buyer and seller. Earnouts are helpful when the buyer and seller have difficulty agreeing on a price since an earnout typically pays back the seller more if the company does well. They are also used when the seller remains involved in the company and is used as a management performance incentive.

Expansion and Maturity

A HoldCo isn't really a HoldCo until it owns multiple companies. Let's outline a few key concerns for HoldCos to consider as they grow.

Strategy, Opportunism + Adaptability

We outlined a few portfolio strategies earlier, and a HoldCo may use multiple tactics as it grows. They will learn through experience, get deeper exposure to new industries, and evolve their investment thesis. It's important to stay open-minded and be on the lookout for new opportunities. Just because something is obvious to you doesn't mean that someone else is already solving that problem. Great HoldCos see unexpected opportunities and respond to what's happening in the real world, rather than forming academic or conceptual plans that make sense on paper but have no grounding in the market.

Additional Acquisitions

HoldCos own multiple companies and one of their primary activities is scouting for new companies to buy. For HoldCos in the SMB space, one new acquisition per year is a healthy pace. This requires 1-2 team members to have at least 50% of their time allocated to searching, due diligence, negotiation, and structuring deals. Finding good companies to buy is not easy, but as you get established and build a name and a network in an industry, it can become easier. In the HoldCo world, "inorganic growth" means growing the group by acquiring new companies.

Organic Growth

When individual companies grow their revenue without taking on additional capital, they are growing organically. HoldCo entrepreneurs may hire a CEO or general manager to run each Operating Company (OpCo), but they will want to work with that operator to fan the flames of growth. If a HoldCo has a promising company with strong growth, it may choose to put time and money into fueling that growth rather than looking for more companies to buy.

Professionalization + Enhancement

A major aspect of running a successful HoldCo is improving the companies in your portfolio. There are many horror stories of private equity buyouts that gut the staff, kill the culture, and mess things up in the name of short-term gains. But this doesn't have to be the case. Many thoughtful HoldCo managers improve the employee experience with better training and support and improved compensation. Although it's probably smart to ask questions and listen before making major changes at a company, there might be major opportunities to add value to a company that has been "on autopilot" for 10 years.

When doing due diligence, seeing the problems with a company can actually be a good thing. If the company is managing to turn a profit despite backward practices, that means there's room to add value, and opportunity to make the company better.

Final Thoughts

A Warning Label to Idealists

A HoldCo is a powerful tool for accumulating capital and building wealth. Mixing HoldCos with social impact missions is an advanced level of play, fraught with potential pitfalls. People will want a piece of the action, and they can be vulnerable to cronyism, "social washing" and self-dealing managers. The social impact HoldCos we studied put significant work into structuring their ownership and governance to address issues of power.

HoldCos as Engines of Shared Value

HoldCos are a powerful tool for building wealth. When their benefits are shared, they are a tactic to help with our massive wealth inequality problem. But how can they feed into deeper systemic change in our economies and communities? Might HoldCos be used as the economic engines within the larger vehicle of transformation? Harvard Business School's Michael Porter advocates strategies where businesses have built shared value: creating economic value that also solves pressing problems in society.[267] Steward-owned HoldCos are a perfect example of a business creating shared value that benefits society, not just shareholders.

Employee-owned holding companies not only help address wealth inequality but also play a vital role in funding civic projects, local infrastructure, and other community needs. HoldCos are a way of distributing the surplus generated in a capitalist enterprise, so how might HoldCos serve as cash cows to drive capital into the real needs of their communities? When America had better wealth equality, some small business owners were active citizens who knew and cared about their neighbors and contributed back to the community through donations to local projects. Nowadays, large multinationals have major market share in our communities, and much of the cash spent there evaporates into the checkbooks of far-off owners who won't recirculate that cash locally. Faceless corporations don't have decision-makers and resource-holders living in the community helping to solve and fund the needs of the community. In fact, those far-off decision-makers are often professional asset managers, not business owners at all.

HoldCos move us beyond the financial precarity of the "non-profit industrial complex" by providing a perpetual source of cash. Communities

---

267   Porter, M. E., & R. Kramer, M. (2011, January). Creating shared value. Harvard Business Review. https://hbr.org/2011/01/the-big-idea-creating-shared-value

are better off if they have their own source of capital to fund necessary civic projects. Instead of applying for grants from global wealth holders, community projects can be funded by the profits from steward-owned local HoldCos.

Whether a local small business is part of a steward-owned HoldCo or not, it's also valuable for small businesses to have local ownership. Local owners are more exposed to the real problems in their communities and can play a more active role in lending a hand. As big business has taken more market share in our economy, it has weakened the role of local business owners as engaged, resourceful citizens.

Industry Clusters and Local Economies

As we saw with Goodworks in Montana, a HoldCo can be used as a vehicle for preserving independent businesses that contribute to the health and local feeling of a region. Similarly, Industrial Commons in North Carolina is using HoldCo strategies in concert with non-profit work to keep textile companies in-state. Industrial Commons employees are joining local community groups like the Lions Club and engaging their fellow local leaders to help shape their region.

HoldCos with steward ownership formats can play a key role in stabilizing necessary infrastructure for the industries and geographies in which they operate. They can partner with civic groups, foundations, and governments to build shared value that benefits local citizens and economies.

How the Story Ends: Terminal Value + Enterprise Value

Companies are frequently valued by speculating on their future value, which creates skewed incentives. Presently, we are heavily incentivized to build companies and then sell them for upside, rather than generating value through growing revenue steadily. The phrase "terminal value" refers to the value of all future cash flows of an investment or business. It represents the value of an investment or business at a future point in time, and a related concept is the "enterprise value" of a firm. It's almost like an assessment of the company's net worth with all health indicators taken into account. This determines the equity value of the company itself, literally the dollar value of the enterprise. When we focus heavily on optimizing terminal value as a number, we can risk undermining the practical foundation of a company. Business owners generally make money in two ways: from the cash profits yielded from delivering value to customers, or from proceeds from selling part or all of the company. When companies are sold, they tend to be bought by larger companies, which further consolidates our economies into the hands of fewer and fewer players.

Steward ownership and shared ownership forms protect against an over-focus on terminal value. Many companies that are converting to employee ownership trusts and perpetual purpose trusts never intend to sell. In fact, some formally bind ownership to stay in the trust and prohibit it from ever being sold.[268] By taking the temptation of a sale off the table, these companies are removing one of the defining rights of capital – the right to treat capital as an object that can be bought and sold as an item. Compare this to equity in a publicly traded company, which is traded daily and is so liquid it can be used as collateral to take out loans. In steward-ownership, you wouldn't be able to take out a loan against the stock since the stock can't be sold, it's of no use as collateral.

By removing the focus from a future buyout or sale, these models foster a more balanced incentive structure that encourages long-term sustainability, employee engagement, and community impact. This approach aligns investors, employees, and stakeholders around the continuous improvement of the business's operations, product quality, and service excellence, rather than gearing towards short-term financial gains or preparing for an exit strategy.

---

268   Johnson, M. (2023, November 30). The emergence of employee ownership trusts in the US – the Aspen Institute. The Aspen Institute. https://www.aspeninstitute.org/blog-posts/the-emergence-of-employee-ownership-trusts-in-the-us/

Opportunities for Funders

Zoe Schlag

Aligning Finance as Appetite Grows

Interest in shared ownership investment has grown rapidly in recent years, from community projects allowing members to invest internally, to pension funds financing employee ownership buyouts. All types of investors, from local non-accredited to large institutional, are recognizing the potential of shared ownership and are keen to invest across various asset classes.

Given this interest, we have an opportunity to shape the role of capital in the evolution and scaling of this space. Effectively supporting shared ownership projects is not just about increasing investment. Equally important is how that capital is structured and deployed. In other words, the structure and incentives of the capital are just as crucial as the amount invested. Consider two hypothetical economies, the same amount of capital invested in shared ownership projects in each could lead to two different outcomes, a short-lived shared ownership bubble or a sustainable, growing economy.

In our experience, we've seen the way incentives determine which scenario will play out. We agree with the framing provided by economist Mariana Mazzucato:[269] "There is a difference between profits and rents – between the wealth generated by creating value and wealth that is amassed through extraction. The first is a reward for taking risks that improve the productive capacity of an economy; the second comes from seizing an undue share of the reward without providing comparable improvements to the economy's productive capacity."

---

269   Mazzucato, M., Kattel, R., & O'Reilly, T. (2021, February 5). Reimagining the platform economy. Project Syndicate. https://www.project-syndicate.org/onpoint/platform-economy-data-generation-and-value-extraction-by-mariana-mazzucato-et-al-2021-02

Although shared ownership models are designed to create and share value between a wider set of key stakeholders, those principles can be undermined by the terms of the capital used to finance the projects. Just as Mazzucato differentiates between how value is generated or extracted, shared ownership models can be formatted to extract value without adding any real productive capacity. To protect against this, we are advocating for financing that builds resilience, incentivizes long-term innovation, and shares that value commensurately. Which economic future we choose to build will depend not only on whether we will meet the market demand for financing for shared ownership but also on whether the terms of our financing work for or against the core goals of the projects.

Over the past few decades, the increasing concentration of ownership, wealth, and power has come at the direct expense of worker and community wealth and has even compromised product quality. 75% of U.S. industries have experienced an increase in concentration since the late 1990s.[270] Wealth inequality has reached staggering heights: While the top 1% owns 30% of American wealth, the "bottom" 50% owns just 2.6%[271]. There has been a measurable negative impact on our communities as a result. Hospitals acquired by private equity firms have produced an increase in patient complications, even among lower-risk patients.[272]

While this is daunting, we have an opportunity to reverse course on these trends due to seismic demographic changes and public sector interest. The "silver tsunami" is a demographic shift that will have an enormous impact. It is the wave of baby boomer small business owners across America who will look to sell their businesses as they retire. This presents

---

270   Grullon, G., Larkin, Y., & Michaely, R. (2019). Are US industries becoming more concentrated?*. Review of Finance, 23(4), 697–743. https://doi.org/10.1093/rof/rfz007

271   Federal Reserve. https://www.federalreserve.gov/

272   Kannan, S., Bruch, J. D., & Song, Z. (2023). Changes in hospital adverse events and patient outcomes associated with private equity acquisition. JAMA, 330(24), 2365. https://doi.org/10.1001/jama.2023.23147

one of – if not the – largest asset transitions in ownership in U.S. history. The public sector is also a huge driver for the uptake in shared ownership approaches. Some estimates put commercial assets owned by the public sector at up to $75T.[273] Shared ownership could very well be the largest Archimedes Lever of our generation to course correct on many of these trends. How we choose to finance shared ownership will impact whether this sector grows steadily without compromising on resilience.

Abundant Opportunities

Shared ownership presents numerous investment opportunities for funders, not only because of upcoming market changes but also due to its adaptability to any economic asset. Consequently, shared ownership assets can lead to the creation of new markets, and financial innovation is relevant at every level. Aligned capital can impact the way employees access their internal capital accounts inside their companies and the ways companies manage liquidity. Across networks of assets, funders can help enable systems like intercompany mutual insurance and loan structures, and urban wealth fund-style municipal solutions.

Funders fueling this work can be valuable in any part of this stack. For instance:

- Institutional investors could offer bonds to finance large-scale shared ownership projects

- Regional banks and Community Development Finance Institutions (CDFIs) could provide loans to finance employee ownership buyouts, protecting quality jobs in their regions and in rural areas

---

273   Detter, D., Pettinari, A., Buiter, W., Howell, A., L. Morse, E., Bilerman, M., & Fölster, S. (2015, June 11). The public wealth of nations. CITI GPS: Global Perspectives and Solutions. https://www.citigroup.com/global/insights/citigps/public-wealth-nations

- Limited Partners (LPs) could invest in a rising tide of shared ownership funds, across employee ownership, community-owned real estate and other models

- Equity investors could invest in new products designed to uniquely serve the needs of the emerging B2B customer base of shared ownership models

- Philanthropic funders could provide loan guarantees to support shared balance sheet innovations

The Shared Ownership Flywheel

Investors new to shared ownership often assume they are taking on more risk due to unfamiliarity and sacrificing higher returns by sharing profits with others. From a first principles perspective, these aren't a given; however, they merit unpacking.

At the center of any shared ownership investment thesis sits an incentive thesis: When stakeholders who significantly influence an asset's long-term value are given a share of the economic upside, they are motivated to drive performance.[274] While much of the economy has already adopted this in the corporate context, the circle of "key stakeholders" has been drawn extremely narrowly. Typically, incentivizing performance with economic interest is available to executive management and senior leadership, while it remains largely inaccessible to the vast majority of workers.

A shared ownership thesis takes the perspective that much of the economy is overvaluing incentivizing CEOs and undervaluing incentivizing the wider workforce. Within employee ownership, the research bears this out: according to research evaluated by Douglas Kruse, "over 100 studies across many countries indicate that employee ownership is generally

---

274 For a deeper explanation of this concept, please see: Shell, J. (2023, February 9). Introducing The Ownership Fund. | Ideas from Social Capital Partners. Medium. https://medium.com/ideas-from-social-capital-partners/introducing-the-ownership-fund-39be3bf11d46

linked to better productivity, pay, job stability, and firm survival."[275] This is the ownership flywheel at work. So while an investor may initially believe they are trading away value by sharing upside, there is a strong case that investors can tap into gains that could not otherwise be realized without extending ownership to a wider pool of key stakeholders. While less well researched than employee ownership, the same incentive thesis could improve outcomes for other asset classes like residential or commercial real estate, among others.

Diligent Shared Ownership Financing: Considerations for Investors

Many interested investors looking to get into shared ownership feel under-equipped to evaluate opportunities. Diligence is perceived as harder and risk profiles seem higher, simply because investors cannot easily identify appropriate market comparables. A lack of comparables on its own should not be evidence of higher risk; rather, a lack of comparables should simply imply a rigorous due diligence process centered on first principles.

Key Principles

Any shared ownership thesis is an incentive thesis, resultantly, any investor evaluating a shared ownership opportunity should evaluate whether the financing structure is working for or against the incentive thesis at play. Therefore, any diligence process should include an analysis of:

- (1) how key stakeholders are included and incentivized,
- (2) whether the incentive thesis linked to shared ownership is likely to unlock the performance benefits of the ownership flywheel, and
- (3) how the capital structure interfaces with those incentives.

Due to the diversity of models and incentives, we are not offering a universal, prescriptive diligence method. However, in general, we encourage investors to evaluate the following dimensions as a baseline:

---

275   Kruse, D. (2022). Does employee ownership improve performance? IZA World of Labor. https://doi.org/10.15185/izawol.311.v2

- Are the incentives material, meaning do they actually matter to the key stakeholders you are looking to bring into the ownership fold?

- Are the incentives within reach, meaning do those key stakeholders see and understand a clear pathway to access those incentives?

- Will the performance gains be realized within a timeframe that aligns with the investment term and liquidity structure, allowing the investment to benefit from the advantages of shared ownership?

Financing Risks to Successful Shared Ownership

Alongside looking for positive signals from the above design considerations, there are also red flags to look out for. Investors evaluating shared ownership opportunities should specifically evaluate:

- Who is taking cash off the table when: How much are investors taking off the table before key stakeholders participating in the shared ownership structure realize any of their benefits? If there is a significant difference, and if so, is there a meaningful rationale and justification around risk to support that?

- Time Horizons: Does the return target and time horizon sit at odds with building long-term value and resilience?

- Liquidity: What happens to shared ownership for an investor to exit? Does an investor exiting require that the asset be bought out of shared ownership?

- Legibility: Is the shared ownership economic model easily understood by everyone? We've seen a lot of complicated structures, and what we come back to time and time again is that stakeholders being able to truly understand the structure matters just as much as the structure itself.

Before concluding this chapter, we will explore how some of the risks and red flags may be buffered against through further structural protections.

Long-Term Resilience through Steward Ownership

So we have discussed how shared ownership offers a structure that can build greater value for more stakeholders. An important complement to this goal is protecting the long-term endurance and outcomes of a company. Implementing steward ownership models can protect long-term business health, resilience, and outcomes, and secure a scenario where businesses are contributing to economy-wide resilience and steady growth. Here we outline why steward ownership enables a risk management function over the long-term, and is a valuable framework to use in combination with shared ownership models.

Steward ownership operates with two key principles: 1) profits serve a purpose, and 2) perpetual independence. The first principle guides a business's governance towards long-term financial well-being and a higher purpose for its profits. This protects the business from the risks of financial engineering and excessive profit extraction, while also providing a governance mechanism for the business to consider the long-term risks of externalities. Functionally, this also often leads to higher rates of reinvestment, research and development, and subsequently innovation, building the long-term resilience of the underlying business.

The second principle of steward ownership enables businesses to remain independent and insulated from the dynamics of their investor bases when those dynamics should not in fact impact the strategy and operations of a business. For instance, the strategic choices made by an investor reaching the end of their fund life may be more influenced by their need to exit their position than what is truly in the long-term interest of the business. Likewise, an investor preparing to raise their next fund may be more interested in being able to demonstrate that the value of their investment has been marked up, even if the strategy to achieve that mark-up is not in the best interest of the business. Steward ownership offers a mechanism to insulate business strategy from dynamics such as these, among others.

These protections offer meaningful improvements to business resilience and focus. There are prominent examples of companies benefitting from steward ownership as a risk management function over time like Bosch and Novo Nordisk, as well as more recently, Patagonia. Research conducted by Steen Thomsen demonstrates that businesses operating under steward ownership have a 6x higher survival rate over a 40-year period[276]. As expounded upon in prior chapters, steward ownership is most commonly implemented through non-profit ownership and trust ownership, especially using perpetual purpose trusts.

Ownership structures determine what a company and its leaders optimize for. In this sense, ownership can be viewed as an optimization protocol. A century ago, businesses were often owned and operated by private individuals. These owners largely viewed their businesses as a going concern, caring most about the business's endurance over the long-term, and making decisions with long-term value as opposed to short term liquidity in mind.

This began to shift with the deregulation of finance that began in the 1970s that subsequently spurred the growth of the financial services industry. As the financial sector grew, the ownership of assets turned over from private ownership by owner-operators to professional managers operating the assets they managed to meet specific time horizons and return targets.

Transferring ownership of assets from an individual owner to a professional manager changes the optimization function that guides decision-making and resource allocation within the business. Private ownership does not have a legally bound investment period or fund life, so private owner-operators have the ability to integrate diverse considerations into how they govern and manage the business. For example, they can consider

---

276   Author page for Steen Thomsen. (2024, March 29). SSRN. https://papers.ssrn.com/sol3/cf_dev/AbsByAuth.cfm?per_id=53665

the relative priority of providing a quality product or service, providing good jobs to their employees, and contributing back to their community. With professional managers, the optimization function is more narrow, constrained by considerations such as fund life, target return profile and the term of their investment.

To illustrate this point, consider one business owned by a private owner who cares about the business' endurance over the long-term. With that perspective, that owner will invest in finding, training, and retaining talent, they will invest in R&D and innovation, they will invest in their brand and therefore pre-emptively manage any negative externalities. Thinking "long-term" is not just lip service – one business we worked with while exiting to employee ownership was motivated by "building a 100-year company."

Now, consider a business bought by a financial sponsor on a tight timeframe to turn around high returns to their investors. That investor may choose to leverage the business at higher levels than a long-term operator, knowing that leverage will increase their Internal Rate of Return (IRR) when they sell a few years later. They may choose to cut research and development (R&D) investment, knowing that while those may be good bets over a ten to twenty-year time horizon, their fund life will require them to exit long before those benefits materialize.

Private equity firms often employ these tactics in leveraged buyouts. While private equity is known for generating high returns, a 2020 Morgan Stanley report found that companies acquired through buyouts are approximately 10 times more likely to file for bankruptcy within 10 years compared to similar companies not involved in such transactions[277]. As a result, private equity can simultaneously be viewed as highly successful for its individual investors, while also externalizing risk beyond its investment term that can negatively impact the business, workers, community, and society at

---

277   J. Mauboussin, M., Callahan, D. (2020, August 4) CFA. Public to Private Equity in the United States: A Long Term Look. Morgan Stanley. https://www.morganstanley.com/im/publication/insights/articles/articles_publictoprivateequityintheusalongtermlook_us.pdf

large. The dissonance that a successful investment can also cause long-term harm results from the fact that our most commonly used investment metrics lack the nuance to differentiate between investment used to build productive capacity, and investment that is acting to increase their profits at the expense of longer-term value. In the example of private equity, we can see a fund successfully return a high IRR, while leaving the business that was the driver of that IRR closer to bankruptcy.[278]

This essay does not argue that we turn back toward private ownership, but rather that we turn toward steward ownership. Where private ownership benefits from owner-operators with a long-term time horizon, it is simultaneously dependent upon an effective benevolent dictator. Where professional management of assets is intended to professionalize governance, strategy, and operations, its constraints can yield unintended consequences for long-term value. Steward ownership offers a legal structure and governance function that directly codifies the best practices of both types of ownership, ensuring businesses are governed and operated professionally, while also ensuring that the governance of the business is oriented toward long-term health, resilience, and sharing those benefits.

Zooming out, an economy operating with the more narrowed optimization function that comes exclusively with professional management of the last fifty years has less ability to contend with complexity and manage externalities. Steward ownership is a valuable tool for governing and managing assets toward protecting and growing long-term value.

Conclusion

We started this chapter by looking at the unique market opportunities and the increase in appetite for shared ownership. We then discussed

---

278   This is not to say that private equity is wholly "bad" – rather, the investment metrics by which we evaluate a fund's performance obscure long-term harmful effects on the business or negative externalities, even while providing a competitive return, and leverage buyouts have an outsized impact on business operations and financial health relative to other asset classes and financial instruments.

the need to course-correct the concerning trend lines including rising wealth inequality, waning community resilience, and accelerating corporate concentration. We have also addressed impending market shifts, such as employee ownership as a scalable approach to address the "silver tsunami", or urban wealth funds to better manage the estimated $75T in publicly-owned commercial assets. With market opportunities such as these in mind, we discussed how both shared ownership and steward ownership can be complementary tools for investors to think about both building value and managing risk.

Together, all these elements present a compelling opportunity for funders looking to accelerate an economy that serves us all and is built for the long-term. As we engage in this opportunity, the imperative is to revisit the fundamentals of how we are choosing to finance our economy to reorient toward long-term stakeholder benefits.

Shared ownership financing will require new models and new thinking. A common misconception is that shared ownership asks investors to simply trade away returns with no commensurate adjustment on risk. In reality, shared ownership and steward ownership both offer the opportunity to build a more prosperous and competitive economy, for the long haul. When evaluating wealth creation, it's important to distinguish between two approaches. One involves balance sheet engineering that doesn't increase productive capacity, while the other utilizes new ownership structures designed to provide broader incentives and more effective long-term risk management. We have an opportunity to reconsider which financing techniques are appropriate for this emerging economic future and which are ripe for retirement. Furthermore, it provides an opportunity to look at risk and return with greater nuance.

As we reshape our economy, it is crucial that financing prioritizes long-term, sustainable growth and the equitable distribution, ensuring that the benefits of our shared prosperity are felt by all stakeholders, now and for generations to come.